7

GREEK
AND ROMAN
JEWELLERY

ROMAN-EGYPTIAN LADY, SECOND CENTURY AD

GREEK
AND ROMAN
JEWELLERY

Second Edition

REYNOLD HIGGINS

University of California Press

BERKELEY and LOS ANGELES

University of California Press
Berkeley and Los Angeles

ISBN 0-520-03601-8

Library of Congress Catalog Card Number : 77-20321

Printed in the United States of America

TO PAT
WITH LOVE

CONTENTS

Contents

Part II Historical

x   Contents

LIST OF TEXT FIGURES

LIST OF PLATES

Frontispiece
Roman mummy portrait probably from the Fayonne, second century
AD. British Museum (Egyptian Department), no. 65346 *Photo:*
British Museum

1 A] Fresco from Pompeii (House of the Vettii) showing Erotes as
  goldsmiths, first century AD. Naples, Museo Nazionale.
  Photo: S. Bruno, *Les Petits Amours de la maison des Vettii.*
  B, C] Bronze die for pressing sheet gold from Corfu, seventh
  century BC. Oxford, Ashmolean Museum, G. 437. *JHS*, XVI
  (1896), p. 323. Length 12.5 cm.
  Photo : Ashmolean Museum.
  D] Gold chain from the Aegina Treasure, seventeenth century BC.
  Micro-photo. British Museum. *BMCJ*, no. 752.
  Photo: British Museum Research Laboratory.
  E] Stone mould for casting earrings probably from Crete, 1600–1450
  BC. Oxford, Ashmolean Museum, G. 707. Boardman, *Cretan
  Collection*, no. 546. Height 3.8 cm; width 3 cm.
  Photo: Ashmolean Museum.

2 Jewellery from Thyreatis, about 2200 BC. Berlin, Staatliche Museen,
  no. 30987. Greifenhagen, *Schmuckarbeiten*, I; pls 1 and 2.
  Photo: Staatliche Museen, Berlin.

3 Cretan jewellery, about 2200 BC. New York, Metropolitan Museum
  (R. B. Seager Bequest, 1926).
  Photos: Metropolitan Museum.

A] Hairpin: spray of leaves from Mochlos. No. 26. 31. 418. Length of each leaf 5 cm.

B] Hairpin: daisy from Mochlos (?). No. 26. 31. 427. Diameter 3 cm.

C] Bead from Mochlos. No. 26. 31. 510. Height 1.3 cm.

D] Pendant on chain, provenance not stated (probably Mochlos). No. 26. 31. 419. Length 9 cm.

4 A] Cretan beads from the Aegina Treasure, about sixteenth century BC. British Museum, no. 749A. *BSA*, LII (1957), pl. 12a. Height 1.2 cm.
Photo: British Museum.
B] Earring from Mycenae, Shaft Grave III, 1600–1500 BC. Athens, National Museum. Karo, *Schachtgräber*, no. 61. Greatest diameter 7.5 cm.
Photo: German Archaeological Institute, Athens.
C] Earring from Mycenae, 1600–1500 BC. Paris, Louvre Museum, Bj 135. Height 2.9 cm.
Photo: Louvre Museum.
D] Pendant with confronted dogs and monkeys threaded with cornelian beads, from the Aegina Treasure, about seventeenth century BC. British Museum. *BMCJ*, no. 765. Diameter of ring 6.5 cm.
Photo: British Museum.

5 A–C] Beads, 1500–1450 BC.
A] Bull's head from Hagia Triada, 1500–1450 BC. Heraklion Museum. Height 2.5 cm.
Photo: Hirmer Fotoarchiv.
B] Lion from Hagia Triada, 1500–1450 BC. Heraklion Museum. Width 2.7 cm.
Photo: Hirmer Fotoarchiv.
C] Toad from Kakovatos, Tholos Tomb A, 1500–1450 BC. Athens, National Museum. Height 1.5 cm.
Photo: Hirmer Fotoarchiv.
D] Wild goat pendant from Crete, about seventeenth century BC. British Museum. *BMCJ*, no. 815. Total height 5 cm.
Photo: British Museum.
E] Necklace of beads in the shape of pomegranates from Mycenae, Shaft Grave III, 1550–1500 BC. Athens, National Museum. Karo, *Schachtgräber*, no. 77. Height 2.6 cm.
Photo: German Archaeological Institute, Athens.

6 A] Pendant, confronted bees, from Mallia, Chrysolakkos, about

seventeenth century BC. Crete, Heraklion Museum. *Études Crétoises,*
VII, pl. 66. Height 4.6 cm.
Photo: Hirmer Fotoarchiv.
B] Pendant, 'Master of Animals', from the Aegina Treasure, about
seventeenth century BC. British Museum. *BMCJ*, no. 762. Height
6 cm.
Photo: British Museum.

7 A] Pendant hanging from silver pin from Mycenae, Shaft Grave III,
1600–1500 BC. Athens, National Museum. Karo, *Schachtgräber*,
no. 75. Height 6.7 cm.
Photo: German Archaeological Institute, Athens.
B] Pendant with human heads (? formerly inlaid, with lapis lazuli)
from the Aegina Treasure, about seventeenth century BC. British
Museum. *BMCJ*, no. 761. Length 10.8 cm.
Photo: British Museum.

8 A, B] Finger ring from Knossos, Ailias, Tomb 7, seventeenth
century BC. Heraklion Museum. External diameter 1.7 cm.
Photo: M. S. F. Hood. Courtesy, British School at Athens.
C] Finger ring inlaid with lapis lazuli from the Aegina Treasure,
seventeenth or sixteenth century BC. British Museum. *BMCR*,
no. 690. Width of shield 1.8 cm.
Photo: British Museum.
D, E] Clothing ornaments from Mycenae, Shaft Grave III,
1600–1500 BC. Athens, National Museum. Karo, *Schachtgräber*,
nos 50, 45. Height 3.5, 4 cm.
Photo: German Archaeological Institute, Athens.
F] Clothing ornament: owl, from Kakovatos, Tholos Tomb A,
1500–1450 BC. Athens, National Museum. Height 2 cm.
Photo: Hirmer Fotoarchiv.
G] Clothing ornament (one of fifty-four identical) from the Aegina
Treasure, about sixteenth century BC. British Museum. *BMCJ*,
no. 723. Diameter 4 cm.
Photo: British Museum.

9 A] Beads from a tomb at Mycenae, about fourteenth century BC.
Oxford, Ashmolean Museum, AE 582–592. Lifesize.
Photo: Ashmolean Museum.
B] Beads from a tomb in the Argolid, about fourteenth century BC.
Brooklyn Museum, no. 35. 780. *Brooklyn Museum Quarterly*, XXII
(1935), p. 112. Width of argonaut bead 3 cm.
Photo: Brooklyn Museum.

10 A] Relief beads (type 5) with traces of enamel from Mycenae,

Tomb 103, 1450–1350 BC. Athens, National Museum. Height about 2.2 cm.
Photo: Tombazi, Athens.
B] Relief beads (type 22) with traces of enamel from Mycenae, Tomb 88, about 1450–1350 BC. Athens, National Museum. Rosenberg, *Zellenschmelz*, p. 22, fig. 6. About lifesize.
Photo: Tombazi, Athens.
C] Relief beads (type 9) with traces of enamel from Mycenae, Tomb 88, about 1450–1350 BC. Athens, National Museum. Rosenberg, *Zellenschmelz*, p. 22, fig. 8. About lifesize.
Photo: Tombazi, Athens.
D] Earring from Knossos, Mavro Spelio, Tomb VII, 1450–1200 BC. Heraklion Museum. *BSA*, XXVIII (1926–7), pl. 18, no. vii. B.1. Length 3.5 cm.
Photo: Heraklion Museum.
E] Cypro-Mycenaean diadem, decorated with stamps intended primarily for making relief beads, from a tomb near Klaudia (Larnaka), 1400–1100 BC. British Museum. *BMCJ*, no. 144. Length 16.1 cm.
Photo: British Museum.

11 A] Finger ring with enamelled decoration from Sellopoullo (Knossos), Tomb 4, 1425–1400. Bezel 1.3 × 2.1 cm; diameter of hoop 2 cm.
Photo: M. R. Popham. Courtesy, British School at Athens.
B] Finger ring from Ialysus, 1400–1150 BC. British Museum. *BMCR*, no. 873. Length of bezel 2.5 cm; diameter of hoop 1.9 cm.
Photo: British Museum.
C] Signet ring with impressed decoration from Mycenae, Tomb 68, 1400–1350 BC (?). Athens, National Museum, no. 4860. *CMS*, I, no. 102. Bezel 2.2 × 1.5 cm.
Photo: German Archaeological Institute, Athens. Courtesy, Mlle O. Sargnon.
D] Signet ring with engraved decoration from Mycenae, Tomb 84, 1400–1350 BC (?). Athens, National Museum, no. 4851. *CMS*, I, no. 119. Bezel about 2.5 × 1.5 cm.
Photo: German Archaeological Institute, Athens. Courtesy, Mlle O. Sargnon.

12 Cypro-Mycenaean jewellery from Enkomi, 1400–1100 BC. British Museum.
Photos: British Museum.
A] Pin. *BMCJ*, no. 546. Length 6.6 cm.
B] Earring. *BMCJ*, no. 376. Diameter 2.4 cm.

C] Earring. *BMCJ*, no. 543. Height 1.9 cm.

D] Earring. *BMCJ*, no. 349. Diameter 2.5 cm.

E] Earring. *BMCJ*, no. 299. Diameter 2.2 cm.

F] Earring. *BMCJ*, no. 470. Height 1.7 cm.

G] Earring. *BMCJ*, no. 525. Height 3.2 cm.

H] Earring. *BMCJ*, no. 328. Height 4.5 cm.

I] Spiral, probably for the hair. *BMCJ*, no. 408. Diameter 3.2 cm.

13 A] Finger ring, ninth century BC. British Museum (Elgin Collection), 1960. 11–1. 36. External diameter 2.2 cm.

B] Hair spiral, eleventh century BC. British Museum (Elgin Collection), 1960. 11–1. 11. External diameter 1.9 cm.

C] Finger ring, about eighth century BC. British Museum (Elgin Collection), 1960. 11–1. 41. External diameter 1.9 cm.

D, E] Earrings from Athens, Agora, Grave H 16 : 6. About 850 BC. Stoa of Attalus Museum. Height 6.5 cm.

Photo: American School of Classical Studies, Athens.

F] Earring from Eleusis, Grave A. 825–800 BC. Athens, National Museum. Width 2.4 cm.

Photo: German Archaeological Institute, Athens.

G] Earring from Eleusis, the Isis Grave. 800–775 BC. Athens, National Museum. Width 3 cm.

Photo: German Archaeological Institute, Athens.

14 A, B] Pair of fibulae, 775–750 BC. British Museum (Elgin Collection), 1960, 11–1. 44 and 45. Width 4.5 cm.

Photos: British Museum.

C] Pair of earrings, 800–750 B C. Los Angeles County Museum of Art. Diameter of cones 2.7 cm; of discs 2.8 cm.

Photo: Los Angeles Country Museum of Art and Jay Bisno.

D] Earring, 800–750 BC. Collection of E. Kofler-Truniger. Diameter of disc 2.7 cm.

Photo: E. Kofler-Truniger.

E] Earring, 800–750 BC. British Museum (Elgin Collection), 1960. 11–1. 18. Diameter of disc 2.9 cm.

Photo: British Museum.

15 A] Necklace from Spata, Tomb 3, eighth century BC. Athens, National Museum, no. 2604. Length 10 cm.

Photo: German Archaeological Institute, Athens.

B–F] Parts of a pectoral ornament inlaid with amber from Eleusis, eighth century BC. Athens, National Museum, no. 147. Three-quarter scale.

Photo: German Archaeological Institute, Athens.

16 A] Earring from Corinth, eighth century BC. Oxford, Ashmolean Museum, 1927. 1329. Diameter of disc 1.6 cm.
Photo: Ashmolean Museum.
B] Gold-plated button from Megara, seventh century BC. Louvre Museum, Bj 137. Coche de la Ferté, pl. 15: 1. Diameter 2 cm.
Photo: Louvre Museum Laboratory.
C] Earring from Lefkandi, 875–850 BC. Eretria Museum. *Lefkandi*, I, pl. 231d. Diameter 1 cm.
Photo: M. R. Popham. Courtesy, British School at Athens.
D] Earring from Lefkandi, 850–825 BC. Eretria Museum. *Lefkandi*, I, pl. 231a. Diameter of cones 1 cm.
Photo: M. R. Popham. Courtesy, British School at Athens.
E] Earring from Lefkandi, 875–850 BC. Eretria Museum. *Lefkandi*, I, pl. 231 a. Diameter of cones 0.7 cm.
Photo: M. R. Popham. Courtesy, British School at Athens.
F] Fibula from Lefkandi, 875–850 BC. Eretria Museum. *Lefkandi*, I, pl. 231c. Length 5.5 cm.
Photo: M. R. Popham. Courtesy, British School at Athens.
G] Finger ring from Lefkandi, 850–825 BC. Eretria Museum. *Lefkandi*, I, pl. 230c. Diameter 1.3 cm.
H] Gold-plated lead spiral from Lefkandi, about 900 BC. Eretria Museum. *Lefkandi*, I, pl. 230l. External diameter 1.1 cm.
Photo: M. R. Popham. Courtesy, British School at Athens.
I] Finger ring from Lefkandi, 850–825 BC. Eretria Museum. *Lefkandi*, I, pl. 230h. External diameter 2 cm.
Photo: M. R. Popham. Courtesy, British School at Athens.
J] Earring from Thebes, eighth century BC. Paris, Louvre Museum, Bj 142. Diameter of cones 5.5 cm.
Photo: Chuzeville.
K] Earring from Lefkandi, 875–850 BC. Eretria Museum. *Lefkandi*, I, pl. 231b. Total height 2 cm.
Photo: M. R. Popham. Courtesy, British School at Athens.

17 A] Pendant from the Idaean Cave, Crete, about 750 BC. Athens, National Museum, no. 11784. *AJA*, XLIX (1945), p. 317. Width 4.5 cm.
Photo: German Archaeological Institute, Athens.
B] Silver pin from Tekke (Knossos), Tomb Q, 800–670 BC. Heraklion Museum. Length 6 cm.
Photo: L. H. Sackett. Courtesy, British School at Athens.
C–F] Jewellery from Tekke (Knossos), Tomb 2, about 800 BC.
Photos: British School at Athens.
C] Lunate pendant with inlaid crystal and amber. Maximum width of main element about 6.5 cm.

D] Quatrefoil pendant. Maximum width about 4.5 cm.

E] Penannular pendant with human head finials and birds within. Width about 5.5 cm.

F] Lunate pendant. Width about 3 cm.

18 A–C] Earrings from Camirus, seventh century BC. *BMCJ*, nos 1173, 1174, 1166. Length 2.6 cm, 3 cm, 5.9 cm.
Photo: British Museum.
D] Rosette from a diadem, provenance unknown, seventh century BC. British Museum. *BMCJ*, no. 1230. Diameter 4.3 cm.
Photo: British Museum.
E] Earring from Camirus, seventh century BC. Boston, Museum of Fine Arts, H. L. Pierce Fund, no. 99. 378. Height 5.5 cm.
Photo: Museum of Fine Arts, Boston.

19 A] Diadem, from Camirus, seventh century BC. British Museum. *BMCJ*, no. 1160. Length 30.5 cm.
Photo: British Museum.
B] Plaque with Astarte bust and lions' masks, seventh century BC. British Museum. *BMCJ*, no. 1152. Height (excluding rosette) 3.3 cm.
Photo: British Museum.
C] Plaque with figure of sphinx and female heads from Camirus, seventh century BC. British Museum. *BMCJ*, no. 1108, Height 3.2 cm.
Photo: British Museum.
D] Plaque with figure of Mistress of Beasts, from Camirus, seventh century BC. British Museum. *BMCJ*, no. 1126. Height of plaque 4 cm.
Photo: British Museum.
E] Plaque with figure of Mistress of Beasts. Two hawks and a rosette on top. From Camirus. Seventh century BC. British Museum. *BMCJ*, no. 1107. Height 5.2 cm.
Photo: British Museum.

20 Rhodian jewellery, seventh century BC.
A] Plaque with figure of a centaur from Camirus. British Museum. *BMCJ*, no. 1115. Height of plaque 5.1 cm.
Photo: British Museum.
B] Plaque with two female heads from Camirus. British Museum. *BMCJ*, no. 1103 (part). Height of plaque 1.8 cm.
Photo: British Museum.
C] Plaque with Mistress of Beasts from Camirus. British Museum. *BMCJ*, no. 1128 (part). Height of plaque 4.2 cm.

D] Plaque with figure of a griffin from Camirus (?). Osborne House, Isle of Wight. Height 3.3 cm.
Photo: Department of the Environment.
E] Plaque with figure of a goddess from Camirus. British Museum. *BMCJ*, no. 1132. Height 3.1 cm.
Photo: British Museum.
F] Plaque with figure of a bee goddess from Camirus. British Museum. *BMCJ*, no. 1118. Height 3 cm.
Photo: British Museum.

21 Jewellery from Ephesus, seventh century BC. British Museum.
Photos: British Museum.
A] Clothing ornament. *BMCJ*, no. 870. Length 1.4 cm.
B] Clothing ornament. *BMCJ*, no. 827. Length 1.5 cm.
C] Clothing ornament. *BMCJ*, no. 876. Diameter 3.5 cm.
D] Earring. *BMCJ*, no. 948. Height 1.7 cm.
E] Earring. *BMCJ*, no. 946. Height 1.9 cm.
F] Earring. *BMCJ*, no. 942. Height 2.2 cm.
G] Clothing ornament. *BMCJ*, no. 894. Diameter 2.1 cm.
H] Clothing ornament. *BMCJ*, no. 877. Height 2.2 cm.

22 Jewellery from Ephesus, seventh century BC.
A] Disc brooch. British Museum. *BMCJ*, no. 1035. Diameter 2.7 cm.
Photo: British Museum.
B] Silver fibula (Asia Minor type). British Museum. *BMCJ*, no. 1089. Width 3.5 cm.
Photo: British Museum.
C] Four pins. British Museum. *BMCJ*, nos 950, 951, 958, 959. Length 5.5, 6.7, 6.1, 6.5 cm.
Photo: British Museum.
D] Brooch in shape of a hawk. West Berlin, Staatliche Museen, Antiken-Abteilung, no. 1963. 6. Height 4 cm.
Photo: Staatliche Museen (Jutta Tietz-Glagow).
E] Brooch in shape of a hawk. British Museum. *BMCJ*, no. 1037. Height 3.1 cm.
Photo: British Museum.

23 Wreath from Armento, about 350 BC. Munich, Antikensammlungen, no. 2335, Becatti, no. 354. Height 36 cm.
Photo: C. H. Krüger-Moessner.

24 A] Pair of earstuds (front and back view) from Rhodes, about 400 BC. British Museum. *BMCJ*, nos 2068–9. Diameter 1.6 cm.
Photo: British Museum.
B] Bronze button with gilt terracotta filling, about 500 BC. British Museum, 1959. 7–20. 1. Diameter 2 cm.
Photo: British Museum.

C] Spiral-type earring from Nymphaeum, fifth century BC.
Oxford, Ashmolean Museum, 1885. 483. Height 3.4 cm.
Photo: Ashmolean Museum.
D] Earring with granulation, from Nymphaeum, fifth century BC.
Oxford, Ashmolean Museum, 1885. 468. Height 5.9 cm.
Photo: Ashmolean Museum.
E] Earring with filigree, granulation and enamel from Eretria,
later fifth century BC. British Museum. *BMCJ*, no. 1653. Height
6 cm.
Photo: British Museum.
F] Silver pendant: cicada, about 400 BC. Louvre Museum, Bj. 740.
Coche de la Ferté, pl. 15:5. Height 1.4 cm.
Photo: Archives Photographiques.

25 Greek earrings.
A] Disc-and-boat type from Madytus, about 330 BC (type starts
about 360). New York, Metropolitan Museum, Rogers Fund,
1906, no. 06, 1217. 3. Height 7.5 cm.
Photo: Metropolitan Museum.
B] Disc and pendant with female head from Crispiano, near
Tarentum, early fourth century BC. Taranto, Museo Nazionale.
Becatti, no. 388. Height 6 cm.
Photo: Hirmer Fotoarchiv.
C–H] British Museum.
Photos: British Museum.
C] Boat type with pendants from Kalymnos, fourth century BC.
BMCJ, no. 1660. Height 4.4 cm.
D] Human head (South Russian type; sometimes an earring, some-
times part of a necklace), fourth century BC. 1934. 11–15. 2. Height
3.2 cm.
E] Spiral type with pyramids of granulation, 450–400 BC. *BMCJ*,
no. 1585. Height 2.1 cm.
F] Pendant type, fifth or fourth century BC. 1920. 12–21. 5. Height
3–6 cm.
G] Spiral type of gold-plated bronze enamelled and with griffin-
head finial from Amathus, fifth century BC. *BMCJ*, no. 1646. Height
2.9 cm.
H] Spiral type, Mainland and Cretan variety, fifth–fourth century
BC. *BMCJ*, no. 1648. Height 2.4 cm.

26 Necklaces from Eretria, fifth century BC. Athens, National Museum.
About $\frac{4}{5}$ scale.
Photo: German Archaeological Institute, Athens.

27 A] Necklace from Nymphaeum, fifth century BC. Oxford, Ashmolean Museum, 1885. 502. Length about 23 cm.

B] Necklace from Nymphaeum, fifth century BC. Oxford, Ashmolean Museum, 1885. 482. Length about 31 cm.
Photo: Ashmolean Museum.

28 Necklace from Tarentum, early fourth century BC. British Museum. *BMCJ*, no. 1952. Length 30.6 cm.
Photo: British Museum.

29 Pendant from Kul Oba, Kerch, fourth century BC. Leningrad, Hermitage Museum. Diameter of disc 7.2 cm.
Photo: Hermitage Museum.

30 A] Bracelet of gold-plated bronze with ram's head finials from Curium, Cyprus, fifth century BC. British Museum. *BMCJ*, no. 1985. Diameter 8.4 cm.
Photo: British Museum.
B] Bracelet with sphinx-head finials from Kul Oba, Kerch, fourth century BC. Leningrad, Hermitage Museum. Diameter 11.5 cm.
Photo: Hermitage Museum.

31 A] Fibula from Ruvo, sixth century BC. British Museum. *BMCJ*, no. 1408. Length 7 cm.
Photo: British Museum.
B] Swivel ring: dancers, from Kerch, Pavlovsky Barrow, about 350 BC. Leningrad, Hermitage Museum. Height of bezel 2.3 cm.
Photo: Hermitage Museum.
C] Fibula, mid-fourth century BC. Louvre Museum, Bj. 833. Coche de la Ferté, pl. 22: 3. Length 8 cm.
Photo: Archives Photographiques.
D] Finger ring with engraved bezel: male portrait, late fifth century BC. West Berlin, Staatliche Museen, no. FG287. Greifenhagen, *Schmuckarbeiten*, II, pl. 54: 11, 17. Height of bezel 1.7 cm.
Photo: Staatliche Museen (Isolde Luckert).
E] Silver fibula: North Greek type, from Budva, Yugoslavia, about fourth century BC. British Museum, 1939. 3–24. 1. Length 6.5 cm.
Photo: British Museum.
F] Finger ring with engraved bezel: seated woman, from Olbia, about 400 BC. West Berlin, Staatliche Museen, no. 31323. Greifenhagen, *Schmuckarbeiten*, II, pl. 54: 7, 13. Height of bezel, 1.7 cm.
Photo: Staatliche Museen (Jutta Tietz-Glagow).

32 Etruscan jewellery.
A] Earstud, inlaid with glass, sixth century BC. British Museum. *BMCJ*, no. 1419. Diameter 6.8 cm.
Photo: British Museum.
B] Earstud, sixth century BC. Munich, Antikensammlungen, no. 2477. Diameter 6 cm.
Photo: Antikensammlungen.

C] Earring, *a baule* type. New York, Metropolitan Museum, Rogers Fund 1959, no. 59. 11. 21. Height 3.4 cm.
Photo: Metropolitan Museum.
D] Hair spiral, seventh century BC. Hamburg, Museum für Kunst und Gewerbe, no. 1960. 92; cat. no. 104. Diameter 2.1 cm.
Photo: Museum für Kunst and Gewerbe.
E] Earring with notched disc from Vulci, seventh century BC. British Museum. *BMCJ*, no. 1310. Diameter 3.8 cm.
F] Clothing ornament, from Caere, seventh century BC. British Museum. *BMCJ*, no. 1265. Diameter 4.1 cm.
Photo: British Museum.

33 Etruscan jewellery.
A] Necklace, seventh century BC. British Museum. *BMCJ*, no. 1453. Length 17.7 cm.
Photo: British Museum.
B] Necklace from Vulci, seventh century BC. Munich, Antiken-sammlungen, no. 2339. Diameter of disc 2.6 cm.
Photo: Antikensammlungen.

34 Etruscan necklace from the Maremma, about 500 BC. British Museum. *BMCJ*, no. 1461. Length 27.6 cm.
Photo: British Museum.

35 Etruscan jewellery.
A] Finger ring, late seventh or sixth century BC. British Museum. *BMCR*, no. 210. External diameter 2.3 cm.
Photo: British Museum.
B] Necklace from Atri (Abruzzi), late sixth century BC. British Museum. *BMCJ*, no. 1460. Diameter of bullae 2 cm.
Photo: British Museum.

36 Pair of Etruscan bracelets (front and back view) from Tarquinii, seventh century BC. British Museum. *BMCJ*, nos 1358–9. Length 16.5 cm.
Photo: British Museum.

37 A] Etruscan bracelet from Praeneste, seventh century BC. British Museum. *BMCJ*, no. 1356. Length (exclusive of heads and clasps) 18.5 cm.
Photo: British Museum.
B] Etruscan bracelet, seventh century BC. Louvre Museum, Bj. 985. Coche de la Ferté, pl. 29: 1 and 2. Length 25 cm.
Photo: Archives Photographiques.

38 A] Etruscan fibula, serpentine type, from Vulci, seventh century BC. British Museum. *BMCJ*, no. 1376. Length 18.6 cm.
Photo: British Museum.

B] Etruscan fibula, leech type, seventh century BC. New York, Metropolitan Museum, Fletcher Fund 1931, no. 31. 11. 1. Length 6 cm.
Photo: Metropolitan Museum.

39 A] Etruscan bolt fibula from Caere, seventh century BC. British Museum. *BMCJ*, no. 1371. Length 9.1 cm.
Photo: British Museum.
B] Etruscan comb fibula, seventh century BC. British Museum. *BMCJ*, no. 1372. Length of tube 12.4 cm.
Photo : British Museum.

40 Etruscan fibula from Caere, Regolini-Galassi Tomb, seventh century BC. Rome, Vatican Museum. Length 31.5 cm.
Photo: Vatican Museum.

41 Etruscan jewellery.
A] Myrtle wreath, about fourth century BC. British Museum. *BMCJ*, no. 2292. Length 27.9 cm.
Photo: British Museum.
B] Wreath from Tarquinii, fourth–third century BC. British Museum. *BMCJ*, no. 2296. Length 31.7 cm.
Photo: British Museum.

42 Etruscan jewellery.
A] Earring from Chiusi, fourth–third century BC. British Museum. *BMCJ*, no. 2264. Height 7.1 cm.
Photo: British Museum.
B] Bulla: Thetis and Peleus, fourth–third century BC. Paris, Louvre Museum, Bj 745. Height 7.6 cm.
Photo: Louvre Museum.
C] Earring from Perugia, fourth–third century BC. British Museum. *BMCJ*, no. 2262. Height 10.7 cm.
Photo: British Museum.
D] Earring, fourth–third century BC. British Museum. *BMCJ*, no. 2256. Height 14.2 cm.
Photo: British Museum.

43 Etruscan jewellery. British Museum.
Photos: British Museum.
A] Earring, fifth century BC. *BMCJ*, no. 2244. Height 2.2 cm.
B] Earring, sixth or fifth century BC. *BMCJ*, no. 2200. Diameter 2.4 cm.
C] Earring, fifth century BC. *BMCJ*, no. 2206. Diameter 1.8 cm.
D] Earring from Populonia, fourth–third century BC. *BMCJ*, no. 2230. Diameter 4.6 cm.

E] Finger ring from Bologna, fourth–third century BC. 1956. 7–18. 1. External diameter 2.5 cm.

F] Finger ring from Populonia, fourth–third century BC. *BMCR*, no. 705. Length 3.2 cm.

G] Finger ring from Tarquinii, fourth–third century BC. *BMCR*, no. 355. External diameter 3.6 cm.

44 Part of an Etruscan necklace of bullae from Tarquinii, fourth century BC. British Museum. *BMCJ*, no. 2271. Diameter of circular bullae 3.5 cm.
Photo: British Museum.

45 A] Diadem with garnet and enamel from Melos, third or second century BC. British Museum. *BMCJ*, no. 1607. Height of centre-piece 1.6 cm.
Photo: British Museum.

B] Wreath diadem with enamel and coloured glass from Canosa, 'Tomb of the Gold Ornaments', third century BC. Taranto, Museo Nazionale. Becatti, no. 353. Length 45 cm.
Photo: Hirmer Fotoarchiv.

C] Diadem from Madytus, late fourth century BC. New York, Metropolitan Museum, Rogers Fund 1906, no. 06. 1217. 1. Length 36.8 cm
Photo: Metropolitan Museum.

46 Diadem from Thesaly, about second century BC. Athens, Benaki Museum. Segall, no. 28. Total length 51 cm; height of knot 4.5 cm.
Photo: Benaki Museum.

47 Hellenistic earrings. British Museum.
Photos: British Museum.

A] Disc and pendant: Victory, from Kephallenia, about third century BC. *BMCJ*, no. 1848. Height 4.1 cm.

B] Disc and pendant: Eros, from Kyme in Aeolis, late fourth century BC. *BMCJ*, no. 1890. Height 4.2 cm.

C] Disc and pendant: enamelled female head, about third century BC. *BMCJ*, no. 1855. Height 5.3 cm.

D] Hoop inlaid with garnets: goat's head, about third century BC. *BMCJ*, no. 1803. Diameter about 2.7 cm.

E] Hoop threaded with onyx: dolphin's head, first century BC–AD. *BMCJ*, no. 2426. Length 3.1 cm.

F] Hoop: lion's head, 330–200 BC. *BMCJ*, no. 1762. Diameter 2 cm.

G] Pendant: siren, from Leukas, about 300 BC. 1920. 5–29. 4. Total height 4.5 cm.

H] Hoop: female head, about third century B C. *BMCJ*, no. 1706. Diameter 2.2 cm.

I] Hoop inlaid with garnet: Eros, from Damascus. About second century B C. *BMCJ*, no. 2327. Diameter 2.7 cm.

J] Hoop, negress head, in garnet, from Kyme in Aeolis, late fourth century B C, or later. *BMCJ*, no. 1709. Height 1.8 cm.

K] Hoop: bull's head, about third century B C. *BMCJ*, no. 2435. Diameter 2.3 cm.

48 Hellenistic earrings.

A] Pendant: ganymede and eagle, from near Salonika, late fourth century B C. New York, Metropolitan Museum, Harris Brisbane Dick Fund 1937, no. 37. 11. 9. Height 5.5 cm.
Photo: Metropolitan Museum.

B] Pendant: enamelled dove, from Artjukhov's Barrow, Taman, second century B C. Leningrad, Hermitage Museum. Height 6.5 cm.
Photo: Hermitage Museum.

C] Pendant: amphora, from Kalymnos, second or first century B C. British Museum. *BMCJ*, no. 2328. Height 6.2 cm.
Photo: British Museum.

D] Elaborate pendants from Kalymnos, late fourth century B C. West Berlin, Staatliche Museen, Misc. 10823b. Greifenhagen, *Schmuckarbeiten*, II, pl. 40: 4. Height 5.7 cm.
Photo: Staatliche Museen (Isolde Luckert).

E] Double bezel setting and pendant Eros from Palaiokastro. Second–first century B C. Hamburg, Museum für Kunst und Gewerbe, no. 1918. 58; cat. no. 25. Height 7.9 cm.
Photo: Museum fur Kunst and Gewerbe.

49 A] Necklace with crescent-shaped pendant from near Damascus, about second century B C. British Museum. *BMCJ*, no. 2718. Length of crescent 3.3 cm.
Photo: British Museum.

B] Necklace from Melos, 330–200 B C. British Museum. *BMCJ*, no. 1947. Length 33.6 cm.
Photo: British Museum.

50 A] Necklace with garnets, etc. from Artjukhov's Barrow, Taman, second century B C. Leningrad, Hermitage Museum. Length about 30 cm.
Photo: Hermitage Museum.

B] Bracelet with garnets, green glass and enamel from western Syria, second century B C. Oriental Institute, Chicago, no. A 29788. Length 6.8 cm.
Photo: Oriental Institute, University of Chicago.

51 A] Gold and crystal bracelet from near Salonika, late fourth century

BC. New York, Metropolitan Museum, Harris Brisbane Dick Fund 1937, no. 37. 11. 11. Height 7.7 cm.
Photo: Metropolitan Museum.

B] Spiral bracelet: tritoness, second century BC. New York, Metropolitan Museum, Rogers Fund 1956, no. 56. 11. 6. Height 16 cm.
Photo: Metropolitan Museum.

C] Spiral bracelet: snake, from western Syria, second century BC. Oriental Institute, Chicago, no. A 29786. Height 14 cm.
Photo: Oriental Institute, University of Chicago.

52 A] Medallion: breast ornament, from Thessaly, second century BC. The Art Museum, Princeton University, no. 38. 49. Diameter 7.9 cm.
Photo: Art Museum, Princeton University.

B] Medallion: hair ornament, from Karpenisi (?), second century BC. Athens, Benaki Museum, no. 105. 42; cat. no. 36. Diameter 11.1 cm.
Photo: Benaki Museum.

53 A] Finger ring: garnet bezel, from Crete, third century BC. British Museum. *BMCR*, no. 714. Maximum width of bezel 3 cm.

B] Finger ring with garnet and amethyst, first century BC. British Museum. *BMCR*, no. 843. Maximum width 3.5 cm.

C] Finger ring: glass bezel, third century BC. British Museum. *BMCR*, no. 725. External diameter 2.3 cm.
Photo: British Museum.

D] Finger ring: enamelled bezel, from Artjukhov's Barrow, Taman, second century BC. Leningrad, Hermitage Museum. External diameter 2 cm.
Photo: Hermitage Museum.

E] Finger ring from Athribis, Lower Egypt, third century BC. British Museum. *BMCR*, no. 958. External diameter 2.4 cm.

F] Pin with garnets and enamel from Artjukhov's Barrow, Taman, second century BC. Leningrad, Hermitage Museum. Length of pin 8 cm; length of pendant 7.5 cm.
Photo: Hermitage Museum.

G] Pin from Syria, about second century BC. British Museum. *BMCJ*, no. 3034. Maximum width 1.1 cm; total height 13.6 cm.

54 A] Earring: hoop and pendant, from Tortosa, Syria, about second century AD. British Museum. *BMCJ*, no. 2422. Height 3.5 cm.
Photo: British Museum.

B] Earring: bar and pendants, from the Hauran, Syria, third century AD. Hamburg, Museum für Kunst und Gewerbe, no. 1966. 29; cat. no. 91. Height 3.2 cm.
Photo: Museum für Kunst und Gewerbe.

PREFACE TO THE SECOND EDITION

In this edition, because of the vast increase in our knowledge in certain areas, Chapters 8–12 have had to be completely rewritten and re-arranged (with the incorporation of an extra chapter), while the others have all been brought up to date as necessary.

A criticism of the first edition was that too many illustrations were drawn from the same source, i.e. the British Museum. I have in consequence spread my net much wider in this edition, and have drawn on many European and American museums.

I have also tried to make this edition acceptable to a wider public by a simplification of language, by the avoidance of archaeological jargon (LMIA, EG, etc.), and by the translation or transliteration of Greek words.

Certain Greek and Bulgarian place-names will be found to be spelt slightly differently, in accordance with changing practice. But consistency has been no more attainable in this edition than in the first. Familiarity and euphony have been my guidelines.

ACKNOWLEDGEMENTS

The acknowledgements expressed in the first edition are, of course, valid for those parts of it – and they are many – which have survived into this edition.

To consolidate my obligations. For help and advice of all kinds, for making material available for study, for assistance with photographs, and for sending me offprints, I am very grateful to: D. M. Bailey, R. D. Barnett, J. Boardman, D. L. Carroll, R. A. G. Carson, H. W. Catling, J. Charlton, E. Coche de la Ferté, J. N. Coldstream, P. E. Corbett, P. Demargne, J. Dörig, A. R. Emerson, X. Gorbounova, D. E. L. Haynes, F. W. von Hase, H. Hoffmann, M. S. F. Hood, the late R. W. Hutchinson, G. K. Jenkins, the late C. Karousos, A. Lembessi, L. Marangou, H. Maryon, W. A. Oddy, R. M. Organ, B. Philippaki, N. Platon, M. R. Popham, L. H. Sackett, T. A. Sakellarakis, A. X. Sakellariou, O. Sargnon, the late D. E. Strong, the late A. Voschinnina, D. M. Wilson.

The British Academy very generously gave me a grant to go to Greece to study material in Greek museums for the second edition.

I am grateful to heads of institutions for supplying photographs and giving permission to publish them. Acknowledgements are made individually in the List of Plates.

Of the text figures, no. 13:3, 5–10, 13, 15–17, 19, 22, 23, 25–7 and 30–4 are by Paddy Deans; nos 15 and 16 by Carey Miller; and the remainder by Peter Toseland.

J. H. W. Axtell and D. W. Akehurst worked out the arrangement of a multiple loop-in-loop chain and made the models on which Fig. 3 is based.

Janice Price, Anna Fedden and Mary Cusack of Methuen deserve my heartfelt thanks for their hard work and patience.

Finally, without the constant help and encouragement of my wife, this book would never have been finished.

ABBREVIATIONS

AA : Archäologischer Anzeiger. Supplement to *JdI*.

AAA : Athens Annals of Archaeology.

ABC : Antiquités du Bosphore Cimmerien, Imperial Archaeological Commission (St Petersburg, 1854). The plates reprinted in S. Reinach's French edition of 1892. Plate refs apply to either edition; text refs only to the 1892 edition.

Aberg, *Chronologie :* N. Aberg, *Bronzezeitliche und früheisenzeitliche Chronologie,* III and IV (Stockholm, 1932, 1933).

AD : Antike Denkmäler.

A. Delt. : Archaiologikon Deltion.

AdI : Annali dell'Instituto di Correspondenza Archeologica.

AE : Archaiologike Ephemeris.

Aegean and Near East : S. S. Weinberg (ed.), *The Aegean and the Near East : Studies Presented to Hetty Goldman* (New York, 1956).

AJ : Antiquaries' Journal.

AJA : American Journal of Archaeology.

Aldred, *Jewels of the Pharaohs :* C. Aldred, *Jewels of the Pharaohs* (London, 1971).

Alexander, *Jewellery :* C. Alexander, *Jewellery : The Art of the Goldsmith in Classical Times* (New York, 1928).

AM : Mitteilungen des deutschen archäologischen Instituts, Athenische Abteilung.

Andronikos, *Vergina :* M. Andronikos, *Vergina,* I (Athens, 1969).

Ann. : Annuario d. R. Scuola Archeologica di Atene.

Ant. class. : L'Antiquité Classique.

Arch. Rep. : Archaeological Reports. Supplement to *JHS*. From 1955.

Artamonov, *Treasures:* M. I. Artamonov, *Treasures from Scythian Tombs* (London, 1969).

Asine: O. Frödin and A. W. Persson, *Asine: Results of the Swedish Excavations 1922–1930* (Stockholm, 1938).

AZ: Archäologische Zeitung.

Barnett, *Nimrud Ivories:* R. D. Barnett, *Catalogue of the Nimrud Ivories . . . in the British Museum* (London, 1957).

BCH: Bulletin de Correspondance Hellénique.

Becatti: G. Becatti, *Oreficerie Antiche dalle Minoiche alle Barbariche* (Rome, 1955).

Beck, *Beads and Pendants:* H. C. Beck, *Classification and Nomenclature of Beads and Pendants* (Oxford, 1928).

Blegen, *Prosymna:* C. W. Blegen, *Prosymna*, I (text) and II (plates) (Cambridge, 1937).

Blegen, *Zygouries:* C. W. Blegen, *Zygouries* (Cambridge, Mass., 1928).

Blümner, *Technologie:* H. Blümner, *Technologie und Terminologie der Gewerbe und Künste bei Griechen und Römern*, III, IV (Leipzig, 1884, 1887).

BMC: British Museum Catalogue.

BMCJ: F. H. Marshall, *Catalogue of the Jewellery, Greek, Etruscan and Roman, in the Departments of Antiquities, British Museum* (London, 1911).

BMCR: F. H. Marshall, *Catalogue of the Finger Rings, Greek, Etruscan and Roman, in the Departments of Antiquities, British Museum* (London, 1907).

B. Met. Mus. : Bulletin of the Metropolitan Museum of Art, New York.

Boardman, *Cretan Collection:* J. Boardman, *The Cretan Collection in Oxford: The Dictaean Cave and Iron Age Crete* (Oxford, 1961).

Boardman, *GGFR:* J. Boardman, *Greek Gems and Finger Rings* (London, 1970).

Boston Bull. : Bulletin of the Museum of Fine Arts, Boston.

Brailsford, *Antiqs of Roman Britain:* J. W. Brailsford, *Guide to the Antiquities of Roman Britain* (London, 1951).

Breglia: L. Breglia, *Le Oreficerie del Museo Nazionale di Napoli* (Rome, 1941).

Brock, *Fortetsa:* J. K. Brock, *Fortetsa: Early Greek Tombs Near Knossos* (Cambridge, 1957).

BSA: Annual of the British School at Athens.

Buchholz and Karageorghis: H. G. Buchholz and V. Karageorghis, *Prehistoric Greece and Cyprus* (London, 1973).

Cesnola, *Salaminia:* A. P. di Cesnola, *Salaminia, Cyprus* (London, 1882).

Cl. Rh. : *Clara Rhodos : Studi e Materiali pubblicatti a cura dell' Istituto Storico-Archeologico di Rodi.*

CMS : *Corpus der minoischen und mykenischen Siegel* (Berlin, 1964 onwards).

Coche de la Ferté: E. Coche de la Ferte, *Les bijoux antiques* (Paris, 1956).

Coldstream, *GG* : J. N. Coldstream, *Geometric Greece* (London, 1977).

Collection Stathatos, I: P. Amandry, *Collection Hélène Stathatos : Les Bijoux antiques* (Strasbourg, 1953).

Collection Stathatos, III: P. Amandry, *Collection Hélène Stathatos*, III. *Objets antiques et byzantins* (Strasbourg, 1963).

Collection Stathatos, IV: O. Picard and J. P. Sodini, *Collection Hélène Stathatos*, IV. *Bijoux et petits objets* (Athens, 1971).

Corinth, XII: G. R. Davidson, *Corinth*, XII. *The Minor Objects* (Princeton, NJ, 1952).

CR : *Comptes rendus de la Commission Impériale Archéologique.*

DA : Daremberg and Saglio, *Dictionnaire des antiquités.*

Dawkins, *Artemis Orthia* : R. M. Dawkins (ed.), *The Sanctuary of Artemis Orthia at Sparta* (London, 1929).

Délos, XVIII: W. Déonna, *Exploration archéologique de Délos*, XVIII. *Le Mobilier délien.*

Desborough, *GDA*: V. R. d'A. Desborough, *The Greek Dark Ages* (London, 1972).

Desborough, PGP: V. R. d'A. Desborough, *Protogeometric Pottery* (Oxford, 1952).

Dohan, *Italic Tomb Groups* : E. H. Dohan, *Italic Tomb Groups* (Philadelphia and Oxford, 1942).

Ebert, *Reallexikon* : M. Ebert, *Reallexikon der Vorgeschichte* (Berlin).

Edgar, *Gr. Eg. Coffins* : C. C. Edgar, *Graeco-Egyptian Coffins, Masks and Portraits* (Cairo, 1905).

Ergon : *To ergon tes Archaiologikes Hetaireias.*

Evans, *Palace* : A. Evans, *The Palace of Minos at Knossos*, I–IV (London, 1921–35).

Evans, *PTK* : A. J. Evans, 'Prehistoric Tombs of Knossos', *Archaeologia*, LIX (1906).

Evans, *TDA* : A. J. Evans, 'The Tomb of the Double Axes, etc.', *Archaeologia*, LXV (1914).

Excav. in Cyprus : A. A. Murray and others, *Excavations in Cyprus* (London, 1900).

Fasti : *Fasti Archaeologici.*

Fontenay: E. Fontenay, *Les Bijoux anciens et modernes* (Paris, 1887).
Forbes, *Metallurgy :* A. J. Forbes, *Metallurgy in Antiquity* (Leyden, 1950).
Frankfort: H. Frankfort, *The Art and Architecture of the Ancient Orient* (Harmondsworth, 1954).
Furumark: A. Furumark, *Myceanaean Pottery : Analysis and Classification* (Stockholm, 1941).

Greifenhagen, *Schmuckarbeiten :* A. Greifenhagen, *Schmuckarbeiten in Edelmetall,* I (*Fundgruppen*), II (*Einzelstücke*) (Berlin, 1970, 1975).

Hadaczek: K. Hadaczek, *Der Ohrschmuck der Griechen und Etrusker* (Vienna, 1903).
Hall, *Sphoungaras :* E. H. Hall, *Excavations in Eastern Crete : Sphoungaras* (Philadelphia, 1912).
Hall, *Vrokastro :* E. H. Hall, *Excavations in Eastern Crete : Vrokastro* (Philadelphia, 1914).
History of Technology : C. Singer and others, *History of Technology,* I and II (Oxford, 954, 1958).
Hoddinott, *Bulgaria in Antiquity :* R. F. Hoddinott, *Bulgaria in Antiquity* (London, 1975).
Hoffman and Davidson, *Greek Gold :* H. Hoffmann and P. Davidson, *Greek Gold* (Mainz, 1965).
Hogarth, *Ephesus :* D. G. Hogarth, *Excavations at Ephesus* (London 1908).
Hood, *APG :* S. Hood, *The Arts in Prehistoric Greece* (Harmondsworth, 1978).

ILN : *Illustrated London News.*
Ippel, *Galjub :* A. Ippel, *Dr Bronzefund von Galjub* (Berlin, 1922).

Jacobsthal, *Pins :* P. Jacobsthal, *Greek Pins* (Oxford, 1956).
JdI : Jahrbuch des deutschen archäologischen Instituts.
JEA : Journal of Egyptian Archaeology.
Jewellery Through 7000 Years : H. Tait (ed.), *Jewellery Through 7000 Years* (London, 1976).
JHS : Journal of Hellenic Studies.
JRGZM : Jahrbuch des Römisch-Germanischen Zentralmuseums, Mainz.
JRS : Journal of Roman Studies.

Karo, *Schachtgräber :* G. Karo, *Die Schachtgräber von Mykenai* (Berlin, 1930).

Kerameikos: K. Kübler and others, *Kerameikos: Ergebnisse der Ausgrabungen*, I, IV, V (1) (Berlin, 1939, 1943, 1954).
Kr. Chr. : Kretika Chronika.
Kythera: J. N. Coldstream and J. L. Huxley, *Kythera* (London, 1972).

Laffineur: R. Laffineur, *L'Orfévrerie rhodienne orientalisante* (Paris, 1978).
Lefkandi, I: M. R. Popham and L. H. Sackett (eds), *Lefkandi,* I. *The Iron Age* (London, 1979). British School at Athens, Supplementary Volume, no. 11.
Lindos: C. Blinkenberg, *Lindos: Fouilles de l'Acropole 1902–14,* I. *Les Petits Objets* (Berlin, 1931).
Lucas, *Materials and Industries:* A. Lucas, *Egyptian Materials and Industries,* 4th ed., revised by J. R. Harris (London, 1962).
von Luschan, *Sendschirli,* V: F. von Luschan and N. Andrae, *Ausgrabungen in Sendschirli,* V (Berlin, 1943).

MA : Monumenti Antichi pubblicati per cura della Reale Accademia de Lincei.
MAAR : Memoirs of the American Academy in Rome.
McIver, *Villanovans:* D. Randall-McIver, *Villanovans and Early Etruscans* (Oxford, 1924).
Marinatos and Hirmer: S. Marinatos and M. Hirmer, *Crete and Mycenae* (London, 1960).
Maxwell-Hyslop, *Western Asiatic Jewellery:* K. R. Maxwell-Hyslop, *Western Asiatic Jewellery* (London, 1971).
MEFRA : Mélanges de l'École française de Rome : Antiquité.
Michel, *Recueil :* G. Michel, *Recueil d' inscriptions grecques* (Paris, 1900).
Minns: E. H. Minns, *Scythians and Greeks* (Cambridge, 1913).
Minto, *Populonia :* A. Minto, *Populonia* (Florence, 1943).
MMS : Metropolitan Museum Studies.
Mon. Piot : Fondation Piot : Monuments et mémoires.
Montelius, *Civ. Prim. It. :* O. Montelius, *La Civilisation primitive en Italie,* I and II (Stockholm, 1895, 1904).
Mylonas, *Taphikos kyklos B :* G. E. Mylonas, *Ho taphikos kyklos B ton Mykenon* (Athens, 1973).
Mylonas, *To dytikon nekrotapheion :* G. E. Mylonas, *To dytikon nekrotapheion tis Eleusinos* (Athens, 1975).

Naukratis, I and II: W. M. F. Petrie, *Naukratis,* Part I (London, 1886). E. A. Gardner, *Naukratis,* Part II (London, 1888).
NS : Notizie degli scavi di antichità communicate alla Reale Accademia dei Lincei.

Ohly: D. Ohly, *Griechische Goldbleche des 8. Jahrhunderts v. Chr.* (Berlin, 1953).

Ohnefalsch-Richter, *Kypros:* M. Ohnefalsch-Richter, *Kypros, the Bible and Homer* (London, 1893).

ÖJH : Österreichische Jahreshefte.

PAE : Praktika tes Archaiologikes Hetaireias.

Palace of Nestor, I, III: C. Blegen and others, *The Palace of Nestor at Pylos in Western Messenia*, I and III (Princeton, NJ, 1966, 1973).

Papavasileiou: G. A. Papavasileiou, *Peri ton en Euboia archaion Taphon* (Athens, 1910).

Pendlebury: J. Pendlebury, *The Archaeology of Crete* (London, 1939).

Perachora, I, II: H. G. G. Payne and others, *Perachora : The Sanctuaries of Hera Akraia and Limenia* I, II (Oxford, 1940, 1961).

Persson, *New Tombs:* A. Persson, *New Tombs at Dendra near Midea* (Lund 1943).

Persson, *Royal Tombs :* A. Persson, *Royal Tombs at Dendra near Midea* (Lund, 1931).

Pfeiler: B. Pfeiler, *Römischer Goldschmuck des ersten und zweiten Jahrhunderts n. Chr. nach datierten Funden* (Mainz, 1970).

Pierides, *Jewellery in Cyprus Mus. :* A. Pierides, *Jewellery in the Cyprus Museum* (Nicosia, 1971).

Pollak, *Samml. Nelidow:* L. Pollak, *Klassisch-Antike Goldschmied-arbeiten im Besitze des Herren von Nelidow in Rom* (Leipzig, 1903).

RA : Revue Archéologique.

R. D. Ant. Cypr. : Report of the Department of Antiquities, Cyprus.

Reichel: W. Reichel, *Griechisches Goldrelief* (Berlin, 1942).

Renfrew, *Emergence:* C. Renfrew, *The Emergence of Civilisation: The Cyclades and the Aegean in the Third Millennium* BC (London 1972).

Richter, *Etruscan Coll. :* G. M. A. Richter, *The Metropolitan Museum of Art : Handbook of the Etruscan Collection* (New York, 1940).

Richter, *Met. Mus. Gk. Coll. :* G. M. A. Richter, *A Handbook of the Greek Collection : Metropolitan Museum of Art* (Harvard, 1953).

Roman Crafts : D. Strong and D. Brown (eds), *Roman Crafts* (London, 1976).

Rosenberg, *Granulation :* M. Rosenberg, *Geschichte der Goldschmiede-kunst auf technischer Grundlage : Granulation* (Frankfurt, 1915).

Rosenberg, *Zellenschmelz :* M. Rosenberg, *Geschichte, etc. : Zellen-schmelz* (Frankfurt, 1921–2).

Rostovtzeff, *Iranians :* M. I. Rostovtzeff, *Iranians and Greeks in South Russia* (Oxford, 1922).

Rostovtzeff, *SEHHW* : M. I. Rostovtzeff, *Social and Economic History of the Hellenistic World* (Oxford, 1941).

Rostovtzeff, *Sk. u. B.* : M. I. Rostovtzeff, *Skythien und der Bosporus* (Berlin, 1931).

SCE : E. Gjerstad and others, *The Swedish Cyprus Expedition* (Stockholm, 1934 onwards).

Schäfer: H. Schäfer, *Königliche Museen zu Berlin : Mitteilungen aus der Aegyptischen Sammlung*, I (Berlin, 1910).

Schefold, *Meisterwerke :* K. Schefold, *Meisterwerke griechischer Kunst* (Basle and Stuttgart, 1960).

Schmidt: H. Schmidt, *Heinrich Schliemanns Sammlung Trojanischer Altertümer* (Berlin, 1902).

Schreiber: T. Schreiber, *Alexandrinische Toreutik* (Leipzig, 1894).

Seager, *Mochlos :* R. B. Seager, *Explorations in the Island of Mochlos* (Boston and New York, 1912).

Segall: B. Segall, *Museum Benaki : Katalog der Goldschmiede-Arbeiten* (Athens, 1938).

Shore, *Portrait Painting :* A. F. Shore, *Portrait Painting from Roman Egypt* (London, 1962).

Siviero: R. Siviero, *Gli Ori e le Ambre nel Mus. Naz. di Napoli* (Florence, 1954).

Stais: V. Stais, *Collection mycénienne du Musée National* (Athens, 1909).

St. e. Mat. : L. A. Milani (ed.), *Studi e Materiali di Archeologia e Numismatica* (Florence, 1899 onwards).

St. Etr. : *Studi Etruschi.*

Survey : M. S. F. Hood, *Archaeological Survey of the Knossos Area* (London, 1959).

Sutherland, *Gold :* C. H. V. Sutherland, *Gold : Its Beauty, Power and Allure* (London, 1959).

Tocra, I: J. Boardman and J. Hayes, *Excavations at Tocra 1963–1965*, I. *The Archaic Deposits*. British School at Athens, Supplementary Volume, no. 4.

Troy : C. W. Blegen and others, *Troy*, I-IV (Princeton, NJ, 1950–8).

Wace, *Chamber Tombs :* A. J. B. Wace, 'Chamber Tombs of Mycenae', *Archaeologia*, LXXXII (1932).

Wilkinson, *Ancient Egyptian Jewellery :* A. Wilkinson, *Ancient Egyptian Jewellery* (London, 1971).

Williams, *Gold and Silver Jewelry :* C. R. Williams, *New York Historical Society. Catalogue of Egyptian Antiquities : Gold and Silver Jewelry and Related Objects* (New York, 1924).

Woolley, *Ur Excavations*, II: C. L. Woolley, *Ur Excavations*, II (London and Philadelphia, 1939).

Xanthoudides: S. A. Xanthoudides, *Vaulted Tombs of Mesara* (London, 1924).

Zahn, *Ausstellung* : R. Zahn, *Führer durch die Ausstellung von Schmuckarbeiten aus der Staatlichen Museen* (Berlin, 1932).

NOTES ON THE TEXT

1. In the absence of any statement to the contrary, it may be assumed that any jewellery is of gold or electrum.

2. When reference is made to burials, the word *tomb* is regularly used to denote something built, or hollowed into a hillside; the word *grave* to denote something dug out of the ground. But consistency has not always been possible.

3. The rendering of Greek proper names is based on the system recommended in *JHS*, LXVII (1947), pp. xix f., and *BSA*, XLIV (1949), pp. 330 f., but consistency is often sacrificed to familiarity or euphony.

4. When a piece is said to be in London, the British Museum is meant. Similarly, for Paris, the Louvre is meant; for New York, the Metropolitan Museum; and when other towns are mentioned the principal relevant museum is meant.

5. The term Classical is used, for lack of a better, in two different senses. In some contexts it denotes the entire civilization of Greece and Rome at all periods; in others it is restricted to the Classical period in Greece *par excellence*, between *c.* 475 and 330 BC. There should, however, be no ambiguity in any individual instance.

6. Dates throughout Chapters 6–16, and elsewhere for all periods other than Roman, are BC, whether or not this is stated.

7. Where a bibliographical reference covers more than one page, in many cases only the first page is quoted.

8. Where no provenance is given, it is not recorded.

INTRODUCTION

Scope and plan

The scope of this survey is rather wider than its title, chosen for the sake of brevity, might suggest. It is, in fact, proposed to consider the jewellery of the Bronze Age in Greece, the Cyclades and Crete, of Iron Age Greece, of Etruria, and of the Roman Empire.

The first five chapters are concerned with descriptions of technical processes and their historical development. The next twelve chapters consist of an account of the jewellery itself, chiefly in chronological sequence. Although successive chapters purport to represent different 'periods', this division is principally a matter of convenience, for in practically no instance does the jewellery of a particular epoch cease abruptly, to be succeeded by a different kind. In ancient jewellery, as in most crafts, new ideas, however suddenly they might be introduced, tended at first to be grafted cautiously on to the existing stock, and only after a certain interval to be used to their fullest extent. Consequently, with a few exceptions, the story of ancient jewellery is one of gradual development rather than of a series of sudden innovations.

The final section of the book comprises a combined bibliography and site list. The primary object of this arrangement is to reduce the number of footnotes, which can be both distracting to the reader and wasteful of space. All important tomb groups and other deposits are included, with bibliographical references, in the site lists, which the reader may consult when any of these deposits are mentioned in the text.

I

Materials

Ancient jewellery was made chiefly of gold, silver and electrum (a natural alloy of gold and silver). This survey will therefore be concerned for the most part with the work of the goldsmith and silversmith; but not with all their work, for such categories as statuettes, plate and ornamental weapons are excluded by virtue of their functions. In another sense this study goes beyond the work of these craftsmen, since base metals, stones and other materials are also considered in so far as they were used in conjunction with precious metals or as substitutes for them.

Types of jewellery

Apart from Minoan Crete, when both sexes (it seems) were equally addicted to the practice, the wearing of jewellery was in Classical antiquity predominantly a feminine preserve. Ancient jewellery consisted of diadems and wreaths (also worn by men); hair ornaments; earrings; beads and pendants; finger rings (also worn by men); bracelets (worn both above and below the elbow); and attachments to clothing. Pins, fibulae, brooches and buttons are in general regarded as jewellery only when made of precious metals. Seal stones are considered chiefly in their capacity as beads, pendants or ring stones, the character of the engraving being outside the scope of a survey of this nature.

Surviving jewellery

In spite of its easily convertible nature, a surprisingly large amount of ancient jewellery of gold and electrum has survived. A certain amount of silver jewellery also exists, but silver is a perishable metal, and (contrary to appearances) may originally have been as popular as gold.

The chief reason for the quantity of the surviving material is the custom of burying with the dead some of their favourite possessions. Jewellery is, however, also occasionally found on habitation sites, especially if, like Pompeii, they have been involved in some sudden disaster. Votive deposits provide another source, but in the course of the ages have usually been stripped of any precious objects. In these several ways much ancient jewellery has escaped the melting-pot which would otherwise have been its fate.

The quantity of available material varies enormously for different periods. In some it is so plentiful that the account has had to be compressed. In others there is so little that every scrap of evidence has been used to the limit. The reasons for this unevenness are several: the actual amount of jewellery in use at a given period; the different burial customs at different times; and the accidents of survival and discovery.

Collections

One of the best collections for the study of ancient jewellery is in the British Museum. It is also one of the best catalogued.

The Louvre possesses another good all-round collection, its chief riches coming from the Campana Collection; it is catalogued, but not worthily. The Staatliche Museen in West Berlin also have a good collection, superbly catalogued in two volumes. Another good general collection is that of the Metropolitan Museum in New York. Part of it comes from the Cesnola Collection of objects from Cyprus. The Cesnola Collection is catalogued; the rest is not. The Museum für Kunst und Gewerbe at Hamburg has a small but choice collection, expertly catalogued. The Munich Antikensammlungen possess some splendid (uncatalogued) examples of Etruscan and Hellenistic jewellery.

Apart from general collections, there are museums of regional or national antiquities in Greece, Italy and elsewhere. The National Museum in Athens is extremely rich in Mycenaean jewellery, most of which has never been adequately published, but which is admirably displayed. The Stathatos Collection, now belonging to the National Museum, contains some superb pieces, and is excellently catalogued. The same is true of the Benaki Museum in Athens.

The Archaeological Museum at Heraklion in Crete contains the greater part of surviving Minoan jewellery. It is admirably displayed and most of the jewellery has been published in excavation reports.

In Italy, the Vatican Museum and Villa Giulia Museum in Rome and the Archaeological Museum in Florence contain much Etruscan and later jewellery. The National Museum at Naples contains Etruscan, Western Greek and Roman jewellery, admirably catalogued. The National Museum at Taranto is particularly strong in Western Greek jewellery. Countless provincial Italian museums contain material– Etruscan, Greek or Roman–from local sources.

The Cairo Museum has much Egyptian jewellery of Ptolemaic and Roman date. This collection is catalogued. Finally, the Hermitage Museum in Leningrad contains some of the finest of all Greek jewellery from South Russian sites, recently published in English.

Forgeries

In many ways forgeries are harder to recognize in goldwork than in any other class of antiquities, owing to the imperishable nature of gold, which shows virtually no signs of wear.

In general, however, it is only worth the forger's while to work on the grand scale, so that his profits may be commensurate with his efforts and the high cost of his material. Certain notorious forgeries of this class are the so-called Thisbe Gems in the Mycenaean style, and the works of Rouchomovsky in the Classical style, of which the so-called Tiara of Saitaphernes in Paris is the best known. Forged Hellenistic medallions, based on those in the Benaki and Stathatos Collections, and bracelets in the same style, are also worthy to be considered in this class. A number of very good forgeries have been identified in a recent American exhibition of Hellenistic jewellery. Other less ambitious efforts in the Classical Greek and Etruscan styles are also known.

By way of warning, it should be stated that more and better forgeries are coming on the market. Until 1933, ancient filigree and granulation could not be imitated at all convincingly, and the efforts in this direction, of which Castellani's are typical, are easily identified. Now, however, Littledale's process of colloid hard soldering is taught in the art schools, and what Littledale did in all honesty others are now doing with intent to deceive.

PART I
TECHNICAL

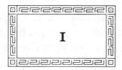

I

ANCIENT METALLURGY

Gold

Gold is the only metal of which appreciable quantities occur in usable metallic form. It is found as reef gold in veins or lodes of quartz, and as alluvial (or placer) gold in certain rivers, the latter being merely reef gold which has been washed and concentrated by the action of water. Both kinds were exploited in antiquity from an early period.

The extraction of the metal consists of separating it from the associated impurities, whether rock or alluvium. Reef gold was extracted in antiquity by hammering the rock and grinding it to powder. The powder was washed with a current of water, which carried off the lighter particles, leaving the gold to be collected on sponges. Alluvial gold was washed in much the same way. In the Caucasus, gold-bearing water was run over a layer of fleeces; the gold, being the heaviest element, sank to the bottom and was held by the grease in the wool. To this process the legend of the Golden Fleece owes its origin.

In its natural state, gold is seldom if ever pure, but is found alloyed with silver, copper and occasionally traces of iron. In earliest times it was used unrefined. When silver was present in appreciable quantities – Pliny says one part in five[1] – the alloy was regarded in antiquity as a different metal, known then as 'white gold' and today as electrum.

The precise date of the introduction of gold refining is not known, but it was evidently not a general practice before Classical times. Refining is a secondary process where gold is concerned, whereas silver refining is essential for the production of the metal and we may therefore conclude that the former process was adapted from the latter. For both

7

metals, it is known as cupellation. The Greek term for this process, *obryza*, is derived from the Hittite, and archaeology and etymology agree in suggesting that refining was first practised in Asia Minor. To separate the gold (and silver, if it is present) from the associated base metals, lead is added to the ore and the whole is melted together in a porous clay crucible (or *cupel*) over a charcoal fire. The lead and the other base metals are then oxidized by a current of air, which blows them off or drives them into the walls of the crucible, leaving a residue of fine gold or, if silver was also originally present, a mixture of gold and silver. Recent discoveries at Sardis in Asia Minor have established that gold refining by cupellation began there as early as 580 BC.

The removal of the silver was effected in two principal ways:

1. The salt process. Salt and some organic material, to act as a reducing agent, are heated in a crucible with the silver–gold alloy. The salt attacks the silver, which is absorbed by the crucible as silver chloride. By a combination of this method and cupellation–that is, by heating the ore with lead, salt and barley husks–Egyptian metallurgists removed base metals and silver at the same time.

2. The sulphur process. The alloy is heated with a sulphur compound such as stibnite (antimony sulphate) and charcoal. The silver is converted to silver sulphide, which floats on the surface as a scum, and is easily removed.

The Romans introduced two further processes. The first is liquation, which was employed as a preliminary to cupellation, and which consists of the separation of metals by fusion. In the second process, amalgamation, gold dust is dissolved in mercury, which is then evaporated, leaving a solid mass of gold.

The Amarna Letters from Egypt of the fourteenth century BC refer to the purity of gold and to its refining and assaying.[2] One of the most popular tests of purity was to rub the gold on a touchstone, and to compare the streak with that made by gold of a known purity.

The final stage in the preparation of gold is to melt it down and cast it in moulds of stone or clay into blocks, or ingots.

SOURCES

There is much uncertainty about the precise sources of gold at any particular period, but the following list includes areas that supplied the Classical world at one time or another.

Greece. There were many gold sources in Macedonia which may well have been exploited as early as the Bronze Age. Production was certainly in full swing under Philip II in the mid-fourth century BC. According to Herodotus the Phoenicians opened rich mines on Thasos about the eighth century BC. These mines have in all probability been identified, but have not been explored. The Thasians also exploited mines in their territory on the Thracian mainland. The Cyclades, which produced silver from an early date, were anciently quoted as sources of gold too. Herodotus refers to important gold mines on Siphnos which were flooded in the fifth century BC. Modern exploration has produced no more than small amounts in the alluvial sand, but Herodotus may yet be proved right. The island of Skyros has also, in modern times, been shown to possess small amounts of alluvial gold, which may have been exploited in antiquity.

The Balkans contained some of the principal sources of gold in Hellenistic and Roman times, especially in Transylvania (modern Romania) and Mount Pangaeum in Thrace. It may well be that the gold-hungry Mycenaeans also drew on these sources.

Noricum (now part of Austria) was one of the principal sources of Roman gold in the second century AD.

Italy. The Pennine Alps supplied Etruria and Republican Rome.

Spain. Spanish gold probably reached Etruria in the seventh and sixth centuries BC and the Western Greeks from the sixth century BC onwards, by way of the Phoenicians, who controlled the mines. Later, after the Second Punic War (which ended in 201 BC), Spanish gold began to flow into Rome and continued to do so in Imperial times.

Gaul and Britain helped to supply the needs of Rome under the late Republic and early Empire.

Syria. Alluvial gold is known to occur in the valley of the River Melas near Alexandretta (now Iskanderun, and part of Turkey). It may have been exploited as early as the Bronze Age. It is interesting to note that the Greek word for gold, *chrysos*, which occurs as early as the Minoan period, is of Semitic derivation.

Asia Minor had limited amounts of gold. The deposits south of the Caucasus supplied Greece in Mycenaean times (if we can believe the legend of the Argonauts), and may have supplied her later. A second gold-bearing area is the River Pactolus, the source of Lydian and later of Persian gold. This area was probably not exploited before the Iron Age and was exhausted by the end of the first century BC. A third source, in the Troad near Astyra, may have satisfied local needs from early times, but was virtually exhausted by the beginning of the Christian era.

Arabia and Bactria supplied the Hellenistic world and Rome under the late Republic and early Empire.

Siberia and the Altai were very rich in gold, which reached the Greek communities of South Russia through the agency of the Scythians.

Egypt was one of the principal sources of gold for the ancient world in the Bronze Age, and an important source thereafter. There were two main gold-producing areas: a plateau running along the west bank of the Nile for some 200 miles, its centre opposite Luxor; and an area in Nubia (now in north Sudan) by the third cataract of the Nile.

Silver

Silver may well have been used for jewellery to the same extent as gold, but, owing to its perishable nature, little has survived. Unlike gold, it seldom occurs in metallic form. The principal source of silver (and of lead) was galena ore. The method of extraction was apparently developed in Asia Minor in the third millennium BC and was gradually disseminated. The ore is crushed, washed and sieved. It is then partially desulphurized by roasting, and the product, litharge, is converted by reduction to a lead–silver alloy with many impurities, such as antimony, copper, tin and arsenic. Silver is obtained from this alloy by cupellation, a process already described in connection with gold. In Roman times, as with gold, cupellation was preceded by liquation. Small amounts of silver were also obtained as a by-product of the refining of gold. The final stage, as with gold, is to cast the metal into ingots.

SOURCES

The following list includes sources of silver for the Classical world.

Greece. There were silver mines in operation in Macedonia, Thrace and the Cyclades from an early date–some as early as the Bronze Age. Those at Laurium in Attica were worked from about the sixteenth century BC. In the early fifth century BC an extremely rich vein was discovered, which was worked intensively until near the end of the century. The mines were worked intermittently until about 100 BC. Thereafter, no attempt was made to reopen them until about the fifth century AD.

Sardinia was probably the principal source of Etruscan, and one of the sources of Roman, silver.

Spain. From the second century BC onwards, Spain was an important source of Roman silver.

Asia Minor, where twenty-six separate ancient deposits have been identified, was the principal source of silver for the ancient world at all times.

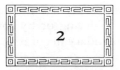

2

BASIC PROCESSES

The workshop

Our evidence for ancient workshops and workshop practice takes several forms: written sources; representations in paintings and sculptures of goldsmiths at work; surviving workshops and tools; and comparative technology. A fresco from Pompeii (Pl. IA) shows cupids at work in a goldsmith's shop of the first century AD.

From the second millennium BC the technical processes of the goldsmith and the silversmith remained basically unchanged throughout the long period with which we are concerned, and indeed far beyond it; and it may be assumed that the tools employed also changed but little, except that after the end of the Bronze Age iron to some extent supplanted stone and bronze.

The source of heat was an open charcoal fire with some means of making a forced draught to raise the temperature, such as a blowpipe or bellows. The work to be heated was held over the fire in bronze tongs.

The principal tools were an anvil of metal or stone; hammers for beating sheet metal and for driving punches and tracers of different shapes and sizes; stamps and cores; moulds for beating and for casting; chisels; engraving-tools of stone or iron; tongs; abrasives; burnishing-stones; scales; pottery crucibles. No files were used, no piercing-saws, no blowlamps, no proper draw-plates, no acid for 'pickling' and no lenses.

The ancient craftsman would receive his raw materials in the form of blocks or 'dumps' of gold, silver or electrum, from which he would fashion the basic elements of his craft: sheet metal, wire and (to a lesser extent) cast metal. Most pieces consist of a number of separately made parts, joined together by soldering or by some other means and frequently embellished by secondary decorative processes.

Sheet metal

Sheet metal is made by setting an ingot on an anvil and hammering it. Whenever the metal becomes hard and brittle, the craftsman anneals it by raising it to a red heat and quenching it in water. In this way the crystals, distorted by the hammering, rearrange themselves so that the metal is again soft and workable.

The metal worked in antiquity in repoussé and related methods is referred to in these pages as sheet metal. It is thin enough to be worked easily but stout enough to withstand ordinary wear and tear. Measured samples of sheet gold from Egypt varied in thickness between 0.17 mm and 0.54 mm.[1]

But gold can be hammered thinner still. Sheets about the thickness of paper (here referred to as gold foil) were used as plating on a base of other metals or glass (see p. 29). And infinitesimally thin gold (say, 0.005 mm), here referred to as gold leaf, was used for gilding (see p. 30).

REPOUSSÉ

Repoussé is a general term for ornamental work produced on sheet metal with a hammer and punches. Strictly, it should apply only to work embossed from the back, while work done from the front is known as chasing; but the term is now generally used to cover both processes and will be so used here.

To make a pattern, or a complete ornament, in relief, the goldsmith drives punches into a piece of metal which rests on a bed of yielding material. For very shallow relief, wood or lead is used; this is the simplest and cleanest method. For most purposes, however, a softer substance is required, which will be firm enough to support the work, but soft enough to give way under the blows of the hammer. Today a bowl of warm pitch is used, but (on the evidence of a find of the fourteenth century BC at Tel el-Amarna in Egypt) it appears that in antiquity a mixture of wax and clay was preferred. Work may be done on either side of the material; the simplest decorative processes consist of patterns of dots or lines produced either from the front or from the back. In a job of any complexity it will be necessary to work from both sides. In general, the outline of a figure is made from the front with a tracer (a punch shaped like a blunt chisel) and the embossing within the outline is done from the back with round-faced punches; finally, subsidiary detail is punched in from the front. Punches of both kinds have been found in a Hellenistic deposit at Galjub in Egypt of about the second century BC.

Repoussé is, as has been said, a process suitable for complete pieces of jewellery and also for subsidiary decoration. In fact it was seldom used in antiquity for either purpose. Instead, several rather more mechanical processes were employed: stamping, striking, working over a core, or working into a mould.

STAMPING

Stamping is a variant of repoussé much used in antiquity for making basic shapes and decorative detail. It has the advantage that patterns may be exactly repeated with a minimum of effort. In its simplest form it is closely related to repoussé, but the ends of the punches are shaped to the pattern which it is desired to reproduce, and they are driven in from the back. Fig. 1 shows a bronze punch for making amphora-shaped pendants of Hellenistic earrings. Mycenaean relief

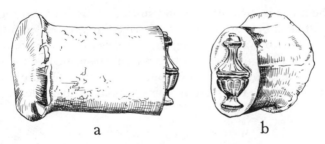

a   b

Fig. 1 Bronze stamp for making amphora-shaped pendants for earrings, second-first century BC.

beads were so made, as can be confirmed from the diadem (shown in Pl. 10 E) which was stamped by means of tools intended for making such relief beads.[2]

STRIKING

Striking is a similar process but the design is cut in intaglio and the punch is in consequence driven in from the front, as in striking a coin. This process was not employed as often as stamping but its use is occasionally attested.[3]

WORKING OVER A CORE

A Greek gold pendant of the sixth century B C from Olbia contains a wooden core, a phenomenon also observed in contemporary Scythian gold ornaments. These objects were evidently hammered or rubbed over a wooden core, which, if the object was in the round, could not subsequently be removed. The metal could also be worked over a core of bronze which was subsequently removed (Fig. 2). If an object of any depth was being made, the metal was probably roughly hammered to the required shape before being set on the core. For reliefs and similar objects, the process presented no difficulties, but objects in the round

Fig. 2 Bronze core for hammering ornaments of sheet gold, about second century B C.

had to be made in two sections and subsequently soldered together. A number of such bronze cores have survived in a hoard from Galjub in Egypt, dating from about the second century B C. Some are for reliefs, and some for parts of figures in the round. Bronze cores for very high reliefs were made in two sections, one for the main feature and one for the background, the two sections being subsequently soldered together.

WORKING INTO A MOULD

Another method of making repetitive shapes was by working a sheet of metal into a mould. The simplest kind of mould consists of a plain concavity, such as was used for making globular beads. A hemisphere is made by driving a piece of sheet metal into the hollow with a round-faced hammer or punch. It is pierced through the centre and is soldered to a similar hemisphere, similarly pierced. Melon beads are made in the same way, from ribbed hollows. But moulds were as a general rule more elaborate than this, and were capable of reproducing patterns and shapes of considerable complexity.

Where the gold was thin, it was perhaps possible to rub it into the mould with a burnishing-stone or a spatula; but sheet gold of the usual thickness must have been hammered or punched, the hammers or punches being made of some fairly soft material such as copper, wood or horn. It is also possible that a *force* was used. In this method, common today, the gold is placed over the mould, and over the gold is set a strip of lead, the *force*. The lead is then hammered into the mould, carrying the gold with it. The details are thus faithfully reproduced and the mould is protected from the direct blows of the hammer or the punch.

The surviving moulds for this process are chiefly of bronze. One of the finest is a four-sided mould from Corfu (illustrated in Pl. I B and C). Another bronze mould comes from Olympia. A stone mould, believed to be for this purpose, was found at Corinth. Moulds of reinforced terracotta, together with a copper hammer, were found at Olympia in 'Pheidias Workshop', and were evidently used for making the gold drapery of the chryselephantine cult statue. Wooden moulds are another possibilty; but if they existed they would almost certainly have perished, and there can in consequence be no certainty on this point.

SUBSEQUENT OPERATIONS

After the stamping or hammering of sheet gold, blemishes were removed and further detail frequently added in repoussé. It was found advantageous to outline figures in relief with a tracer, a process clearly discernible in Rhodian plaques of the seventh century. Occasionally, in the best of the Rhodian plaques, embossed figures were cut and soldered to a separate background, a technique which gave an even clearer outline.

Wire

Throughout most of antiquity wire was made by twisting a block of metal until it was more or less round in section and finally rolling it between plates of stone or bronze. It was also occasionally made by hammering a block of metal. A third method, related to the use of the medieval draw-plate, is believed to have been used occasionally in Hellenistic and Roman times. In this method a roughly shaped wire is pulled through holes of decreasing thickness in a plate of bronze or iron.

A fourth method, employed for making really thick wire, is to cast it.

Hollow wire, or tube, is made by hammering strips of sheet metal into grooves in a block of wood or metal; or the strip may be wrapped round a mandrel (a length of wire) and driven into a groove. When the tube is complete, the mandrel is withdrawn.

For ornamental work, wire was frequently given a more interesting form by twisting a single strand, by twisting two or more wires together, or by winding thin wires in a tight spiral to form a thicker wire.

Beaded wire was made, it is thought, by soldering together in a line a quantity of separate 'beads', and rolling the resulting wire between flat surfaces. When more pressure is applied, the beaded wire becomes spool wire.

Wire was used at various times for finger rings, hair rings, earrings, bracelets, pins and fibulae; to attach the various elements of composite ornaments; for filigree; and for chains and straps.

Chains played a very important part in ancient jewellery. They were used primarily as necklaces and for carrying pendants.

The simple chain was used at all periods and needs no description. It is composed of a series of links, made by inserting a section of wire in the previous link, bending it round, and soldering the ends together.

Such a chain is perfectly satisfactory from a structural point of view, but more decorative effects can be obtained from another kind, the so-called *loop-in-loop* or *square* or *upset* chain, a variety used in the Classical world from about 2500 BC onwards. Its first attested use here is in the Prepalatial jewellery of Mochlos. Further east, it is found in jewellery at Ur from about 3000 and its origins should probably be sought in that quarter.

In contrast with the simple chain, in which each link is made separately as the work progresses, the loop-in-loop variety is made from previously prepared links. It is found in varying degrees of complexity.

1. In the single form (Fig. 3a) the first link is compressed to an elliptical shape and folded in half. The next link is similarly compressed, threaded through the looped ends of the first, and in its turn folded in half. This process is continued until the chain is complete. Chains of this nature have a remarkably square section, which accounts for one of the names by which they are known. From a structural point of view, they may be said to have two principal faces and two sides.

2. A similar but more compact chain is made by threading each successive link through the looped ends of the two preceding. This may be called a double loop-in-loop chain (Fig. 3b).

3. What is frequently miscalled a cord is made by cross-linking a double loop-in-loop chain so that, instead of two, it has four, six or even eight principal faces (Figs 3c and d). Such chains are always made from double rather than single loop-in-loop, to conceal the tangle of crossing wires in the interior. The characteristic herringbone pattern has led to the often-expressed belief that such chains are plaited. Apart from the fact that close inspection leaves no doubt of the method of manufacture, plaited chains (if such existed) would completely lack the flexibility which is a characteristic of these examples.

Straps, also frequently miscalled plaited or braided, are made from several lengths of loop-in-loop chain, interlinked side by side. Such straps could no doubt have been made as early as the corresponding

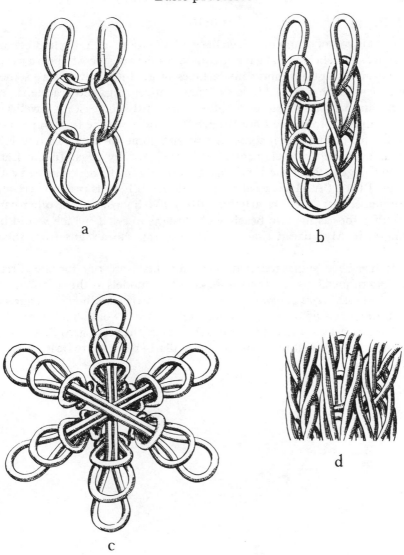

Fig. 3 Stages in the development of the loop-in-loop chain: (a) single; (b) doubled; (c) doubled sextuple, end view, in process of manufacture; (d) doubled sextuple, completed, side view. Drawn from models.

chains, but in fact are first seen in the Classical world in Rhodian jewellery of the seventh century BC (see p. 114). They were popular for necklaces in Etruscan, Hellenistic and Roman jewellery, and were occasionally used for Hellenistic diadems.

Casting

For motives of economy, jewellery was seldom cast from precious metals, since sheet metal gave adequate results at less cost. There were, however, exceptions, and some articles of gold and silver were sometimes cast, such as pins, fibulae, earrings, finger rings and bracelets.

A number of soft stone moulds, apparently for casting jewellery, have survived from the Late Bronze Age and from the Roman period. Some are in one piece, some in two and some in three. In multiple moulds the separate elements were connected by pegs. In the Late Bronze Age most of the surviving moulds are for finger rings and earrings (Pl. 1 E). A Mycenaean ring mould from Eleusis presents certain problems. Part of it is clearly for casting two hoops, but the other part is either for casting two bezels with designs in relief (which would be unique in Mycenaean rings) or for pressing the designs from sheet gold.

It has been suggested that these moulds were not for the direct casting of metal objects but for making wax models as the first stage of the 'lost wax' (*cire perdue*) process. Most experts are, however, agreed that direct casting of metal is more likely, since it would have been very difficult to get the wax to flow through some of the very narrow channels. Stones such as steatite are in fact particularly resistant to heat.

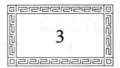

DECORATIVE PROCESSES

The decorative processes at the goldsmith's disposal fall under three general headings: they may involve the addition of the same metal, the addition of other substances, or the removal of metal.

In the first category are filigree, granulation, and the soldering on of minor ornaments; in the second, enamel, inlay and related processes; in the third, engraving, carving and piercing. For convenience a fourth process, by which objects of other materials are overlaid with gold or silver, is included in this chapter.

Filigree and granulation

Filigree and granulation are two closely related processes for decorating goldwork by the application respectively of wires and grains of gold. Silver can be treated in the same way, but in fact these techniques were virtually restricted in antiquity to gold and electrum.

FILIGREE

The commonest form of filigree consists of wires soldered in patterns on a background. The wires may be arranged singly, in twists or in plaits, and they may be plain or beaded. From the nature of the material the most popular patterns are circles, spirals and straight lines. Such patterns as could not easily be made freehand were probably made with jigs: blocks of wood studded with pins round which the wire is bent. In this way any pattern can be exactly repeated.

Usually the wires themselves created a satisfactory pattern, but sometimes the effect was heightened by the addition of enamel.

A rarer, and technically more difficult, variety of filigree consists of openwork patterns without a background. This variety was especially popular in Etruria in the seventh and sixth centuries BC (see Pl. 37 B).

GRANULATION

Although both processes arrived in Greece at about the same time, granulation probably originated later than filigree, from which it is apparently derived. Both depend on the same basic principles, but granulation demands a far higher standard of technical skill. It may be described as the making of patterns with minute grains of gold soldered to a background. In the Late Bronze Age the grains measured as little as 0.4 mm in diameter. In the finest Etruscan work even smaller grains were used; many measure 0.25 mm and some as little as 0.14 mm. A vast quantity of such grains would be needed to decorate a piece of jewellery. That illustrated in Pl. 19 E has been calculated to contain over 2600.

It is not known for certain how the grains were prepared in antiquity. Three separate methods, all perfectly possible, have been suggested:

1. Small pieces of gold of roughly equal size (filings or pieces cut from a wire or a sheet) are laid separately in a clay crucible on a bed of ash or powdered charcoal, and alternate layers of gold and charcoal are built up until the crucible is full. It is then brought to a bright red heat, which melts the gold into minute spheres, separated from each other by the charcoal. When the crucible has cooled the charcoal is washed away and the grains remain.

2. Molten gold is poured into water from a height of several feet.

3. Molten gold is poured into a container of charcoal.

It will probably be necessary to grade the grains for size by passing them through meshes of various gauges.

Simple patterns can be made by attaching the grains directly to the surface of the metal, but for most granulated work a transfer method, such as is used today, must have been necessary. The pattern is first engraved on a plate of stone or metal, and the grains are set in the engraved areas. A drum is made by sticking a sheet of paper over the end of a tube; in antiquity papyrus or leather would have served. The paper is covered with an adhesive and is lowered on to the engraved plate to pick up the grains, which are treated with the soldering mixture described below and placed on the surface to be decorated. The paper is now soaked off and the work is ready for soldering. An additional advantage of the transfer method is that the same pattern can be repeated as often as required.

Grains can be used with much greater freedom than filigree. They can be *massed* to cover an entire ornament or part of one. They can also be used to make simple linear patterns or geometrical shapes; such treatment may be called *decorative* granulation. Finally, granulation may be employed in three rather more elaborate ways: the *outline* style in which lines of grains are used as an adjunct to embossed forms; the *silhouette* style, in which figures are rendered with solid masses of grains; and the *reserved silhouette* style, a very rare technique in which the background is filled in with grains, while the main features are embossed but are otherwise left undecorated. The best example of this last technique is found not in a piece of jewellery but in a stand for a glass flask, in Paris.[1] The two latter processes invite comparison respectively with the black-figure and red-figure vase-painting styles. The resemblance may in fact be the result of conscious imitation by the goldsmith of the vase painter's methods.

COLLOID HARD SOLDERING

The art of granulation finally died out in Europe about AD 1000. In the nineteenth century attempts were made to revive it, but the difficulty always lay in the method of attaching the grains. Castellani tried, without success, to achieve the desired result by normal methods of soldering; but the solder always flooded and the flux boiled up and displaced the grains. In this century various fairly satisfactory methods of brazing and 'sweating' have been employed, and it is quite possible that they were used in antiquity: the former for the earliest and coarsest granulation, the latter for the superfine work of Greeks and Etruscans in the eighth and seventh centuries BC. But for granulation of medium quality, it became increasingly clear that the ancient craftsmen must have used an entirely different method.

In 1933 Littledale patented a process of hard soldering which he entitled *colloid hard soldering*.[2] Using this process (one well within the powers of an ancient craftsman), he succeeded in reproducing exactly some of the most complicated of the surviving pieces of ancient filigree and granulation.

Instead of using a prepared solder, he succeeded in making the solder in the joint. The process which he evolved is based on the fact that when copper is heated in contact with gold (or, for that matter, silver) the melting-point of the two metals is lower than that of either of the metals separately.

A copper salt—preferably copper carbonate—is ground up and mixed with an equal quantity of vegetable or fish glue. The mixture is diluted with water to the consistency of a thin paste; this forms a strong adhesive, which is used to attach the grains or wires. The work is then heated over a bed of hot charcoal. At 100°C the copper salt changes to copper oxide; at 600°C the glue turns to carbon; at 850°C the carbon absorbs the oxygen from the copper oxide and goes off as carbon dioxide, leaving a layer of pure copper between the parts to be joined; at 890°C the copper and the gold melt and the joint is made. The proportion of gold to copper in the joint varies according to the temperature to which the work is raised. Since the melting-point of fine gold is 1063°C, there is a generous range up to which it may be safely heated. The higher the temperature, the more the surrounding gold alloys itself with the copper and the less visible the joint. Since, moreover, ancient goldwork nearly always contains a certain amount of copper as a natural impurity, it is easy to understand how the nature of this form of soldering remained for so long undetected.

The process can be used equally well for silver, but the scarcity of surviving silver jewellery precludes any estimate of the popularity of filigree and granulation in that medium.

Since Littledale, our knowledge of the techniques of granulation has been carried forward by the work of Diane Lee Carroll and other scholar-craftsmen.

HISTORICAL

Filigree and granulation are first found in the Aegean world shortly after 2000 BC, when they occur on jewellery from Minoan tombs in the Mesara (see p. 57).

These techniques had a long tradition in Mesopotamia, Syria and Asia Minor. The Royal Tombs at Ur, of about 2500 BC, produced filigree work of an advanced kind and the crude beginnings of granulation.[3] In the Treasures of Troy II of about 2200 BC and in jewellery from Byblos of about 2000 is similar filigree and fully developed granulation.[4] We may therefore conclude that filigree existed in Western Asia by 2500, and that granulation reached its full development not long after. For geographical reasons, the direct source from which these processes reached Crete must have been either Asia Minor or Syria. That the ultimate source was Mesopotamia is suggested by the discovery at Knossos of a Babylonian cylinder seal with granulation, of a class dated 'before Hammurabi', who lived in the eighteenth or seventeenth century BC.[5] Surprisingly, these processes do not have an early history in Egypt, where granulation is not recorded before about 1900 BC.[6]

In the Bronze Age, granulation is found in Crete from about 1900 to 1100, and in Greece from about 1600 to 1100. It was never really common, but becomes comparatively plentiful in Greece in the fifteenth century.

Filigree, after its first appearance about 2000 BC, is found again in Crete in the seventeenth century, and perhaps lasts into the sixteenth; but after that it appears scarcely to have been used in Minoan or Mycenaean goldwork until the final phase, about 1200–1100.

The most complicated forms of granulation have not as yet been found in jewellery of this date from Crete and Greece, where the goldsmiths appear to have restricted themselves to the massed, decorative and outline varieties. But, since the silhouette style was known in Egypt in the fourteenth century (where it occurs in jewellery from Tutankh-amun's Tomb),[7] it may yet prove to have been practised in the Aegean at an early date.

The Dark Ages lasted from 1100 to 900 BC. Shortly after 900, granulation and filigree were again practised in Greece, and from about 700 BC in Etruria. The source from which these processes came is not absolutely clear, but Phoenicia is a strong candidate, as it was the source of most of the Oriental influences in Greece and Etruria at this date. Apart from a certain amount of jewellery from Sinjirli of about 700 BC,[8] evidence from these regions at the relevant period is almost nonexistent. However, Phoenician jewellery of the sixth century (from Aliseda and Tharros) shows granulation and filigree of all the varieties found in Greece and Etruria slightly earlier.[9]

In Greece, granulation was used between 900 and 600 in the massed, decorative and outline styles. Filigree was probably used principally as a surround for enamel and seldom as a decorative process on its own.

From 600 to the end of the first century BC filigree gradually (but never completely) replaced granulation. Filigree was used both as a decorative process on its own, and as a surround for enamel, while granulation was used to make only the simplest patterns.

In Etruria these processes reached a very high stage of development in the seventh and sixth centuries BC, after which they gradually died out. Granulation was practised in the massed, decorative, outline, silhouette and reserved-silhouette styles. Filigree is found in its usual form and also in openwork technique.

In Roman jewellery filigree and granulation are found, but neither process was popular, and granulation especially became extremely coarse. In the West filigree of a kind never completely died out; granulation lingered on on the fringes of the Western world, in Scandinavia and Eastern Europe,[10] and finally died out about AD 1000, to be revived in our own era. In the East, filigree continued in many areas down to our own day,[11] while granulation just survived, unnoticed by Western craftsmen, in parts of Western Asia and India.[12]

Enamel

TECHNICAL

Enamel is a coloured glass fused to a metallic base. Gold and electrum were the metals generally enamelled; silver occasionally; bronze in Romano-Celtic jewellery.

Five varieties of ancient enamelling may be recognized:

1 *Cloisonné*. The enamel is set in areas on the surface bounded by strips of metal arranged in cells, or *cloisons*, to form a pattern.

2 *Filigree*. A variation of cloisonné enamel, in which the metal strips are replaced by filigree wire.

3 *Repoussé*. The enamel is set in depressions punched in the background and surrounded by granulation.

4 *Champlevé*. The enamel is set in depressions carved out of the background.

In these varieties broken or powdered glass (in antiquity a soda-lime glass) is placed in the areas to be decorated and the work is fired. When the glass reaches melting-point it fuses and penetrates the surface of the metal, which has been rendered soft and porous by the heat. The work is then slowly cooled. In Romano-Celtic champlevé, use was sometimes made of glass cut to fit, as for inlay, and melted only just sufficiently to ensure adhesion. This fact is clearly demonstrated by the employment for this purpose of previously prepared mosaic glass.

5 *Dipped*. A metal armature is made and, when heated, is dipped in molten glass. Some of the glass adheres to the metal and is then shaped by normal glassworking methods while in a viscous state (Pl. 48 B).

HISTORICAL

Two kinds of enamelling, cloisonné and repoussé, are found in Minoan and Mycenaean jewellery.

Cloisonné enamelling in dark blue and turquoise green occurs in finger rings from about 1425 until shortly before 1100 (Pl. 11 A) The process was evidently invented in Egypt, for its use is attested at Dahshur as early as the nineteenth century BC.[13] It is closely related to the technique of inlaying jewellery with sections of stone and (later) glass, cemented in place, and was probably derived from this process. If a craftsman accidentally overfired a piece containing a glass inlay, he would unwittingly have converted the glass inlay to an enamel.

In the break-up of the Mycenaean world in the twelfth century the technique of cloisonné enamelling was transported to Cyprus. It is found in six finger rings from a tomb at Kouklia (old Paphos)[14] and in a gold sceptre from a tomb at Curium.[15] The sceptre is surmounted by a sphere on which are two figures of hawks. The sphere and the birds are decorated with mauve, green and white cloisonné enamel.

Repoussé enamelling, in dark blue only, also makes its first appearance about 1425. It has not yet been identified outside the Aegean world and was probably a Minoan-Mycenaean invention, adapted from cloisonné work. It did not have a long life and seems to have died out by 1300.[16]

The materials used are similar in appearance to those used for glass relief beads (see p. 40) and the same materials were probably used for both purposes. Sir Harry Garner established by experiment that the relief-bead glass, which melts partially but sufficiently at 850°C, could have been used as enamel.

In the Dark Ages, between 1100 and 900 BC, no enamel is known in Greek lands, nor is it to be expected. Surprisingly, it has not as yet been found in Greek jewellery of the eighth and seventh centuries BC but makes its appearance in the early sixth century in Greek and, shortly after, in Etruscan work. This time it takes the form of filigree enamel. The process can be traced back into the seventh century in a piece of jewellery from Ziwiye in Azerbaijan, a diadem with rosettes whose petals are decorated with filigree enamel.[17] The art of Ziwiye at this date is remarkably mixed, but was composed basically of Assyrian and Scythian elements. The diadem is certainly Assyrian rather than Scythian, and we may, with all due caution, suggest Assyria as the home of filigree enamelling in the seventh century BC.

Definite evidence of enamel is found in Greek goldwork of the first half of the sixth century; a chryselephantine statue from Delphi, and a diadem from Kelermes in South Russia. As at Ziwiye, rosettes with filigree-enamelled petals are found. Enamel of the same kind is also found at this time in goldwork probably made by Greeks in Etruscan factories and in South Russian goldwork almost certainly made by Greeks for Scythian customers.

From the sixth century onwards, filigree enamel was regularly used in Greek jewellery; in the second century true cloisonné enamel makes a brief appearance—it is found in Artjukhov's Barrow—and is then lost to sight again; in the third, the second and probably the first centuries, dipped enamel was used for specialized purposes, such as earring pendants and decorations on diadems.

The colours used in Greek enamel are white, deep blue, deep green and pale greenish-blue.

Another process, akin to cloisonné enamelling, was practised in Hellenistic and Roman times.[18] Strips of metal were bent to form decorative patterns or letters of the alphabet, and were pressed in a background of heated glass. A dated example of this technique, a ring with a sandal-shaped bezel, comes from Artjukhov's Barrow, of the second century BC (Fig. 25). In an extension of this process, the metal was bent to the outline of a figure, which was filled with powdered glass and placed on a background of glass. Both were now heated. When the background was sufficiently soft, the metal was pushed into it, carrying the powdered glass, which was now partially fused.

In Etruria, apart from the Graeco-Etruscan work already mentioned, enamel is found in genuine Etruscan work in the sixth and perhaps the fifth century, but it had a limited vogue and was not popular for long. It apparently owed its introduction to Greece, and never became truly naturalized. It is, however, again found in the second century BC, when Etruscan art became, for all practical purposes, Hellenistic.

Enamel was scarcely used in Roman goldwork, being superseded by the inlaying of stones and glass. It does, however, occasionally occur in the West, where Celtic influence may be assumed. Champlevé enamel was, however, used to a great extent in Romano-Celtic bronze ornaments, principally brooches. The brooches are attractively set with brightly coloured enamels, many of them patterned in mosaics, like contemporary glass vessels.

Niello

Niello is a matt black substance, composed of one or more metallic sulphides, used for the decoration of gold and, more commonly, silver. It is set in recesses cut in the surface of the metal. A black substance, which may or may not be niello, is found in Syrian metalwork as early as the twentieth century BC and in Egyptian and Mycenaean in the fifteenth and fourteenth centuries.[19] It was used to decorate weapons and plate, but not apparently jewellery, and is therefore outside the scope of this survey.

After a gap of many centuries, a substance identified with certainty as niello was used in Classical lands; it is a silver sulphide, and is found in Hellenistic and Roman silver plate and in late Roman and Byzantine jewellery. Two gold rings from the Beaurains Treasure, of about AD 300, and silver fibulae of the fourth century AD are among the earliest examples of its use in jewellery. According to the most likely theory, it was placed in powder form in the recesses in the metal. The work was then gently heated and the powder, becoming plastic well below its melting-point, was rubbed to the correct shape.

It was not until the eleventh century AD, well beyond our period, that a niello suitable for fusion to metal was employed.

Inlay

TECHNICAL

Another method of polychrome decoration, more frequently employed in antiquity than enamel, is the inlaying of jewellery with coloured stones, glass and other substances. The inlays are cut to shape and cemented in cells formed by strips of metal soldered to a background. The cement was composed of resin with a calcareous filler such as powdered limestone or gypsum. It was probably applied in a molten state. In certain examples inlay is very close in appearance to enamel but the difference is one of technique: inlay is cut to shape and fixed; enamel is fused *in situ*.

The cells with inlay may be adjacent, to form a continuous pattern, they may form a pattern without being adjacent, or they may exist in isolation. In the last category there are examples where the stone or other substance has little immediate background and is clearly of more importance than the surrounding metal; inlay in such cases is perhaps not the correct term, but, for convenience, it will be so used here.

The surface of the inlay is generally cut flush with the top edge of the cell; sometimes, however, when the cells are not contiguous, the inlay is cut *en cabochon*, to rise above the cell, and the cell is turned inwards at the top, to hold the inlay more securely. This system is frequently found in ring bezels.

HISTORICAL

The inlaying of jewellery has a long history in Mesopotamia, where it is found in the Royal Graves at Ur of about 3000 BC,[20] and in Egypt.[21] In Syria it is first found in jewellery from Byblos of about 2000 BC, and may well have been practised there earlier.[22] In the Aegean it is first attested about the seventeenth century, but here too it may have an earlier history. The earliest examples, in Minoan rings from the so-called Aegina Treasure, are very close to the jewellery from Ur both in the method of inlay and in the choice of lapis lazuli as the material.

We may therefore place the ultimate origins of this technique in Mesopotamia.

In the Dark Ages, the art of inlaying fell out of use. It was reintroduced into Greece, almost certainly by Phoenician craftsmen, about 800 BC. Shortly after, about 700 BC, it was introduced into Etruria, doubtless from the same source. In Greece it is particularly common in jewellery from Attica and Crete of the eighth century. The inlays are frequently in cloisons bounded by granulation, set a little apart from each other and arranged in patterns. In the seventh century inlay was still used, but to a decreasing extent, and before the end of the century it had almost died out in Greece. In Etruria its use is less frequent, but it lingered into the sixth century and then died out. The materials for inlay in Greek and Etruscan jewellery of this period are principally rock crystal, amber and glass.

Inlay is not regularly found again in Greek jewellery until the later fourth century BC, when Alexander's conquests again brought to Greece the fashions and luxuries of the East. Seal stones were henceforth set in rings, and from this date provide virtually the only form of seal. In other forms of jewellery garnets and cornelians were at first used almost exclusively. In the second century BC they were supplemented by other stones, and glass. For a short time in the second century glass inlay was employed in a manner very like later cloisonné enamel; but in general the preference was for a broader treatment, with single stones, or small groups.

In Etruria, inlay did not become popular until Etruscan jewellery proper had given place to Hellenistic, in the second century BC. In Roman jewellery, however, the position was different. Stones and glass were extremely popular, and were frequently set in small clusters comprising different materials and different shapes. Towards the end of the period, in the third century AD, the stones had become definitely more important than the settings.

Other attachments

BEADS

Beads were occasionally attached by wires to jewellery, especially in Hellenistic and Roman times. Cornelian was most commonly used in this way; in Late Hellenistic times pearls were also used.

SCULPTURAL

In the Hellenistic period stones were occasionally carved as human or animal heads and attached to the ends of hoop earrings or necklaces (see Pl. 47 J).

Cutting processes

ENGRAVING

Engraving on gold was practised sporadically from Late Minoan times onwards. Catchplates of fibulae were treated in this way (see Pl. 14 A and B). Bezels of gold and silver rings were also frequently engraved. Late Minoan and Mycenaean rings were sometimes engraved in solid gold; more often the bezel was of embossed sheet gold, with details subsequently engraved.

In the Bronze Age, engraving was probably done with a flake of obsidian or a copper tool, for bronze is too brittle for such work. In the Iron Age, iron tools were used; a graver (or burin) such as is used today, and a *scorper* for the so-called *tremolo line*.[23]

CARVING

Gold was occasionally worked with a chisel in stone-carving technique. Certain Greek ring bezels of the fifth century BC provide examples of this rarely used process.[24]

PIERCING

Towards the end of the Roman period the custom became popular of making patterns in sheet gold by cutting out portions of the metal with a chisel. The process, known to the Romans as *opus interrasile*, is occasionally found much earlier in Early Etruscan work (see Pl. 32 E), but was not in general use before the second century AD.

The result, which can be pleasing, gives a lace-like effect (see Pls 59 and 63 A). Byzantine jewellery shows a further development of this process.

Plating and gilding

GOLD PLATING

Gold foil is pressed over a prepared core of some other material, from which it takes its shape. Where the base is metallic, such as silver or bronze, the gold can be hammered over it; where the base is of other material, such as glass, the metal is merely bent over. This technique is early, and soon died out. It is found on Mycenaean bronze rings and on Geometric pins.

GILDING

Two processes were used in antiquity.

1 Gold leaf was attached to a base with an adhesive. This process was used over metal and terracotta.

2 In Roman times a development of this process, known as cold mercury gilding, was applied to copper (it was not suitable for bronze). Mercury is rubbed on the surface and gold leaf is pressed over it. True mercury gilding, also known as fire gilding, is a post-Roman development.

SILVER PLATING

The process is similar to gold plating.

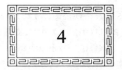

JOINING AND FINISHING

Joining

After the basic and decorative work is finished, there is still much to be done. The various components must be joined together (for few articles of jewellery are made in one piece), and tool marks and other blemishes obliterated.

MECHANICAL

Although soldering was the principal means of attaching the various components of a piece of jewellery, mechanical methods were occasionally used, especially at times and in places where the more difficult processes of soldering were not regularly employed.

Folding. In Late Palatial times the back and front of a piece of jewellery were occasionally attached by folding the one with the other (see Pl. 4 D). It is possible that on occasions the joint was strengthened by burnishing.

Riveting. This clumsy process was seldom used for jewellery, but is occasionally found in Early Etruscan pieces.

Attachment by wires or ribbons. A primitive process used in the Late Palatial period in Crete (see Pl. 4 D) and occasionally later.

SOLDERING

Soldering is a method of joining two pieces of metal by running between them a molten metal or alloy (the solder), the melting-point of which is lower than that of the metal to be joined.

31

Solders are classified as *hard* or *soft*. Hard solders require more heat than soft ones, but make a stronger joint. So far as ancient jewellery is concerned, soft solder (a mixture of lead and tin) may be ignored. It is used today for none but the cheapest jewellery, and there is no evidence that it was used at all in antiquity for jewellery, although the Romans are known to have used it on silver plate.

The ancient goldsmith had at his disposal two entirely different methods of hard soldering. Colloid hard soldering, which has already been considered in connection with filigree and granulation, was also used for major joints, when an invisible finish was needed.

When the finished appearance was less important, the craftsman would use normal hard soldering, a process also known as *brazing*. At first he probably took a piece of naturally alloyed gold whose melting-point was found by experience to be lower than that of the gold to be joined. Later, a piece taken from the gold to be joined was alloyed with silver, copper or a mixture of silver and copper, to lower its melting-point. Pliny recommends six parts of gold to one of silver, which gives a melting-point of 970 C as against 1063 C for pure gold.[1] Alternatively, pure silver, whose melting-point is 961 C, could be used for soldering gold; but its use, though occasionally found, was not common because of the very noticeable joint. For soldering silver, an alloy of silver and copper was used; Theophilus recommends two parts of silver to one of copper.[2]

But all metals except absolutely pure gold oxidize when they are heated, and oxide prevents the solder from flowing over the join. It is therefore essential to prevent oxidization during heating and to dissolve any existing oxides. The material used for this purpose is known as a *flux* because it enables the solder to flow where it is required. Today borax is used in hard soldering. There is some disagreement as to whether it was used in antiquity, but the general view is that it was not. Theophilus recommends the burnt lees of wine, which would produce an effective flux composed of bitartrate of potash, or cream of tartar.[3] Natron, which is known to have been used for many purposes, could also have been used.

To effect a join, the surfaces are coated with flux, and chips of solder are placed between them. The work is then secured with wire and placed over a charcoal fire. The heat of the fire is intensified by a blowpipe or bellows, and when the correct temperature is reached the solder melts and runs into the joint. The work is immediately removed from the fire and allowed to cool; or it is overfired (that is, heated still further for a short time) and is then removed. The higher the temperature to which the work is raised, short of melting it, the stronger will be the joint, for the solder will penetrate further into the adjacent surfaces.

When the work has a cooled the solder will have set and the joint is made. Nothing remains but to remove the binding-wire, to clean off any remaining flux and to remove blemishes. The removal of flux is today effected by 'pickling' in an acid solution; in antiquity it was done mechanically by scraping.

Hard soldering of gold and silver was known in Mesopotamia from the third millennium BC.[4] In Classical antiquity it is first found in Minoan jewellery of about 2400 BC and, apart from the hiatus of the Dark Ages, was regularly practised in Classical lands thereafter. An example of rather clumsy Minoan soldering is shown in Pl. 1 D.

WELDING

Under this term are comprised three distinct processes.

1 *Pressure welding*. A method of joining metal by pressure or percussion alone. Gold is the only metal which reacts in this way when cold. Although pressure welding has been but rarely identified, it was almost certainly practised in the early periods and in the Dark Ages for objects such as finger rings (Pl. 13 A).

2 *Sweating together or surface welding*. The two elements are heated to a point somewhat below melting-point, when they become tacky at the surface, and are brought together. The opposing surfaces interpenetrate one another to a slight degree and adhere on cooling. This process is usually dismissed by scholars because of the difficulty of reaching the exact temperature with the primitive apparatus in use in antiquity, but if it was used for certain forms of granulation (see p. 21) it could conceivably have been used on occasions for making major joins.

3 *Fusion welding* or *autogenous welding*. The surfaces to be joined are actually melted and run together with the possible addition of more molten metal of the same kind to reinforce the joint. This method was used in antiquity with bronze and iron, but is quite unsuitable for fine work in gold or silver, and cannot have been used in ancient jewellery.

Finishing

STRENGTHENING

Closed shapes made from two pieces of sheet metal soldered together were frequently filled with some other substance to give them solidity and weight. Magnetite sand was used in Mycenaean times as a filling for gold pendant ornaments and probably for the larger signet rings, which were certainly made to be filled with something.[5] Pitch was used in Hellenistic hoop earrings.[6] Wax, earth and (apparently) resin are mentioned as fillings in Hellenistic temple inventories.[7]

POLISHING

Irregularities in the metal are removed by abrasives such as sand or emery working on soft wheels. The abrasives used are increasingly fine until an almost completely smooth surface is attained. The final polish is given by rubbing with burnishing-stones. Agate is much used today for this purpose, and could well have been so used in antiquity.

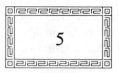
MATERIALS OTHER THAN GOLD
AND SILVER

Some mention has already been made of the use of materials other than gold or silver. In this chapter the use of such other materials, whether independently or in association with precious metals, will be considered in greater detail.

Stones and related materials

Stones and similar natural objects served two principal purposes in ancient jewellery. (1) They were used in direct association with gold or silver as inlay, as ring stones, or as attachments to metal jewellery. (2) They formed independent articles of adornment, such as beads and pendants, signets, bead seals, finger rings or bracelets.

In Greek and Roman times, and probably also in the Bronze Age, stones were used as much for their magical as for their decorative qualities. It appears that each stone had its own peculiar powers.[1]

In the Bronze Age, stones were used principally for beads and pendants, bead seals, signets and pinheads, and for inlay. Finger rings were occasionally made completely of stone, and one example of an engraved ring bezel is known. Favourite stones are rock crystal, amethyst, cornelian, chalcedony, agate (for seals), jasper (chiefly for seals) and lapis lazuli. Inferior beads and seals were made of steatite.

In the Orientalizing period (900–600 BC) hard stones were again used for beads and as inlay. Amber and rock crystal were popular. In the Archaic and Classical periods (600–330 BC) stones were scarcely ever inlaid in jewellery and are altogether rare, except as seals, for which cornelian, agate and chalcedony were principally used. In Etruria, between 800 and 330 BC, the same is roughly true.

35

In the Hellenistic period, garnets and cornelians were especially popular for decorating jewellery. From about 200 B C pearls and emerald became popular. An Early Hellenistic bracelet of rock crystal is known (Pl. 51 A).

In the Roman period the same stones were used as in the Late Hellenistic, and in addition the hardest stones–diamonds, sapphires, aquamarines and topazes–are found. Nicolo was especially popular for ring bezels. Turquoises were occasionally used. Complete finger rings of cornelian and chalcedony are also found.

There follows a list of the stones principally used in ancient jewellery. The hardness indicated is that of the Mohs scale.

AGATE

The ancient *achates*. A variegated chalcedony, found in layers, frequently with inclusions. The layers vary in opacity and in colour. They are opaque or translucent, white, grey, blue, brown, yellow or red. When the layers have irregular outlines, the simple term *agate* is used. Where there are moss-like inclusions the term is *moss agate*. Where the layers are regular, and the stone is cut transversely, it is called *banded agate*. When the same stone is cut horizontally, as in the cutting of cameos, it is known as *onyx* or (if one layer is sard) *sardonyx*. *Nicolo* is a variety of onyx where one layer is black or dark brown and the other bluish-white. Most periods, chiefly seal stones.

AMBER

The ancient *electrum*. A reddish-yellow translucent fossilized resin. Hardness 2–2.5. From the Baltic. Most periods.

AMETHYST

The ancient *amethystus*. A violet-coloured transparent quartz. Most periods. When used in Minoan and Mycenaean jewellery it probably came from Egypt. Pliny says that the best came from India; the next best from Arabia, Armenia, Egypt and Galatia; and the worst from Thasos and Cyprus.

AQUAMARINE

The ancient *beryllus*. A greenish or bluish variety of beryl. Roman (rare).

BERYL

A double silicate of beryllium and aluminium. Transparent. Two forms: *emerald* and *aquamarine*. Hardness 8.

CHALCEDONIC SILICA (CHALCEDONY)

A microcrystalline or cryptocrystalline silica (dioxide of silicon). Translucent. Hardness 6.5. The term includes *chalcedony* proper (see below), *agate*, *cornelian* and *sard*, and *heliotrope*.

CHALCEDONY

A term used generally for all chalcedonic silicas, and specifically for one variety, the ancient *jaspis*; smoky, milky-white, yellowish or bluish in colour. Popular in most periods for seals, rare in jewellery.

CHRYSOLITE (PERIDOT)

The ancient *topazon* or *chrysolithus*. A silicate of magnesium and iron. Yellowish-green, transparent to translucent. Hardness 6.5–7. Roman (rare).

CITRINE

A yellow quartz. Roman.

CORNELIAN (SARD)

The ancient *sardius*. A reddish or brownish chalcedony. Most periods. Some authorities use the term *cornelian* for the red varieties, *sard* for the brown, but the distinction is frequently hard to draw, and here the term *cornelian* is used for both varieties.

CRYSTAL

See 'Rock crystal'.

DIAMOND

The ancient *adamas*. A form of carbon. Colourless and transparent. Hardness 10. Roman (rare). From India; possibly also the Urals.

EMERALD

The ancient *smaragdus*. A green variety of beryl containing chromium. Late Hellenistic and Roman. From the Sikait-Zubara region of the Red Sea Hills in Egypt, 250 km south-east of Luxor. Frequently used in its natural hexagonal crystals. Many true emeralds in Roman jewellery are frequently miscalled *plasma*.

GARNET

The ancient *anthrax, carbunculus*. A group of closely related silicates of various minerals. The variety used is the so-called *almandine garnet*, an iron-aluminium compound. Hardness 6.5–7.5. Hellenistic and Roman. The source is given, erroneously, by Pliny as Alabanda in Asia Minor.[2] The true source was almost certainly India.[3]

JASPER

A quartz, impregnated with much impurity, chiefly clay and oxide of iron. Opaque, with vivid colours, especially black, red, green and yellow. Rare in jewellery, but popular for seal stones, especially Minoan and Roman. Probably from Egypt.

LAPIS LAZULI

The ancient *cyanus, sapphirus* (?). A silicate of sodium, lime and aluminium with some sodium sulphide. Deep blue, with spots of pyrites and white inclusions. Opaque. Hardness 6. From Afghanistan. Chiefly Minoan and Mycenaean, but also used for inferior Roman seals.

PEARL

The ancient *margarita*. Hardness 2.5–3.5. Late Hellenistic and Roman. From the Persian Gulf.

PERIDOT

See 'Chrysolite'.

QUARTZ

A crystalline silica (dioxide of silicon). Hardness 7. Many varieties. (1) Transparent: *rock crystal, amethyst, citrine*. (2) Opaque: *jasper*.

ROCK CRYSTAL (CRYSTAL)

The ancient *crystallus*. A transparent colourless quartz. Most periods. From Crete; Chalcidice; Mytilene. Pliny says the best came from India, then Asia Minor, Cyprus and the Alps.

SAPPHIRE

The ancient name is not known. A transparent blue corundum, sesquioxide of aluminium. Hardness 9. Roman. Probably from India.

SARD

See 'Cornelian'.

SARDONYX

A variety of agate. Chiefly used for seals. Greek, Etruscan and Roman.

STEATITE (AGALMATOLITE; SOAPSTONE)

The ancient *steatitis*. A massive variety of talc, hydrated silicate of magnesium. Opaque; greasy to the touch. White and pale colours: grey, blue, yellow, brown, green. Hardness 1. Chiefly used for seal stones. Frequently confused with serpentine.

TURQUOISE

The ancient *callais* (?). Phosphate of aluminium containing copper. Pale blue; opaque. Hardness 6. From Persia and Sinai. Roman (rare).

TOPAZ

The ancient *topazon*, or *chrysolithus* (?). Silicate of aluminium containing fluorine and hydroxyl. Yellow; transparent. Hardness 8. Roman.

Ivory and bone

Ivory and bone were used for pins at all periods; for seals in Crete, 2500–2000; and for seals, beads and brooches in the Orientalizing period.

Glass

Ancient glass is a compound of silica, lime and soda in the following proportions: silica 57–72 per cent; lime 3–10 per cent; soda 9–21 per cent. It is best considered in two parts: first, for the Mycenaean period; second, for all subsequent periods.

MYCENAEAN

The glass used in Mycenaean jewellery falls into three categories:
(1) beads (including occasional seals); (2) plaques and pendants; and
(3) inlay. Enamel, which might be considered a fourth category, has
already been discussed on pp. 24 ff.

Beads. Glass beads first appear in the sixteenth century BC, in Crete,
and continue until the end of the Bronze Age. They were mostly spherical or elongated in shape, but tubular, multitubular, disc-shaped,
club-shaped, lentoid and other forms are also known. The colours are
frequently unidentifiable, owing to the extent to which glass decays in
damp ground, but blue, greyish-black, white and yellow were popular,
either alone or in combination. A number of glass beads from the beginning of this period are so like contemporary Egyptian beads–in particular, certain multitubular and eyed varieties–that they must be either
Egyptian imports or local imitations. It is therefore highly probable
that the art of making glass beads was learnt from Egypt. A factory for
making, *inter alia*, beads of this nature was discovered in the Palace at
Thebes, which was destroyed about 1400 BC. Some beads were no
doubt moulded; others were cut from canes.

Plaques and pendants. Moulded plaques and pendants are first found
in Mycenaean tombs of the second half of the fifteenth century BC, and
they continued in use until about 1100. They take the form either of
square plaques with figures and patterns in low relief or of relief beads.
All are perforated for suspension or for attachment. The plaques have
floral and marine motifs, sphinxes, genii and the like, and were apparently sewn to clothing. The beads are the exact doubles of the gold
ornaments described on pp. 76 ff. and like those were worn, strung together, round the neck or the wrist.

The colours are dark blue and, less commonly, pale greenish-blue,
in imitation of lapis lazuli and turquoise respectively. The colouring
agents for the dark blue were cobalt and copper; for the greenish blue,
copper alone.[4] The pendant ornaments, especially in the later periods,
were sometimes covered with gold foil, to imitate closely the more precious pendants of sheet gold. The effect aimed at so frequently in the
Bronze Age was a polychromy of gold and other colours.

Ornaments of this class were cast in steatite moulds, of which a fair
number have been discovered–at Mycenae, Knossos and elsewhere.
The suspension holes for the pendants were frequently made by inserting a pin into a specially cut channel in the mould; when the glass had
cooled, the pin was removed, leaving a hole.

The ornaments were usually made in open moulds, and have flat
backs. Certain types of pendant, however, have modelled backs, and
were made in double moulds, of which one example (from Palaikastro)

survives. These moulds were equipped with a pour-hole, and were keyed together with pins.

Ornaments of this nature are not found in Greek lands until about a century after the first appearance of glass beads; unlike the beads, they do not seem to have Egyptian prototypes. Their origins are, in fact, probably to be found in Syria, where moulded plaques of the same general type may go back to the beginning of the second millennium B.C.[5]

Inlay. Glass was used for inlay in the sixteenth century (see p. 69); the colours were those of the plaques and pendants, dark blue and pale greenish-blue. This technique was soon superseded by enamel.

POST-MYCENAEAN

After the Bronze Age, glass was used less for plaques and pendants, more for other purposes, in particular for beads and seal stones. All conceivable colours are now found and, in Roman times, all possible degrees of density, ranging from complete transparency to complete opacity.

1. *Beads.* Glass beads are found after the Bronze Age, throughout the period covered by this book.

2. *Seals.* From the sixth century onwards casts were taken in glass of engraved gems and used as cheap substitutes for precious stones. Clay moulds for the manufacture of such casts are known.[6] In Roman times glass seals are particularly common, a variety imitating banded agate being especially popular.

3. *Amulets.* In Ptolemaic and Roman Egypt amulets and other ornaments of glass were popular. A factory of Ptolemaic date contained moulds of terracotta for such fine work, and of limestone for larger work, not jewellery.[7]

4. *Fibulae.* A number of Early Etruscan fibulae have attachments of sand-core glass.[8]

5. *Inlay and bezel setting.* This use of glass is found in Greek and Etruscan Orientalizing, in Hellenistic and in Roman jewellery, and is described above (see p. 27).

Faience and blue compound

Faience (also known as *glazed composition* or *glazed frit-ware*) consists of a body of powdered quartz covered with a layer of glaze. Glazes were of many colours but commonly green or greenish-blue. The body is composed of 94–9 per cent quartz sand, 0–1 per cent soda (natron) and 2 per cent lime. The glaze is a soda-lime glass. 'Blue compound' (sometimes called 'frit' or 'paste') is a double silicate of lime and copper lightly fired and powdery blue in colour. Unlike faience, it is homogeneous throughout, and is composed of 10–14 per cent lime, 2–7 per cent soda (natron), 60–70 per cent quartz sand and 20 per cent copper.

Apart from these differences in composition, faience and blue compound are very similar in appearance and in function, and are best considered together. Objects of these materials, chiefly beads and amulets, were made for the most part in terracotta moulds, but beads were apparently sometimes modelled freehand.

Coloured and white faience beads are found in Crete as early as 1800 BC and are almost certainly of local manufacture.[9] From about 1500 BC the industry appears to have been established on the Greek mainland.

These materials reappear for a short time on Greek and Etruscan sites in the seventh century BC, in the form of beads, scarabs and amulets. One centre of manufacture would appear to be Naucratis, where clay moulds for scarabs of this type have been found.[10] The Phoenician homeland and Phoenician settlements on Greek sites, in particular Rhodes, have also been plausibly suggested.[11] The fashion for ornaments of this material in Greece and Etruria did not outlast the sixth century BC.

Terracotta

Gilt terracotta was occasionally used for imitation jewellery, especially in the fourth and third centuries BC.

Base metals

IRON

Iron was used (probably for magical purposes) in Minoan and Mycenaean rings,[12] for pins and finger rings in the Dark Ages, and occasionally gold plating, gliding and silver plating.

BRONZE

Apart from its regular use for pins and fibulae, bronze was used for finger rings, earrings and occasionally beads, and served as a basis for gold plating, gilding and silver plating.

LEAD

Cheap imitations of jewellery were cast from lead, probably in large quantities, but, owing to their perishable nature, few survive.

PART II
HISTORICAL

CHRONOLOGICAL TABLE I
THE BRONZE AGE

DATE	CRETE		CYCLADES	GREECE	TROY	CYPRUS	EGYPT		DATE
3000							Archaic	Dynasty I	3000
2900									2900
2800	EM I	Pre-	EC I	EH I	I	Chalco-lithic		II	2800
2700								III	2700
2600								IV	2600
2500		pal-						V	2500
2400							Old King-dom		2400
2300	EM II		EC II	EH II	II	E. Cyp. I		VI	2300
2200		atial			III	E. Cyp. II			2200
2100	EM III		EC III	EH III	IV	E. Cyp. III	1st Inter-mediate	VII-X	2100
2000	MM I					M. Cyp.	Middle King-dom	XI	2000
1900		Early Pal-atial	MC I		V			XII	1900
1800	MM II		MC II	MH			2nd Inter-mediate		1800
1700	MM III	Late Pal-atial	MC III					XIII-XVII	1700
1600	LM Ia		LC I	LH I	Early Mycen-aean	VI			1600
1500	LM Ib		LC II	LH II			New King-dom	XVIII	1500
1400	LM II			Empire		L. Cyp. I			1400
	LM IIIa	Post-pal-atial		LH IIIa					
1300	LM IIIb		LC III	LH IIIb	VII A	L. Cyp. II			1300
					VII B1			XIX-XX	
1200	LM IIIc			LH IIIc	VII B2	L. Cyp. III			1200
1100				Submycenaean				XXI	1100
	Subminoan								
1000									1000

In Crete the left column contains Evans' system; the right, the more recently devised system, adopted in this book. MM II is found only at Knossos and Phaestos; LM II is found chiefly at Knossos. In the Cyclades the subdivisions of the Late Cycladic period are seldom used; the LM and LH systems are used instead. In Greece MH is not yet susceptible of division into phases.

Abbreviations: EM = Early Minoan. MM = Middle Minoan. LM = Late Minoan. EC = Early Cycladic. MC = Middle Cycladic. LC = Late Cycladic. EH = Early Helladic. MH = Middle Helladic. LH = Late Helladic E. Cyp. = Early Cypriote. M. Cyp. = Middle Cypriote. L. Cyp. = Late Cypriote.

CHRONOLOGICAL TABLE II
1100–600 BC

DATE	ATTICA	CRETE	CYPRUS	EGYPT	DATE
1100	Submyc.		L. Cyp. III	Dynasty	1100
1050		Subminoan		XXI	1050
1000	PG		Cypro-Geometric I		1000
950		PG	Cypro-Geometric II		950
900					900
850	EG I / II			XXII	850
800	MG I	PG. B	Cypro-Geometric III		800
750	MG II	Geometric		XXIII and XXIV	750
700	LG I / II				700
650	Protoattic	Orientalizing	Cypro-Archaic I	XXV	650
600				XXVI	600

Based on Coldstream, *GG*.

Abbreviations: Submyc. = Submycenaean.
PG = Protogeometric.   EG = Early Geometric.
MG = Middle Geometric.
LG = Late Geometric.

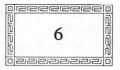

6

GREECE AND THE CYCLADES

3000–1700 BC

EARLY HELLADIC
AND EARLY CYCLADIC 3000–2000 BC

Introduction

In their early phases, the principal Bronze Age cultures of the Aegean were closely related. Those of the Cyclades and mainland Greece (the Early Cycladic and Early Helladic) were, however, closer to each other than to that of Crete (the Early Minoan or Prepalatial), and so it will be best to consider first the jewellery of the Cyclades and the mainland, and to reserve that of Crete for separate treatment.

Little is known of the origins of the two cultures under review, but it seems probable that about 3000 BC the Cyclades were settled (many of them for the first time) by immigrants from Anatolia, who brought with them a bronze-using civilization of a high order. Some of these people soon moved on to settle on the Greek mainland, where they mingled with the Neolithic inhabitants to found the Early Helladic culture.

These cultures were in close contact with Anatolia and in intermittent contact with Crete. About 2000 BC (in some areas rather before), when both cultures had reached a remarkably high level, they ended; the Early Helladic as a result of invasion and wholesale destruction, the Early Cycladic apparently as a result of annexation from Crete.

The inspiration of Early Helladic and Early Cycladic jewellery came chiefly from Western Anatolia. To the so-called Troadic culture of this region belong the rich hoards of jewellery from the destruction layers of

47

Troy II (about 2200 BC) and the contemporary destruction layers of Poliochni on Lesbos. This jewellery, which appears to be partly of native Anatolian and partly of Mesopotamian inspiration, reached the Greek world in a somewhat watered-down form. The familiar shapes were perpetuated, but the techniques were more primitive. Nothing is found more advanced than wire-work, elementary repoussé and casting. Filigree and granulation, although used at Troy, were unknown in Greece and the Islands.

The surviving Early Helladic material is restricted to five sources: a tomb on the Amphaion Hill north of ancient Thebes, of about 2500–2200 BC; poor tombs at Zygouries, near Corinth; the site of Asine; fairly prosperous tombs on Leukas; and a rich collection (in Berlin), believed to come from the Thyreatis, on the borders of Argolis and Laconia (2500–2200 BC). The Thyreatis jewellery gives some idea of the possessions of the aristocrats who inhabited the palaces at Tiryns and Lerna.

The Early Cycladic material, so far as precious metal is concerned, is restricted to Amorgos, where it was fairly plentiful; and to Chalandriani (on Syros) and Naxos. Pendants of stone and pins of bronze were, however, very common in the Cyclades. In addition, a set of gold beads of Cycladic character was found in a tomb of around 2200–2000 BC at Archanes on Crete together with other Cycladic objects.

The jewellery

DIADEMS

Silver diadems decorated with figures in dot-repoussé come from Chalandriani and Zygouries; they seem to be local imitations of a common Minoan type (see Fig. 5). There is a similar diadem of silver, but undecorated, from Apeiranthos, in Naxos Museum (unpublished). Another type, also of silver, with the top cut in a zigzag pattern, comes from a tomb on Amorgos.

HAIR SPIRALS

Spirals of wire were common as hair ornaments in Western Asia,[1] and are found in tombs on Leukas.

EARRINGS

Tapered hoops come from tombs on Leukas; they are presumably derived from Anatolia, since similar earrings occur in Troy II.

At Zygouries one earring was found in Tomb 7 and one in Tomb 20. The former is a wedge-shaped sheet of gold hanging from a silver hoop, which was evidently inserted in the lobe; the latter is a gold disc with a loop at the top and a square hole in the centre. The presence of two singleton earrings suggests that they may have been worn singly by the Early Helladic people.

BEADS AND PENDANTS

Spherical and biconical beads come from Leukas; the latter have analogies in Troy II, Ur and Brak.[2] Silver barrel beads, fluted diagonally, come from a tomb at Amorgos; a type which is echoed in a pinhead from Alaja Huyuk, of about 2200 BC.[2] A necklace of 200 silver beads was found in a grave at Louros (Naxos), of about 2600–2500.

From the tomb at Thebes come three remarkable gold pendants embodying a barrel bead, a vertical rod, a spectacle spiral and two floral clusters.

From Thyreatis come a number of beads and pendants (Pl. 2):

1. Barrel or biconical beads (at the ends of the necklace).

2. Beads composed of concentric hoops of wire with eyes at two opposing points on the circumference, to allow for a cord. From some of these hang a chain, at the bottom of which is a wedge-shaped pendant, possibly representing an axehead. The hoops are represented in Troy II, and evidently reached Greece from that quarter.[4] The wedge-shaped pendant also occurs in Crete (see p. 56).

3. A cylinder surrounded by a wire cage. This type is unique, but has some affinity with the cage on the Mallia jewel (Pl. 6 A).

4. An elaborate ornament made by crossing two spectacle-spiral tubes of the kind discussed on p. 67. This composite type has not been recorded elsewhere but is surely, like the single variety, of Anatolian inspiration.

5. A pendant in the shape of an axehead.

6. A somewhat similar pendant, but instead of an axe-blade a pair of testicles or perhaps the body of an insect is represented. Similar pendants in stone come from Early Cycladic tombs on Paros.

BRACELETS

A spiral of silver wire, round in section and thickened at the ends, comes from Leukas. Similar ones come from Troy II (about 2200) and Brak (about 2100).[5] Also from Leukas, and also paralleled in Troy II,[6] is a spiral of silver wire, square in section, and twisted.

PINS

Pins have been found in large quantities in Early Cycladic burials, and a few come from the mainland. From the discovery of a pin on the shoulder of a skeleton at Chalandriani, it has been established that some at least were used to secure the dress on the shoulders. In five tombs in the same cemetery pins were found in pairs, a fact which strongly suggests that they have served the same purpose.

The pins were usually of bronze or bone, and only occasionally of precious metals, but all kinds may with advantage be considered here. The affinities of all of them are with Anatolia.

1. With a spherical head. In silver, from Chalandriani. In bronze, from Chalandriani; Zygouries, House D; Asine. The type is found in Troy II and III.[7] A variety in silver with projections from the sphere comes from Naxos (unpublished, in Athens). It could well derive from a type found at Alaja.[8]

2. With a conical or pyramidal head. In bronze, from Chalandriani (Fig. 4 e); Zygouries, House A; and Asine. The type is found in Troy II-V.[9]

3. With a hemispherical head. In bronze, from Zygouries, Tomb 20.

4. With a double-spiral head. In silver, from Zygouries, Tomb 20. In bronze, from Naxos (unpublished) and Chalandriani (Fig. 4 b). This is a widespread Middle Eastern type, represented at Troy II (about 2200); Alaja (about 2200); Tarsus (1900–1650); and Tepe Hissar.[10]

Fig. 4 Early Cycladic pins from Chalandriani, Syros: (a) bone; (b) bronze; (c) silver; (d) bronze; (e) bronze.

5. With a cage-like head. In bronze, from Chalandriani (Fig. 4 d). The type is found in Troy III.[11]

6. With a head in the form of a jug. In silver, from Chalandriani (Fig. 4c). A gold miniature jug in the Thyreatis Treasure (Pl. 2) looks as if it once formed the head of a similar pin. Jug-headed pins also come from Naxos and Troy II.[12]

7. With a head in the form of a sheep on a platform. In silver, from Amorgos; compare the later gold pin from Mycenae (pp. 70–1). Pins of this type are probably western Asiatic in inspiration if not in manufacture.[13]

8. With a head in the form of a bull's head. In gold, from Thyreatis (Pl. 2). The closest parallel to this charming pin comes, surprisingly enough, from Chagar Bazar, and is dated about 2900 BC.[14]

9. With a head in the form of a bird. In bone, from Chalandriani (Fig. 4a) The type is found in bronze at Thermi I, and at Alishar (1900–1600 BC).[15]

MIDDLE HELLADIC 2000–1700 BC

Introduction

Since Middle Cycladic jewellery has yet to be discovered, this section will be concerned only with Middle Helladic.

Around 2000 BC the rich Early Helladic civilization gave place to an impoverished culture, probably associated with the arrival of the first Greeks. Greece was plunged into some three centuries of poverty, which lasted until contacts with Crete and Western Asia were renewed about 1700 BC, to give rise to the Mycenaean culture. Although, in terms of pottery, the Middle Helladic period still had about a century to run, in terms of culture it may be said to have ended at this date.

As might be expected, Middle Helladic jewellery is extremely rare, and what has survived tends to be of base metals. Some of the jewellery here ascribed to this period may in fact have been made rather after 1700 BC in areas where there were as yet no Mycenaean contacts; but in the present state of our knowledge it is not possible to be more precise.

The jewellery

RINGS AND SPIRALS

Rings and spirals for the adornment of the hair, and hoop earrings, are found in gold, silver, gold-plated bronze, and bronze. It is not always possible to decide the function of a particular piece, but it is probable that both articles are represented among surviving jewellery. The graves in which they have been found are: Sesklo (Graves 25 and 28) and Dimini (Grave 61); Zygouries, Grave 1; Argive Heraeum, Graves 17 and 18; Asine, Grave MH 98; Drachmani (ancient Elatea); Aphidna (Graves 1 and 3); graves at Eleusis; and Burial 23 at Hagios Stephanos.

BEADS

Simple shapes are found in bronze, crystal, cornelian, steatite and faience.

PINS

Bronze pins with biconical heads occur at Sesklo, Grave 25; Hagios Stephanos, Burial 23; and graves at Eleusis. A bronze bird-headed pin comes from a Middle Helladic level at Lerna.

Three bone pins from Gonia (Grave 7) were definitely hairpins, since they were found behind the skull of what was probably a female skeleton. Similar pins from Lerna doubtless served the same purpose.

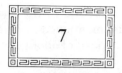

CRETE: PREPALATIAL

3000–2000 BC

Introduction

The Prepalatial (or Early Minoan) culture of Crete is believed to have been introduced about 3000 B C by immigrants from Western Asia. The main centres of civilization were in Eastern Crete, where there is evidence of fruitful contacts with Egypt and Western Asia. The period ended peacefully about 2000, with the shift of power and wealth to the new cities of the centre and south.

Gold jewellery is plentiful in tombs on the island of Mochlos in Eastern Crete, of about 2300–2100 B C; and is also found, but less frequently, in the tombs of the Mesara. The contrast between the richness of Mochlos and the poverty of the Mesara tombs at this date may be explained to a certain extent by a difference in funeral customs. At Mochlos, previous interments were perhaps not robbed of their valuables to the same extent as in the Mesara. But there are other reasons for believing that Eastern Crete at this date was the richer area.

The jewellery consists principally of diadems, hair ornaments, beads and pendants, bracelets and clothing ornaments. Dress pins, so common in the Cyclades and on the mainland, are notably absent. The techniques are elementary, but they are used skilfully. The basic materials are sheet metal, cut into shapes and occasionally decorated with patterns of dot-repoussé; wire and chains. The chains are both simple and loop-in-loop (see p. 16). Gold foil was also used as a covering for objects of other material; it was decorated more elaborately than the sheet-gold, being considerably easier to work.

The antecedents of this style go back ultimately to Mesopotamia, for the best parallels are to be found in the jewellery from Ur, of about 2700–2500 BC, and will be mentioned in detail below. The same types recur at Tell Asmar in a deposit of about 2300–2200.[1] Syria must have been the route by which Mesopotamian influences reached Crete; and jewellery from Brak of about 2200–2100[2] is in fact very like that from Tell Asmar. Syria was from earliest times influenced by Mesopotamian art, but we may imagine this influence to have been intensified by Sargon's conquests of about 2300 BC.

In contrast to this characteristic Minoan style, a tomb at Archanes, of about 2200–2000 BC, has yielded a necklace of beads of strong Cycladic affinities, quite unlike those from Mochlos. They may well be imports from one of the Cycladic islands.

The source of Cretan gold at this date is not known, but it could have been a rich alluvial deposit in the Melas valley near Antioch in North Syria.[3]

The jewellery

Unless otherwise stated, the pieces described below come from Mochlos. Objects from the tombs of the Mesara, which came into use in this period and continued into the next, are in general included only when their early date is guaranteed by resemblances to the jewellery from Mochlos. Most extant Prepalatial jewellery is in Heraklion, but there is also a little in New York.

DIADEMS

Diadems, from Tombs 2, 6 and 19, are cut from sheet gold, and decorated in dot repoussé with simple patterns or figured scenes (Fig. 5). Although found in tombs, they were evidently made in the first place to be worn by the living, for a number showed signs of repeated use.

Fig. 5   Diadem from Mochlos, Tomb 2, about 2200 BC.

They measure between 20 and 30 cm in length, by about 3 cm in height. The original home of such diadems is in Mesopotamia, for a comparable piece comes from Ur and is dated about 2500.[4] A more elaborate version, equipped with three antenna-like crests, was found recently in a re-excavation of Tomb 6. Similar diadems in silver come from the Cyclades and the Greek mainland (see p. 48). A rather more complicated gold diadem with attached gold leaves comes from Lebena and probably dates from about 2000 BC.

HAIR SPIRALS

Hair spirals are not certainly attested, but spirals in silver and bronze, from Kavousi, could have been used either as hair spirals or as earrings.

HAIRPINS

Exquisite hairpins in the form of a crocus, a daisy or a spray of leaves were found in Tombs 2, 6 and 19 (see Pl. 3 A and B). They are made very simply from sheet gold and wire, but are most attractive.

EARRINGS

There are no known Prepalatial earrings, unless we accept the spirals from Kavousi mentioned above.

BEADS

In this period we find globular beads (Tomb 2); collared globular in gold foil (for covering other materials) and chalcedony (Tombs 4 and 19, and see Pl. 3 C); disc-shaped, in gold and faience (Tombs 21 and 6); and thin cylinders like Egyptian mummy beads.

Another shape is the drum, decorated in repoussé with simple floral patterns, in Tombs 1 and 19 (Fig. 6). The shape is derived from fish vertebrae, which were strung together and worn as necklaces. This type of bead, which includes some of the most advanced examples of Prepalatial jewellery, had a long subsequent history (see p. 64).

Fig. 6   Drum bead from Mochlos, Tomb 1.

Biconical beads like those from Leukas (see p. 49) are found in gold in Tomb 21, and in silver at Krasi; and what looks like an ancestor of the later amygdaloid bead comes from the lower deposit of Platanos, Tholos A.

In addition, an attractive dash of colour is provided by beads of simple shapes in steatite, cornelian, amethyst, crystal, faience and shell, notably from Tombs 6 and 19 and from Kavousi.

PENDANTS

Pendants are popular, especially on chains, which are sometimes simple, sometimes loop-in-loop. The pendants frequently take the form of leaves, of which three kinds may be recognized: small leaves, large leaves decorated with dot repoussé, and sprays. Examples come from Tombs 2, 4, 6, 19 and 21 and from the Tholos at Hagia Triada. Another distinctive pendant is a crinkled cone, from Tomb 2 and from the lower deposit of Platanos, Tholos A. A third example, probably from Mochlos, is illustrated in Pl. 3 D. Triangular ornaments, possibly representing axes, come from Tomb 2 and from Hagia Triada and Trapeza; and two splendid pendants from Sphoungaras, near Gournia, take the form of ivy leaves on long chains.

Mention should also be made of a club (or phallus) in silver from Tomb 6; possibly a Cycladic import, for pendants of this shape in stone are common in Cycladic tombs. Finally a chalcedony bird comes from Tomb 4, a bronze lion from Tomb 6, and an ivory pig from Kavousi.

BRACELETS

Bracelets of gold or silver wire come from Pyrgos and Krasi. Another variety comes from Tombs 2, 16 and 19; all that survives is a gold foil covering for some other material (possibly leather), now vanished. They are decorated with embossed patterns, a simple enough process where the metal is as thin as it is here.

FINGER RINGS

Only one example is known, of silver wire, from Krasi.

CLOTHING ORNAMENTS

Ornaments of sheet metal were used for sewing to the dress. Examples from Tombs 2 and 19 take the form of stars, discs and strips.

CRETE: EARLY PALATIAL

2000–1700 BC

Introduction

About 2000 BC the first Cretan palaces were built, at Knossos, Phaestos, Mallia, Zakro and probably at other sites yet to be identified. The civilization based on these royal palaces was essentially an elaboration and a refinement of the Prepalatial culture; it ended with the destruction by earthquake of all the palaces about 1700 BC.

In view of the high level of the Early Palatial culture, one would expect corresponding masterpieces of jewellery, and such there undoubtedly were, but by ill luck very little has survived, and in consequence the history of the jewellery of this phase cannot be traced with any clarity.

Our principal sources are the collective tombs of the Mesara, where a little material has been left by subsequent looters. Exceptionally, the upper level of Tholos A at Platanos has yielded a fairly rich deposit of jewellery of about 2000–1900, sealed by the collapse of the roof. A few commoners' tombs in the Ailias Cemetery at Knossos make an additional contribution.

This period sees technical innovations of the highest importance. Filigree makes its first appearance about 2000 BC, granulation a little later. These closely related processes, long popular in Western Asia, reached Crete from Mesopotamia, by way of Syria (see p. 22).

Diadems were still used, but were less popular as grave furniture than before. Hairpins continue; and hoop earrings make their first appearance. Finger rings with round and oval bezels came in during the eighteenth century, and about the same time we first meet pins which may reasonably be regarded as dress pins. Beads and pendants in this period were little more than continuations of earlier varieties.

The jewellery

DIADEMS

Compared with Prepalatial usage, diadems of this period are less common and less ornate. Examples (mostly fragmentary) come from Platanos, Kalathiana and Koumasa. They are mostly plain, except for a little decoration in dot repoussé. One of the few complete examples, from Koumasa, in somewhat like the diadem from Lebena (p. 55) and can only be slightly later. It rises to a high peak in the centre, and is decorated with two rows of dots, increased to three over the peak. A fragmentary object from Kalathiana, probably a diadem, is decorated with dot rosettes and cut-out patterns, an unusual technique at this period.

HAIR SPIRALS

These articles are rare, but a bronze specimen comes from an eighteenth-century deposit in Tomb XVII at Mavro Spelio (Knossos) and thus establishes their continued existence.

EARRINGS

Open hoop earrings, generally tapering at the ends, make their first appearance. They occur in gold-plated bronze in a tomb at Mallia and in silver-plated bronze at Vorou in the Mesara.

BEADS AND PENDANTS

Globular beads are found in Tomb XVII at Mavro Spelio (Knossos) in amethyst, crystal and faience. A melon bead and a grain-of-wheat bead from a tholos tomb at Hagia Triada probably belong to this period.

From the upper level of Tholos A at Platanos, of about 2000–1900 BC, came twenty-two hollow beads, mostly collared-globular, slightly more elaborate versions of those from Mochlos. Two of them were decorated, rather clumsily, with spiral patterns in filigree.

A cylindrical bead with better filigree, also in spirals, of about the nineteenth century comes from a tomb at Kalathiana (Fig. 7).

Fig. 7   Bead with filigree spirals from Kalathiana, 1900–1800 BC

Pendants (frequently on chains) in the form of leaves and flowers continue from the previous period. As befits this more advanced epoch, they are more substantial and more elaborate in conception and execution. Examples come from the upper level of Tholos A at Platanos.

A bead in the form of a central tube with spectacle spiral drawn out from either end, and variations on this theme, were common in Anatolia, Mesopotamia and Syria (Fig. 11a). Although none has been found *in corpore* in Crete, a terracotta representation from Palaikastro (Petsofa) of 2000–1700 is evidence that the bead itself was known.[1] The type occurs again in sixteenth-century burials at Mycenae and Pylos, and will be considered in the following chapter (see pp. 67–8).

An embossed pendant in the form of a woman's breast comes from a burial deposit at Phaestos (Hagios Onouphrios). Finally, a minute pendant in the form of a lion, its mane indicated in granulation, comes from a tomb at Koumasa (Fig. 8). It was probably made in the nineteenth century.

Fig. 8   Bead in form of lion from Koumasa,
1900–1800 BC.

BRACELETS

Bracelets are rare, but examples made of bronze wire are not unknown. They are represented at Platanos, in Tholos A.

CLOTHING ORNAMENTS

Strips and discs of thin gold, formerly sewn to clothing, are recorded from the upper level of Tholos A at Platanos.

FINGER RINGS

What was later to be the standard Minoan ring, with an oval bezel at right angles to the hoop, makes its first appearance at Knossos in the eighteenth century BC. A bronze example is recorded from Ailias Tomb 5.

Rings with round bezels are also found. A bronze example comes from Vorou Mesaras (eighteenth century or earlier) and one with a silver hoop and an iron bezel from Knossos, Ailias Tomb 5 (eighteenth century).

CRETE, LATE PALATIAL, AND
EARLY MYCENAEAN 1700–1450 BC

Introduction

The great Cretan palaces, destroyed by earthquake about 1700 B C, were immediately replaced by yet finer buildings, inaugurating an even more magnificent way of life; and intensified contacts with Egypt and Western Asia produced a culture more brilliant than before.

This period ends about 1450 BC with the destruction of all the palaces except Knossos and most of the smaller centres, for reasons which are still uncertain. We do know, however, that Knossos was occupied intact by invaders from the Greek mainland.

The principal sources for Cretan Late Palatial jewellery, though more plentiful than before, are disappointingly few. Most important is a communal tomb belonging to the Palace at Mallia and known today as Chrysolakkos (the 'gold-hole'), which, although badly looted, has yielded some fine gold jewellery. On the evidence of pottery, the tomb was in use between 1900 and 1600 BC. The valuables, however, probably all belong to the latter part of this period, say 1700–1600, because of the custom of robbing earlier corpses on the occasion of later interments.

The Aegina Treasure in London is another important source. Although found in the form of tomb robbers' loot, it was almost certainly used by, and buried with, Cretan settlers on Aegina between 1700 and 1500 BC.

Secondary sources are the Royal Temple Tomb at Knossos and a tomb at Poros near Heraklion, both sixteenth century; Tomb 5 at Hagia Triada, 1500–1450; Tomb 22 at Mochlos, sixteenth century; and two houses at Palaikastro, 1500–1450.

Finally, frescoes of ladies in all their finery from the houses at Akroteri on Thera (destroyed about 1500 BC) give some idea of the vanished riches of Cretan Late Palatial jewellery.[1]

The Greek mainland must also be considered in the context of the Late Cretan Palaces. Here Cretan influence began to be felt, especially at Mycenae, during the seventeenth century BC, and was intensified in the sixteenth.

The bulk of the jewellery comes from the fantastic riches of the Shaft Graves at Mycenae: the sixteenth-century Grave Circle A, excavated by Schliemann in 1876, and the less rich and (in part) rather earlier Grave Circle B, excavated by Papadimitriou and Mylonas in 1952–4. The jewellery of the Shaft Graves, like the other objects, has been, and remains, the subject of much scholarly controversy. It appears, however, that some of it was pure Cretan; some was made by Cretans for the Mycenaean market; some by Mycenaeans from Cretan models. Eastern and northern influence, and perhaps imports, have also been identified.

Similar jewellery has come to light in smaller quantities in tombs in the neighbourhood of Pylos, at Corinth and Argos, and on the island of Skopelos.

The jewellery

DIADEMS

Diadems were worn by both sexes. They are found principally in Shaft Graves at Mycenae of the seventeenth and sixteenth centuries. The commonest variety is represented in Graves I, II and IV of Circle A and in Graves Alpha, Gamma, Epsilon, Lambda, Xi, and Omicron of Circle B at Mycenae; and in contemporary tombs at Corinth, Argos, Pylos (Englianos), Peristeria Tomb 3, and Skopelos. It is oval or pointed oval in shape; in the more elaborate versions the ends terminate in loops formed by drawing out the metal into a thin wire and turning it back on itself. Decoration takes the form of embossed circles and other simple patterns. The edges of these diadems are frequently strengthened with bronze wire. They are sometimes enriched by leaves or rosettes attached to their upper edge. The ultimate origins of these diadems must lie in Assyria, for a remarkably similar diadem occurs in a tomb at Assur of about 2000,[2] but it is not clear whether the fashion reached Greece direct from Asia or by way of Crete.

Another type of diadem comes from Shaft Grave IV at Mycenae. It is considerably narrower, and is decorated in dot repoussé with floral motifs and simple geometric patterns. From it hang, on chains, three plaques decorated in a similar way. Two undecorated diadems from the Aegina Treasure represent the basic form of this type.

A third type comes from Grave Upsilon of Grave Circle B at Mycenae. It is composed of a bronze band on which were set three leaves of gold, kept in place by three bronze pins.

Finally, two Mycenaean diadems were accidentally found in 1939 between Tiryns and Nauplia on the north-west slope of Mount Hagios Elias. They were never published, and vanished during the war.

HAIR RINGS AND SPIRALS

A group of silver rings (probably hair rings) was found in the Minoan settlement on Thera (Akroteri). In Shaft Grave Xi at Mycenae a small girl was buried, with coils of narrow gold bands in her hair.

HAIRPINS

A silver hairpin in the form of a shepherd's crook comes from Tomb IX at Mavro Spelio (Knossos). It cannot be directly dated, but is decorated with crocus patterns in a seventeenth-century pottery style, and should thus fall in that century.

Another type, in the form of a flower, is a lineal descendant of Prepalatial pins. It comes from Mallia (Chrysolakkos) and was probably made in the seventeenth century BC.

EARRINGS

The tapered-hoop type continues in Crete from the previous period. It is represented at Knossos in two seventeenth-century tombs: Gypsades Tomb 18 (silver) and Ailias Tomb 7 (bronze). On the Greek mainland similar hoops (evidently of Cretan inspiration) are recorded, in gold, silver and bronze, from Shaft Graves Xi and Upsilon at Mycenae and Grave 3 at Corinth.

In the sixteenth century in Crete the hoop was enriched with a granulated pendant. These so-called mulberry earrings occur in gold, electrum and silver, with a long and with a short 'mulberry'. Prototypes for both varieties are common in Syria (at Alalakh and Ugarit),[3] and Cyprus sees a parallel development (see pp. 86–7). Both varieties occur in a sixteenth-century burial at Poros near Heraklion. Two stone moulds for casting the long-mulberry variety are known, from Mochlos and the Mesara,[4] and one for the short-mulberry variety, probably from Crete (Pl. 1 E).

A house at Palaikastro destroyed about 1450 contained a pair of gold mulberry earrings embodying the next stage of development. The mulberry is composed of much finer granulation and is equipped with a knob finial. This form, considerably enlarged, was to flourish in the next period in Crete as the 'super-mulberry'.

A bead in the shape of a human head in the seventeenth-century Jewel Fresco from Knossos is equipped with three linked hoops in each ear (Fig. 9). If this head represents current practice, such earrings may be recognized in a set of gold wire hoops in the Aegina Treasure, of approximately the same date.

Fig. 9 Bead from the Jewel Fresco at Knossos, 1700–1600 BC.

A pair of scalloped hoops decorated with coarse granulation occurs in Shaft Grave III at Mycenae (Pl. 4 B). We may assume that they belonged to one of the three women in this grave, the other occupants being two children. They were worn suspended from rings of thin gold wire inserted in the lobe of the ear. On the evidence of a contemporary fresco from Thera, this type must surely be of Cretan origin.[5]

Two pairs of much more elaborate hoops from the Aegina Treasure, of about the seventeenth century (Pl. 4 D), must surely be earrings since it is hard to see what else they could be. They are identical front and back and are made from two embossed sheets of gold (probably mould-pressed) cut out and folded together. Within a hoop in a form of a double-headed snake are a pair of greyhounds, and below them a pair of monkeys. From the circumference hang fourteen pendants on gold chains; seven represent owls and seven are discs. Cornelian beads are threaded in various places, to add a touch of contrasting colour. Earrings of this kind, but less elaborate, are worn by a woman on a contemporary fresco from Thera.[6] The scheme of the monkeys and dogs was probably inspired by Egyptian art, for a somewhat similar arrangement occurs on a pectoral of the Twelfth Dynasty.[7]

Northern influence, or even importation, is indicated by a number of hoop earrings made from wire of angular section, with subsidiary spirals, either complete or rudimentary, which occur at Mycenae in Shaft Graves III and Omicron (see Pl. 4 c).[8]

Normal beads

Globular beads abound. A collared globular bead (descendant of Pre-palatial and Early Palatial examples) makes a final appearance in Tomb 22 at Mochlos.

Melon beads are also common. They occur in the Aegina Treasure, in Tomb 22 at Mochlos and in the Royal Temple Tomb at Knossos. Similar beads occur in lapis lazuli in Tholos Tomb B at Kakovatos. Beads of the shape of a grain of wheat are found at Mallia (Chrysolakkos) and the Royal Temple Tomb at Knossos. Biconical beads occur in the Aegina Treasure and in Tholos IV at Pylos (Englianos).

The cylinder with filigree spirals continued from the previous period; an example is found in Tomb 22 at Mochlos. A cylinder with spiral flutings comes from the Royal Temple Tomb at Knossos, and a granul-ated cylinder comes from the Acropolis Treasure at Mycenae. Closely related to this type is a cluster of large grains soldered together, as represented in Tholos Tomb A at Kakovatos.

The drum shape is found in Tomb 22 at Mochlos. A set of drum beads with a pendant leaf ornament from Tholos IV at Pylos (Engli-anos) should probably, on technical grounds, also be dated to the sixteenth century.

The flattened cylinder was popular, especially for seals. It occurs in gold in the sixteenth century, notably in Shaft Grave III at Mycenae.

The amygdaloid (almond shape) is another seal shape also used for pure jewellery. It occurs with a median rib in the Royal Temple Tomb at Knossos. It is found with fluted edges in several materials: at Hagia Triada in gold; in Tholos Tomb B at Kakovatos in lapis lazuli.

Miscellaneous beads and pendants

Identical beads of gold, lapis lazuli and cornelian in the shape of a hand holding a woman's breast occur in the Aegina Treasure.

A gold heart-shaped pendant comes from the Ivory Deposit of the Palace at Knossos, of the seventeenth century. Similar hearts in corne-lian, amethyst and rock crystal are also reported from Knossos, Palai-kastro and elsewhere in Crete.

Finally, an orthodox pendant with extremely unorthodox details, from Hagia Triada, perhaps of the early fifteenth century, consists of a minute amulet in the shape of a heart with magical objects in relief on it: a scorpion, a snake, a spider, a starfish, a snail and a hand. A similar pendant has recently been excavated at a shrine on Mount Iuktas.[9]

Relief beads

The forerunners of the mass-produced relief beads of the Mycenaean Empire (see Fig. 13) were made in Crete between 1700 and 1450 and imitated in Mycenaean Greece as follows:

1 Lotus. From Mallia (Chrysolakkos).
2 Double lily, from Knossos (Ailias, Tomb 7).
3 'Waz-lily'. So named by Evans from a motif which combines the Egyptian papyrus (*waz*) and the lily. A double version occurs in faience in the Temple Repositories of the Palace at Knossos (Fig. 10) and in gold in Shaft Grave III at Mycenae. The latter object is in fact not a bead but a clothing ornament, but is copied from a bead.

Fig. 10 Faience bead, double 'waz-lily', from Knossos, 1700–1600 BC.

4 Volute and bar. From Mochlos, Tomb 22.
5 Ivy and bar. From Mochlos, Tomb 22.
6 Flower or shell. From Tholos Tomb B at Kakovatos, in lapis lazuli.
7 Pomegranate and bar. From Mycenae, Shaft Grave III (Pl. 5E).
8 Papyrus. From the Royal Temple Tomb, Knossos.
9 Palm leaves. They come from Shaft Grave Omicron at Mycenae, and from the Aegina Treasure (Pl. 4A). This type is an early example of the interlocking variety of relief bead. A more elaborate variety with disc pendants like those in Pl. 4D comes from Kythera.

Small animal pendants

A standing lion, its mane richly granulated, was found in the Palace at Knossos in association with the Hieroglyphic Deposit, and so dates around 1700 BC. Lions couchant occur in several varieties. Two kinds are found in Shaft Graves III and IV at Mycenae and (slightly later) in Tomb 5 at Hagia Triada (Pl. 5B).

A gold bull's head occurs in the same Hagia Triada tomb (Pl. 5 A); a similar head in amethyst comes from Tomb 22 at Mochlos; and a recumbent calf comes from the Royal Temple Tomb at Knossos.

A fish comes from the Ivory Deposit of the Palace at Knossos, of the seventeenth century, and a toad, with warts indicated in granulation, from Tholos Tomb A at Kakovatos, of the early fifteenth century (Pl. 5 c).

Elaborate pendants

The most striking pieces of jewellery of the early part of the Late Palatial period are embossed pendants of great elaboration and sometimes of considerable size. Some probably hung from pins, like that in Pl. 7A, while others would have been suspended from cords.

1 An exquisite pendant comes from Mallia (Chrysolakkos) and dates from about the seventeenth century BC (Pl. 6 A). Two bees are posed heraldically over a honeycomb; above their heads is a cage containing a gold bead. From the jewel hang three discs. Filigree and granulation are used with great effect: filigree on the bodies of the bees, the honeycomb and the discs; granulation on the discs. Wire of much the same kind as the filigree is used for the bees' legs and for the cage above their heads. The main body of the ornament is embossed from a sheet of gold. The piece is hollow, with a flat back.

2 A contemporary pendant similar in technique and in certain details, but without filigree or granulation, comes from the Aegina Treasure (Pl. 6 B). A man stands holding a bird in either hand. Behind him are two curved objects resting on three lotus flowers. He wears a tall headdress, earrings, bracelets, a tunic, drawers, an apron and a tight belt. From the ornament hang five gold discs, with dot-repoussé in imitation of granulation. The influence of Egyptian art has long been observed, but the subject and the details are purely Minoan. He represents a Minoan nature god, lord of birds, beasts and vegetation, the less common male counterpart of the Mistress of Beasts. This pendant was worn suspended by a cord or a wire which ran through a horizontal hole along the top of the headdress.

3 A recumbent figure of a goat in London, from Crete, has discs as on the foregoing piece, and is clearly related to it (Pl. 5 D). In style it agrees closely with a sealing from Phaestos of 1800–1700.[10]

4 Another piece from the Aegina Treasure comprises a curved plate of gold terminating in human heads in profile (Pl. 7 B). Below it hang ten discs, as on nos 2 and 3; above the heads are loops for suspension. This piece was evidently worn on the breast, suspended from a cord running round the neck. The heads are in the Cretan style of the seven-

teenth century. [11] The eyes and eyebrows were formerly inlaid, probably with lapis lazuli.

5 In another pendant from the Aegina Treasure the principal element is a lion's head rising from a collar decorated with filigree. Below the collar a hollow receptacle hangs by a pin; some object of a perishable nature (faience or ivory?) was threaded on the pin and is lost. Two pendants representing birds and two representing eggs hang on loop-in-loop chains from the collar; three more birds hang on similar chains from the receptacle. Stylistically, the birds put this ornament in the same class as the earrings described above (p. 63). The lion's head is pierced horizontally to take a cord.

WIRE BEADS, ETC.

A group of gold wire jewellery, composed almost entirely of spirals, is best considered separately. Apart from the exceptional twelfth-century examples from Kephallenia (see p. 76), this group is confined to a few royal graves of the sixteenth century BC. Some of the examples may well have been imported from Western Asia, but others are apparently local copies and adaptations.

The tombs concerned are Shaft Graves III and Omicron at Mycenae, Tholos Tomb IV at Pylos (Englianos) and a shaft grave at Thebes. The jewellery consists of two different kinds of spectacle-spiral beads, sextuple-spiral beads, spectacle-spiral pendants, spiralled bracelets, and spiralled hair rings.

To take the beads first, in the original type (Fig. 11 a), a double spiral is drawn out from either end of a central tube. It flourished between 2300 and 2000 BC in Anatolia, on the Lower Euphrates, and in Mesopotamia, where it probably originated.[12] It has not been found in the Aegean area, but was presumably known there, for the multiple-spiral bead from the Thyreatis (Pl. 2) is an elaboration of it.

In the second type of bead (Fig. 11 b), represented at Mycenae and Pylos, the ends of the spirals are bound round the ends of the tubes. This type occurs principally between 1500 and 1000 BC and had a pretty wide

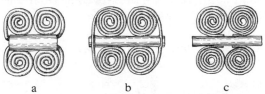

a   b   c

Fig. 11   Three varieties of spectacle-spiral bead:
(a) the original type; (b) and (c) as represented in
the Shaft Graves at Mycenae.

currency in the Middle East, in Mesopotamia and Iran and on the Lower Euphrates.[13]

The third type of bead (Fig. 11 c) differs from the other two in that the ends of the spirals are soldered externally along the sides of the tube—a labour-saving version which lacks the refinement of the second type. The type is rare. It is found at Kultepe in Central Anatolia about 1900;[11] in a terracotta copy at Petsofa near Palaikastro in East Crete, of 2000–1700 (see p. 59); and in Shaft Graves III and Omicron at Mycenae.

These beads are the only elements of the wire jewellery for which we can build up any sort of pedigree. By combining the evidence, we may suggest that all three types evolved in Mesopotamia and spread up the Euphrates into Anatolia, from where they reached the Aegean: the first around 2300 BC; the second and third between 1700 and 1550 BC.

Spectacle-spiral pendants are found only in Shaft Grave Omicron at Mycenae. They have a very long history in Western Asia and the Balkans, and it is impossible to say from which direction this fashion reached Mycenae.

The other varieties of wire jewellery have no counterparts in the Middle East, They could be Mycenaean creations, based on the quadruple-spiral bead; or, alternatively, they might equally well be of Balkan inspiration.

First come sextuple-spiral beads, a variation on the third type of quadruple-spiral beads, but with three spirals on each side. They are represented in both Mycenae Shaft Grave circles and at Pylos.

Then come four different varieties of bracelet composed of spirals arranged in different ways. All four occur in Shaft Grave III at Mycenae; one also occurs in Shaft Grave Omicron.

Lastly, only from the shaft grave at Thebes, come one complete example, and fragments of others, of a spiralled hair ring with two tight spirals attached to it at right angles.

BRACELETS

Bracelets of sheet gold decorated with rosettes come from Shaft Graves IV and Alpha at Mycenae. A simpler version from the Aegina Treasure could be a Cretan prototype.

In addition, simple bracelets of bronze wire are represented at Knossos, in Ailias Tomb 7, of the seventeenth century.

FINGER RINGS

The standard Cretan finger ring with a simple oval bezel at right-angles to the hoop (see p. 59) is first recorded in gold in the seventeenth century in Tomb 7 (Larnax 6) of the Ailias cemetery at Knossos (Pl. 8 A and B). Such rings continue in Crete and in Greece down to the end of the Bronze Age, about 1100 BC, and even occasionally beyond it.

Rings with circular bezels (cf. p. 59) also survive. One such, with the bezel engraved with characters in the Linear A script, comes from Knossos, Mavro Spelio, Tomb IX, and has been dated stylistically to the seventeenth century.

Four finger rings from the Aegina Treasure belong to the seventeenth or the sixteenth century. All are inlaid with lapis lazuli. One has a bezel in the form of a double axe (Pl. 8 C); one in the form of a reef knot; a third is inlaid throughout with fluted lapis lazuli; the fourth with a meander pattern. A somewhat similar ring, inlaid with glass, comes from a tomb at Poros, near Heraklion, where it was found in a context of the sixteenth century.

Signet rings begin perhaps as early as the seventeenth century BC, but are not common till the sixteenth. A gold ring in London has a circular bezel with an engraving of two Cretan wild goats mating.[15] It looks at first sight like a finger ring, but is in fact too small to be worn on the finger and must be a signet. It is dated stylistically about 1600 BC.

A true finger ring of the same date from a tomb at Sphoungaras in East Crete has a double hoop of bronze and an engraved bezel of roek crystal. This use of an engraved ring-stone is apparently unique so early and anticipates by many centuries the custom of Classical Greece.

The surviving gold signet rings of this period are best represented not in Crete but at Mycenae. It is quite probable that the two gold rings from Grave Circle A at Mycenae were made expressly for Mycenaean patrons, but there can be no doubt that they were made by a Cretan. The 'Lion-Hunt' and the 'Battle in the Glen' are too well known to need description here.

CLOTHING ORNAMENTS

From Crete

Strips of thin gold, and discs with rosette patterns, probably sewn to clothing, are found at Mallia (Chrysolakkos). A number of discs from the Aegina Treasure decorated with dotted rosettes (Pl. 8 G) and a relief of a goddess in typical Minoan dress from Gournia (early fifteenth century) would have served the same purpose.

From Greece

Clothing ornaments are very common in the Shaft Graves at Mycenae.

They take three main forms: (1) discs; (2) cut-out reliefs, often very like contemporary relief beads; and (3) belt ornaments.

1 *Discs*. Many varieties, with embossed decoration, occur in Shaft Grave III at Mycenae; popular motifs are a butterfly, an octopus and geometric patterns. The designs are predominantly, but not exclusively, Cretan.

2 *Cut-out reliefs*. The following subjects are represented in Shaft Graves III and IV at Mycenae. A shrine; a goddess in Minoan dress like the one from Gournia; a naked Oriental goddess with doves; a butterfly; an octopus; a sphinx; a griffin; heraldic arrangements of cats and deer (Pl. 8 D and E); and a copy of a 'waz-lily' bead. There is a strong stylistic homogeneity about these ornaments, but influences from several directions can be seen. Syria is suggested by the naked goddess; Anatolia by the deer; Crete by the Minoan goddess, octopus and waz-lily. The work is rather crude, and it would possibly be correct to regard these pieces as genuine Mycenaean creations of an eclectic nature.

In addition, confronted butterflies, a swallow, an owl and a conch shell come from Tholos Tomb 3 at Peristeria, and owls also come from Tholos IV at Pylos (Englianos) and Tholos Tomb B at Kakovatos (Pl. 8 F).

3 *Belt ornaments, etc.* Button-like objects from Shaft Graves IV, V and Omicron at Mycenae had apparently decorated shield straps.

DRESS PINS

Pins of great elaboration are found in the Shaft Graves at Mycenae. Most, if not all, were used for fastening drapery or diadems.

A silver pin of shepherd's crook type comes from Grave III (Pl. 7A). From the head is suspended a gold embossed ornament of a woman wearing Minoan dress and holding in her hands a double chain or garland. On her head are two superimposed pairs of volutes; above these are three pairs of branches curving outwards and downwards and ending in papyrus flowers and fruits; above these are three erect papyrus flowers. The type of the pin and the representation of the goddess (for such she must be) are purely Minoan, but a certain coarseness of the workmanship may indicate mainland work. The papyrus ornament is Egyptian in origin but reached Mycenae by way of Minoan art, where it was common.

Bronze pins with heads of rock crystal are found in Graves III and Omicron. They were used as dress pins.

A gold pin with a head in the form of a sheep of the argali variety on a platform comes from Grave IV. It is remarkably like the silver pin from Amorgos, some three to four centuries older (see p. 51). Both are probably imports from Anatolia, of which area the argali is native.

Another pin from the same grave has a head in the form of a deer's horn. It could have the same origin as the argali pin.

A third pin, from Grave III, with a heraldic arrangement of deer, comes from the same mould (or stamp) as a number of clothing ornaments from the same tomb. Like them, it could well be a local product.

THE MYCENAEAN EMPIRE

1450–1100 BC

Introduction

By 1450 BC the only surviving Cretan Palace was that at Knossos, which, it appears, was taken over by Mycenaean invaders from the Greek mainland, who soon ruled all Crete from their Knossian headquarters. But not for long, for about 1375 that palace too was destroyed (we do not know by whom) and Crete became a second-class and somewhat inward-looking member of the Aegean world.

On the mainland, the capture of Crete would seem to have initiated a sort of Mycenaean Empire, which was to persist intact until about 1200, and, in a rather fragmented state, for a further century after that. The culture of this Empire, which, in some form, extended from Asia Minor and the Levant in the east to Sicily and Southern Italy in the west, was remarkably uniform for some two and a half centuries.

The last century of the Mycenaean age, from 1200 to 1100, is marked by a general decrease in wealth; but (in some areas) there were attempts at recovery, accompanied by a resurgence of Oriental influence, and the development of local styles.

The jewellery of the Mycenaean Empire differs in many respects from its forerunners. Diadems and pins no longer occur, and earrings are virtually restricted to Crete. The principal articles are beads and pendants of many kinds, including the typical relief beads; clothing ornaments, many of them replicas of the relief beads; and finger rings, some for use as seals, others for adornment only. Granulation was much used, and enamel was introduced about 1425. In addition to gold, lapis lazuli, rock crystal and faience were popular throughout the

72

period, as was glass, cast in moulds to resemble closely the relief beads.

For some two and a half centuries, we can find practically no changes in Mycenaean jewellery. The beads, particularly the relief beads, continue in almost exactly the same forms, the only difference being that as gold became scarcer glass gained in popularity, both for complete beads and as a core for a covering of gold foil.

In the twelfth century, in many areas jewellery is confined to glass relief beads. In other regions, such as Crete, Ialysus in Rhodes, Naxos, Perati in Attica, and Kephallenia, gold jewellery continued to be made – partly in the old tradition, partly in a new style owing much to Western Asiatic, Cypriote, and occasionally northern influence.

Remains of no less than three Mycenaean goldsmith's shops have been discovered in the ruins of two successive palaces at Thebes. One, from the earlier palace, is dated about 1400–1350 BC. The other two, from the later palace, are about a century later.

The number of surviving steatite moulds for the casting of glass jewellery gives some indication of the popularity of this class of ornament. Apart from the main centres at Mycenae and Knossos, moulds have been found at Palaikastro in Crete, on Chios, and in Asia Minor.

The abundant jewellery from Cyprus of 1400–1100 BC calls for special mention; it is discussed in detail below (pp. 86–7), and is illustrated in Pls 10 E and 12. It is a mixture of Minoan-Mycenaean, Syrian and Egyptian elements.

In Crete, jewellery of this period has been found principally at Knossos. The Isopata Royal Tomb, a rich source, comes at the very beginning. A little later, about 1400, is the very rich Tomb 4 at Sellopoullo. Tombs at Phaestos (Kalyvia Cemetery) are roughly contemporary. Slightly later, about 1350–1300, are two undisturbed burials in Tholos Tombs 1 and 4 at Archanes. The lady buried in Tholos 4 wore a rich selection of the sort of jewellery made familiar in Mycenaean frescoes: a diadem of gold and glass beads; gold hair spirals; gold rosettes attached to her dress; two necklaces of gold, glass and faience beads. And in her jewel box was a third necklace of assorted beads, mostly of gold. The thirteenth century, much poorer in jewellery, is represented by tombs at Olous and a lady's jewel box in a tomb at Pachyammos. The twelfth-century revival is represented by tombs at Mouliana and Photoula near Praisos.

On the Greek mainland, Mycenae itself is a very rich source of Empire jewellery. Of the chamber tombs, one in three of those excavated contained gold jewellery: a high percentage. Most of it cannot be dated because the tombs excavated by Tsountas in the 1880s have not been properly published. The few dug later by Wace seem to have remained in use over a long period, and, between them, to have contained jewellery of 1450–1200. Other rich sources are tombs at the Argive Heraeum, Dendra, Pylos, and the Vapheio Tomb near Sparta.

Between 1200 and 1100 BC jewellery is rare in Mycenaean lands, with a few surprising exceptions: Ialysus in Rhodes, Naxos, and Perati in Attica.

The jewellery

DIADEMS

Gold diadems, though common in the previous period (see pp. 61–2), are very rare in the Mycenaean Empire. Three are, however, recorded in the twelfth century: plain strips, perforated at each end, from New Tombs 20 and 32 at Ialysus and a diadem mentioned but not described from Kamini Tomb 1 on Naxos. Cypriote influence, if not importation, is probable.

HAIR SPIRALS

Spirals of gold or silver were used both to decorate the hair and as finger rings. It is only where the spirals have been found in burials in their original position on the body that we can be certain of their function. Those certainly used as finger rings are mentioned below, on p. 84. A greater number could have served either purpose. Examples in gold are found in Tomb 7 at Katsamba, in the Kalyvia cemetery at Phaestos, Tholos 4 at Archanes, the lady's tomb at Pachyammos, Tomb 25 at Mycenae, Tombs 11, 16 and 92 at Perati and New Tomb 87 at Ialysus. A silver spiral was found at Aplomata Tomb 2 on Naxos. Spirals of doubled gold wire, from the Tiryns Treasure, not unlike the Athenian Dark Age spirals (see p. 89), should probably be regarded as northern imports of the twelfth century BC.

HAIRPINS

Shepherd's crook pins (probably for the hair rather than the dress) continued in restricted use in Crete until about 1400 BC. Examples are recorded in gold from the Isopata Royal Tomb at Knossos; in silver from another tomb at Knossos (*Survey*, no. 149); and in glass from Tholos 4 at Archanes.

EARRINGS

Earrings are common to Crete, but much less so in Mycenaean territory. Mulberry earrings continue from the previous period. A pair of the long variety comes from a tomb on Samos of the fourteenth century. A pair of the short variety comes from a tomb at Miletus of the thirteenth or twelfth century and a singleton from the tholos tomb at Kamilari near Phaestos (fourteenth century). An aberrant pair of short-mulberry earrings, with overlapping wires at the upper edge of the hoops, comes from Aplomata Tomb 3 at Naxos, of the twelfth century.

But the Cretan earring *par excellence* of the period 1450–1200 is what may be called the super-mulberry (Pl. 10D), a greatly enlarged version (about 3.5 cm long) of the type represented at Palaikastro shortly before 1450 (see pp. 62–3). Examples have been found in Mavro Spelio Tomb VII and on the Kephala Ridge at Knossos; in the tholos tomb at Kamilari; in Tombs 22 and 16 at Olous; and there are further (unpublished) examples in Heraklion from other Cretan sites.

Finally, two Cypriote bull's head earrings found their way to Greece; one in Perati Tomb 11 (twelfth century BC), the other in the Tiryns Treasure.

BEADS AND PENDANTS

Miscellaneous

Beads and pendants are particularly common on Mycenaean sites, and occur in many varieties. They were made in gold, stone and glass. A necklace from Asine, Tomb 5, shows how the colours were arranged. Frescoes and other representations also illustrate the arrangement of beads.[1] The commoner varieties occur in so many tombs that it would be tedious to enumerate them all, and the reader is advised to work from the site lists on pp. 207–10 if a complete record is required.

Globular beads, in gold and many other materials, are numerous. A large globular bead richly decorated with circles and lines in fine granulation (Fig. 12), which is almost restricted to the later fifteenth century, is typical of Mycenaean jewellery at its best. It is found in Sellopoullo Tomb 4 at Knossos; Mycenae, Tomb 515; the Vapheio Tomb; and Dendra, Tomb 10.

Melon beads are found in Tomb 10 at Dendra and in the lady's tomb at Pachyammos. Beads in the shape of a grain of wheat are found in Tomb 10 at Dendra in gold and elsewhere in gold, glass and faience.

Fig. 12   Spherical bead from the Vapheio Tomb, about 1425 BC.

From the fifteenth century onwards a granulated cylinder was popular. It is found in the Acropolis Treasure at Mycenae; at Ialysus, in New Tomb 61; in Tomb 1 at Perati, and elsewhere, so that it survived in use for some three centuries. Closely related in appearance to this type is a cluster of large grains soldered together, a variety represented in Tomb 103 at Mycenae, the Vapheio Tomb, and the Tholos at Dendra.

Biconical beads are rare but the type (a northern one) is represented in gold at Kephallenia.

The club was a frequent form for pendants from the fifteenth century onwards. It was made not only in gold but in rock crystal (Knossos, Zapher Papoura, Tomb 97) and glass.

The crocus is related to the club. It is found from the fifteenth century onwards in gold (Knossos, Isopata Royal Tomb) and glass.

Gold-foil beads in the form of a triglyph occur in Aplomata Tomb 2 on Naxos, of the twelfth century. A Syrian origin is probable.[2]

The drum shape continues, and is found in the Tholos at Dendra. The flattened cylinder also continues, especially for engraved gems. A superb gold seal with a griffin in intaglio on the front and an enamelled net pattern on the reverse comes from Tholos IV at Pylos (Englianos). It is dated stylistically about 1400.

The fluted amygdaloid is another seal shape, also used for jewellery, which continues from the previous period. It is found in gold in Zapher Papoura Tomb 99 at Knossos, in lapis lazuli in the Isopata Royal Tomb at Knossos, in gold foil and glass at Spata, and in cornelian in Tomb 518 at Mycenae.

The wheel bead, sometimes also called a lantern bead, was a popular Syrian and Egyptian type in faience.[3] It is also found on many Greek sites in faience and in Tomb 2 at Mycenae in gold.

Wire cage beads in two or three registers, with blue glass interiors, occur in Isopata Tomb 1 at Knossos and in Tholos Tombs 1 and 4 at Archanes. And a spectacle-spiral bead very like earlier examples from Mycenae and Pylos (see p. 67) is recorded from Kephallenia.

A pendant pomegranate occurs at Mycenae in Tomb 518, and in the Prinaria Deposit. A finer example comes from Old Tomb 67 at Enkomi; it is paralleled by another from Enkomi, in Nicosia.

A gold figure of a duck, with granulation, was found in the destruction levels of the Palace at Knossos, and should date from the early fourteenth century BC.

Relief beads

These, the most characteristic ornaments of Minoan-Mycenaean jewellery, consist principally of stylized representations of marine and vegetable life and of objects of a religious nature, stamped in shallow relief out of sheet gold. The ornament was completed by the addition of a backing of sheet gold, soldered on, the space between the two sheets being filled with magnetite sand. The finest examples were decorated with details in granulation and occasionally with touches of blue repoussé enamel.

Counterparts of many of these ornaments were made from glass, either dark blue, to imitate lapis lazuli, or (less commonly) pale greenish-blue, to imitate turquoise. The beads were cast in steatite moulds, of which a number have survived (see p. 40). Beads of this class were also occasionally made in lapis lazuli and blue compound, and glass beads were covered with gold foil to imitate sheet gold.

The rare early relief beads have been discussed above (p. 65). Between 1450 and 1400 BC something like mass-production seems to have been introduced. Virtually all the best-known types evolved during this half-century. This is a rich period for jewellery, and to it should be ascribed the finest examples, decorated with granulation and enamel. The tombs most productive of such pieces are Sellopoullo Tomb 4 at Knossos, Tholos 1 at Archanes, the Tholos at Volo, Tomb 10 at Dendra, and Tombs 88 and 103 at Mycenae.

During this half-century we find examples of gold beads reproduced exactly in glass, but they are not as yet very numerous.

In the fourteenth century, gold beads of good quality were still being made, but were being supplemented to an increasing extent by glass. In the thirteenth and twelfth centuries, sheet gold was still used, but less often; the beads tended to be of glass, some covered with gold foil. The Tholos at Menidi and the tombs at Spata, Ialysus and Perati provide classic examples of this development.

It should be emphasized that from 1400 BC onwards very few new motifs are found. It is an astonishing phenomenon that, for some three centuries or more, objects stylistically identical continued to be made. Can it be that the inventive spirit responsible for their production was extinguished in the destruction of Knossos?

There follows a list of the types of relief beads, with only the most significant of the contexts in which they have been found. They are illustrated in Fig. 13, under the numbers allotted to them here. A few are also shown in Pls 9 and 10. In Pl. 10 E is a Cypriote diadem; the patterns on it were made with stamps intended for making relief beads.

1 Rosette. The commonest variety. Particularly fine examples come from Zapher Papoura Tomb 66 at Knossos (gold, forty-six examples); Mycenae, Tomb 515 (gold); Argive Heraeum (Prosymna), Tomb 41 (gold and glass); and the Tholos at Dendra (gold). In the last-named

1

2

3

4

5

6

7

8

9

10

11

12

13

14

15

16

17

18

19

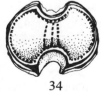

Fig. 13   Types of Mycenaean relief beads,
1450–1150 BC.

tomb an entire necklace of thirty-six rosette beads was discovered; the beads were of two sizes, eighteen large and eighteen small.

2 Bracket, or curled-leaf.[4] A common variety in glass; only rarely found in gold. It is not certain what is represented. The brackets frequently have gold or glass discs attached to them by fine wires. A variant in glass was found in 'Tsountas's House' at Mycenae, in which the upper part is replaced by the head and breast of a goddess of Asiatic type. Examples come from Tombs 24, 55 and 68 at Mycenae (gold); Tomb 515 at Mycenae (gold and glass); the Tomb of the Genii at Mycenae (glass); Tomb 6 at Argos (gold); and (in glass) from many other tombs in the Argolid and elsewhere. Moulds for the casting of this design in glass come from Mycenae (three examples) and Knossos.

3 Volute with bar, 1. A particularly fine example, of gold with touches of enamel, comes from Tomb 88 at Mycenae. Other examples come from Tomb 37 at Argive Heraeum (glass) and Phaestos, Kalyvia (glass).

4 Volute with bar, doubled. A second volute is added to the underside of type 3. A rare type, represented in the Tholos at Volo (gold and glass) and in Tomb 524 at Mycenae (glass).

5 Volute with rosette (Pl. 10 A). The bar of type 3 is replaced by a rosette. A rare type, represented in Tombs 102 (gold) and 103 (gold, enamelled) at Mycenae. In the former the rosette curls to the right, in the latter to the left.

6 Volute with bar, 2 (Pl. 9 A and B). A common type. Select examples come from Mycenae, Tombs 25, 28, 31 and 68 (gold); the Tholos at Dendra (gold); Tomb 2 at Dendra (glass); the tomb at Spata (glass and gold foil); and Perati, Tomb 45. A mould for casting this type in glass comes from Mycenae.

7 Bud. A rare motif, also found in vase painting (Furumark, Motive 62). Examples come from tombs at Mycenae; the Tomb of Clytaemnestra (gold); the Treasury of Atreus and the Tomb of the Genii (glass).

8 Argonaut. A common type, also represented in vase painting (Furumark, Motive 22). Examples come from Mycenae: Tombs 102 (gold), 103 (gold) and the Prinaria Deposit; from Tomb 6 at Argos (gold); and from Tomb 2 at Dendra (gold). A mould for casting this type in glass comes from Knossos.

9 Double argonaut, 1 (Pls 9 B and 10 C). A common type, represented in Tomb 88 at Mycenae (gold, enamelled); the Tholos at Volo (gold, enamelled); at Knossos, Isopata Tomb 2 and Zapher Papoura Tombs 7 and 36 (gold); in Tholos 4 at Archanes (gold and glass); in the Tholos at Menidi (glass); and in Tomb 74 at Perati (glass).

10 Double argonaut, 2. As type 9, but with an extra tentacle. A very

rare variety, represented in Tomb 88 at Mycenae (gold, with spaces for enamel).

11 Cockle (Pl. 9 B). The type is represented in Tholos B at Kakovatos (gold); Tomb 8 at Mycenae (gold and blue compound); Tomb 2 at Dendra (glass); and the Tholos at Menidi (gold foil and glass). A mould for casting glass ornaments of this type comes from Knossos.

12 Lily, 1. A rare type, first found in Minoan vase painting of the seventeenth century. The method of wearing such beads is shown on an ivory engraving from Kakovatos. Examples come from Tomb 76 at Mycenae (gold) and the Tholos at Dendra (gold).

13 Lily, 2. A simplified version of type 12. Represented in Tombs 88 and 91 at Mycenae (gold); Dendra, Tombs 10 (gold) and 2 (glass); Argive Heraeum (Prosymna), Tombs 41 (gold) and 33 (glass). A mould for casting ornaments of this type in glass comes from Knossos.

14 Lily, 3 (Pl. 9 A and B). This type is composed of the upper part of type 13, elaborated and made interlocking. It is represented in Tombs 68, 78, 103 and 520 at Mycenae (gold); and in Tombs 8 and 10 at Dendra (gold).

15 Lily, 4. Like type 14, but with a small projection on each volute. The motif also occurs in vase painting (Furumark, Motive 47: 2). It is represented in the Tholos at Volo (gold) and at Phaestos, Kalyvia (glass).

16 'Waz-lily'. A common motif, ultimately of Egyptian origin, which goes back to the seventeenth century (see p. 65). It is represented in Tombs 88 and 91 at Mycenae; in Tomb 2 at the Argive Heraeum (gold); in Tomb 10 at Dendra (gold); and in the Tholos at Menidi (glass). A mould for casting this type in glass comes from Mycenae.

17 Double 'waz-lily' (Pl. 9 A). A rare type, represented at Mycenae in Tomb 68 (gold) and in the Treasury of Atreus (glass).

18 Papyrus, 1. A motif of Egyptian origin, also found in vase painting (Furumark, Motive 11). It is represented in Tomb 44 at the Argive Heraeum (gold); in the Palace at Thebes (gold); and at Spata (gold foil and glass).

19 Papyrus, 2. A degenerate version of type 18. A common type, also represented in vase painting (Furumark, Motive 25). Select examples come from Tholos 1 at Archanes; the Tholos at Kamilari; the lady's tomb at Pachyammos; Tombs 88 and 91 and the Prinaria Deposit at Mycenae (gold); Tombs 520 and 523 at Mycenae (glass); and Tomb 2 at Dendra. A mould for the casting of this type in glass comes from Mycenae.

20 Papyrus, 3. A rare, and probably late type, found in the Tholos at Menidi (gold foil and glass) and at Spata (glass). A mould for the casting of this type in glass comes from Mycenae.

21 Ivy, 1. A rare type, also represented in wall painting and vase painting (Furumark, Motive 12). It occurs in Tomb 10 at Dendra (gold) and Spata (glass). A double mould for the casting of this type in glass was found at Palaikastro.

22 Ivy, 2 (Pl. 10B). A simplified version of type 21, also found in vase painting (Furumark, Motive 12:8). It is represented at Mycenae in Tombs 88 and 103 (gold, enamelled); in the Tholos at Volo (gold); and at Gournes (glass).

23 Double ivy. A stalked and duplicated version of type 22. A rare type; it occurs in Tomb 88 at Mycenae and Tholos III at Pylos, Englianos (both gold, enamelled).

24 Ivy, 3. An interlocking version of type 22. A common type. Select examples come from Mycenae, Tombs 88 (gold) and 520 (glass); and from the Tholos at Dendra (gold and glass).

25 Wallet. Originally Egyptian, it occurs with a flat or a scalloped top. It was found in Tomb 103 at Mycenae (gold); in Tomb 2 at the Argive Heraeum (gold); in Tomb 10 at Dendra (gold); and at Spata (gold foil). A mould for casting this type in glass comes from Mycenae.

26 Beetle. A rare and probably late type. It occurs at Spata (gold foil).

27 Jug (Pl 9 A). A common type, representing a sacred Minoan motif, which is recorded as early as Early Palatial times; a stone amulet in this form comes from Hagios Onouphrios. Examples come from the Palace at Thebes (gold); the Tholos at Menidi (gold foil and glass); and Old Tomb 4 at Ialysus (gold foil and glass).

28 Figure-of-eight shield. A sacred Minoan motif. Examples come from Tomb 518 at Mycenae (gold); Tomb 3 at Prosymna (gold); Tholos nos III and IV at Pylos, Englianos (gold); and from Tholos 4 at Archanes (rock crystal). A mould for casting this type in glass comes from Knossos.

29 Altar or basin. A sacred Minoan motif. Examples come from the Tholos at Dendra (gold); the Tholos at Menidi (gold); and Spata (glass).

30 Helmeted head. A rare type, recorded only from the shaft grave under the Palace at Pylos (gold).

31 Bee. Examples come from Tomb 8 at Mycenae (gold), Menidi (gold) and Koukaki, Athens (gold). There is a mould for casting this type in glass (in Boston).

32 Bull's head (Pl. 9B). A stylized version of an old-established type of pendant (cf. Pl. 5 A). Examples come from Koukaki (Athens), and New Tomb 42 at Ialysus (gold).

33 Single axe. A rare type, represented in gold in two Athenian tombs: Koukaki and Philopappos.

34 Double axe. A rare type, represented at Enkomi in Cyprus (gold).

NECKLACES

Necklaces are occasionally found composed of loop-in-loop chains so tightly linked as to be frequently mistaken for plaited cords (see Fig. 3). One such example comes from Tomb 55 at Mycenae. Others come from Tomb D at Kephallenia and Aplomata Tomb 2 at Naxos (both twelfth century).

BRACELETS

Bracelets are only once recorded in this period. The Tiryns Treasure contains sets of spirals of doubled wire in three different sizes. The smallest have been interpreted as hair spirals (see p. 74); the two largest sizes are probably bracelets. There is good reason to believe that spirals of this form are in the first instance imports from central Europe via the Balkans.[5] We should probably date these spirals in the twelfth century rather than in the eleventh with the Athenian spirals (p. 74) because they resemble the gold 'wheels' in the Tiryns Treasure which are dated to the twelfth century by the amber beads which decorate them.

FINGER RINGS

Finger rings were used for decoration or as signets. They may be divided into three main classes: (1) simple hoops and their derivatives; (2) rings with an oblong bezel at right-angles to the hoop (the standard Minoan-Mycenaean form); (3) rings with bezels of other shapes.

1. *Hoops and coils.* Plain hoops of gold or silver occur in Tomb 11 at Mycenae, in New Tomb 53 at Ialysus, and elsewhere. Coils were used as hair spirals and as finger rings (see p. 74); but examples from Sellopoullo Tomb 4 and Zapher Papoura Tomb 99 at Knossos, from their position on the corpses, were certainly finger rings. More elaborate coils, of twisted wire, from Tomb 42 at Mycenae and Tomb 9 at Perati, were probably also finger rings.

2. *With oblong bezels.*

(a) With plain bezel. Rings of this type, in gold, gilt bronze, silver, and bronze, first found in Crete in the eighteenth century (see p. 59), continue in Crete and in Greece down to the end of this period and (in Crete) beyond it. They frequently have a raised spine down the centre of the bezel (Pl. 11 B).

(b) With inlaid bezel. A gold ring with traces of ivory inlay in the bezel was found in a lady's jewel box in a thirteenth-century tomb at Pachyammos.

(c) With enamelled bezel. The earlier fashion for inlaying the bezel with precious stones or glass (p. 69) is now superseded by enamelling. One such ring comes from Sellopoullo Tomb 4 at Knossos (Pl. 11 A), three from the Kalyvia Cemetery at Phaestos, and one from the Tholos at Volo; all these probably date from about 1400 BC. One from New Tomb 31 at Ialysus is a little later, and examples are recorded as late as the twelfth century from New Tombs 17 and 61 at Ialysus and (probably) Aplomata Tomb 1 at Naxos. A set of six enamelled rings from a twelfth-century tomb at Kouklia (Old Paphos) in Cyprus is also probably Mycenaean work.

(d) With granulation and filigree on bezel. Two gold rings from the Tiryns Treasure and two from twelfth-century tombs in Eastern Crete (Mouliana and Photoula, near Praisos) have the standard oblong bezel, decorated with serpentine patterns in filigree flanked by granulation. This aesthetic scheme is new to the Aegean and was probably introduced from Cyprus in the twelfth century.

(e) Signet rings. These continue from the previous period right down to 1100. As before, they are sometimes cast solid in gold, but more frequently made hollow from sheet gold and filled with magnetite sand. In a very unusual type of signet ring the bezel has a base metal core, plated with precious metals in two sections, so that the scene is divided horizontally.[6]

In the fifteenth century even finer rings were made than in the sixteenth. The study of the designs is beyond the scope of this survey, but a few superlative examples may be mentioned. The finest is perhaps the large ring from the Tiryns Treasure. Other superb examples come from the Tholos at Dendra and Isopata Tomb 1 at Knossos.

The ring illustrated in Pl. 11 c comes from Tomb 68 at Mycenae and was probably made about 1400. It represents a heraldic composition of griffins on either side of a Minoan column.

The ring in Pl. 11 D comes from Tomb 84 at Mycenae and was probably also made about 1400. It represents a man tending a plant on an altar, while behind him stands a Cretan wild goat, the agrimi; behind the goat is a tree. The clean lines of this design show clearly that it is engraved in solid gold.

Occasionally signet rings were carved entirely out of a block of stone. Examples are recorded in rock crystal, chalcedony, agate and red jasper.[7]

3 *With other sorts of bezel.* From the Vapheio Tomb comes a ring with an inlaid circular bezel and another with an enamelled rosette as a bezel and an enamelled hoop; the enamel is blue and green. Finally, there are three rings with unusual bezels. One from Mavro Spelio Tomb VII at Knossos has a gold bezel in the form of five chrysalids. The ring cannot be directly dated, but the chrysalids appear to be

contemporary with a solitary one from Tomb 518 at Mycenae (fifteenth century). The second ring has a heart-shaped bezel (probably representing an ivy leaf) formerly inlaid, but the inlay is now missing. It comes from Tholos IV at Pylos. The third ring, from Thebes, has a bezel in the form of a bee.[8]

CLOTHING ORNAMENTS

Cut-out clothing ornaments are also found in later Mycenaean deposits. Rosettes in particular are very common throughout this period. An unusual kind of double argonaut comes from the Tomb of Clytaemnestra at Mycenae; a butterfly from the Tomb of Clytaemnestra and Tomb 102 at Mycenae and from the Tholos at Volo; and a sacral ivy from Tomb 1 in the Agora at Athens.

Belt ornaments have also been recognized. A cone with spiral decoration, possibly representing a snail, is very common. A set from a tholos tomb at Pylos (Rutsi) had evidently been sewn to a belt, and such was probably always the purpose of these cones. Like the relief beads, they were also made in glass. An unusually fine kind of rosette probably also served as decoration for a belt or girdle. One such example comes from Tomb 31 at Mycenae, and a set of eight comes from Tomb 10 at Dendra.

Appendix: Cypro-Mycenaean jewellery 1400–1100 BC

DIADEMS

Diadems are common (Pl. 10 E). They are composed of strips of thin sheet gold stamped with rosettes, palmettes and spirals, or with impressions from stamps intended primarily for making relief beads; occasionally they are decorated freehand in repoussé. Although the patterns are frequently of Mycenaean origin, the diadems themselves are not of Mycenaean but of Asiatic inspiration. They bear no resemblance to those from the Shaft Graves at Mycenae; moreover, by the time they first appeared in Cyprus, diadems had been obsolete in Greece and Crete for a century.

FUNERARY MOUTHPIECES

We may claim a similar origin for oval ornaments of thin sheet gold. They are frequently decorated in the same way as the diadems, but some, with embossed representations of lips, reveal their purpose, which was to cover the mouth of the corpse. A mouthpiece of this nature, evidently exported from Cyprus, was found in Tomb IX of the Mavro Spelio cemetery at Knossos.

SPIRALS

Spirals of wire are common in Cypriote tombs of this date (Pl. 12 I). They were probably used indiscriminately as hair ornaments, earrings and possibly even nose rings. They have a long history in the Aegean and Western Asia (see p. 48).

EARRINGS

Many types are known, some of Mycenaean, some of Syrian origin.

1 Spiral. For these ornaments, see above.

2 Tapered hoop (Pl. 12 B and E). This Asiatic type was probably introduced into Cyprus from Syria about 1400. It survived in Cyprus through the Dark Ages and was reintroduced from there into Greece about the seventh century.

3 Tapered hoop made of twisted strips of gold (Pl. 12 D). This type is not Minoan or Mycenaean, and must be either a local Cypriote or a Syrian creation.

4 Leech (Pl. 12 H). An elongated version of the tapered hoop. A non-Mycenaean type, which reached Cyprus in the twelfth century.

5 'Short mulberry' (Pl. 12 F). An Asiatic type also found in Crete (see p. 62). Like the simple tapered hoop, it lasted through the Dark Ages in Cyprus and reappeared in the Greek repertoire in the seventh century.

6 'Long mulberry' (Pl. 12 C). Another Asiatic type also found in Crete (see p. 62). Some examples are equipped with wire spirals at the top of the pendant on either side, to give the appearance of a rudimentary bull's head.

7 Hoop or spiral with a bull's head pendant (Pl. 12 G). A stylized rendering of a bull's head, stamped from sheet gold, is pierced at the top on either side to receive a thin wire, which is bent to form a hoop or a spiral: a local Cypriote creation. Two earrings of this type found their way to Greece: one occurs in a twelfth-century tomb at Perati in Attica, the other in the Tiryns Treasure.

BEADS AND PENDANTS

Many beads and pendants are of known Mycenaean types; others are of Egyptian origin.

FINGER RINGS

Rings with circular bezels inlaid with coloured glass are particularly common. The type is of Minoan-Mycenaean origin, for it occurs in the Vapheio Tomb. Other rings, with no such antecedents, are found; they are probably of Syrian origin. A set of rings from a tomb at Kouklia were decorated with cloisonné enamel. The same tomb also contained a gold signet ring with an engraved bezel of lapis lazuli.

PINS

Most Cypro-Mycenaean pins are not of Mycenaean but of Syrian origin, with an ornate head, sometimes of blue compound, and an eyelet hole (for a safety chain) halfway down the shaft (Pl. 12 A). The shepherd's crook pin, a Minoan type (see p. 62), is also occasionally found in Cyprus.

FIBULAE

Two gold fibulae of the arched type in London come from Maroni; they are dated typologically in the twelfth century or slightly later.[9] This is a pure Greek type of fibula, but examples in precious metals are not as yet attested outside Cyprus.

II

THE DARK AGES 1100–900 BC

General introduction

About 1100 BC the Mycenaean world collapsed, to be succeeded by some two hundred years of poverty and near-barbarism, whose only progressive feature was the gradual replacement of bronze, for certain purposes, by iron. In terms of pottery (our only reliable guide) the Dark Ages cover the Submycenaean, Subminoan and Protogeometric periods.

Contacts with Egypt and Western Asia were effectively broken, but there is evidence for a limited amount of trade with Cyprus to the east and the Balkans to the north.

Most surviving Dark Age jewellery is of bronze, occasionally of iron; but a little gold is found, especially around the middle of the eleventh century. The traditional sources of gold were evidently no longer available, and goldsmiths may well have been reduced to melting down jewellery and plate from rifled tombs of the Late Bronze Age. The Aegina, Tiryns and Mycenae Acropolis Treasures are probably hoards amassed in the Dark Ages for just this purpose.

What little jewellery survives is of the simplest kind, but it is far from uniform in appearance, and is best considered under five regional headings: Attica; the Peloponnese; Central and Northern Greece; Crete; and the Islands and Eastern Greece.

In all these areas the darkness lightens around 900 when restored contacts with the East gradually opened up new horizons for Greek craftsmen and their customers.

ATTICA

Introduction

The principal source for Dark Age Attica is the Cerameicus Cemetery in Athens. From it we learn that jewellery of bronze was in use throughout the eleventh and tenth centuries, but in gold is only recorded between about 1070 and 1030 BC.

The jewellery

HAIR SPIRALS

As in the Mycenaean Empire, spirals of gold and bronze were used for decorating ladies' hair. Some (for example at Salamis, and Cerameicus Graves PG5 and 25) continued the established pattern and are indistinguishable from Minoan and Mycenaean examples. Others, of a Central European (Lausitz) pattern,[1] represent a new departure, whereby a gold wire was bent double and then spiralled. An early example of this type, almost certainly an import from Central Europe, occurs in the Tiryns Treasure (see p. 74); but the home-produced article is not found in Greece before about 1070 and it was never common. It is recorded in the Cerameicus in Graves SM46 and PG22 and in the Elgin Collection in London (Pl. 13 B). A slightly more elaborate form occurs in Cerameicus Grave SM N 136 in which the wires at one end, though still lying side by side, are twisted to give a herringbone effect.

BEADS

Gold beads are rare in Dark Age Attica, but a necklace of short cylindrical gold beads occurs in Cerameicus Grave SM N 136.

BRACELETS

Bracelets of bronze are occasionally found. A girl in Agora Grave Q8:6 wore a spiral bracelet on each wrist.

FINGER RINGS

Finger rings were popular in bronze and were also made of iron, but are not so far recorded in precious metals. The typical Mycenaean finger ring survives in bronze, slightly modified in that the bezel is pointed at both ends. Other simple shapes are also found in bronze: spirals and plain hoops. Spirals from Cerameicus Grave PG 39 and Agora Graves F9:1 and Q8:6 were almost certainly used as finger rings. A further variety, a hoop with an S-spiral bezel, is a northern type, first found in the so-called Aunjetitz culture of Central Europe.[2] The rings with pointed oval bezels belonged, with one exception, to women; the other varieties were worn by both sexes.

PINS AND FIBULAE

These articles were popular in bronze. In this material they are articles of necessity rather than luxury, but are perhaps worthy of a passing mention. The fibulae (worn chiefly by women) are principally of the Mycenaean arched type, but the pins (worn only by women) are a new departure, and constitute the start of a long unbroken series. They were worn in pairs, one on each shoulder, and their presence is evidence for the introduction of the classical peplos, or Doric chiton. The ancestry of these pins can be traced northwards to Vergina in Macedonia and thence to the transitional Aunjetitz–Lausitz culture of Central Europe.[3]

THE PELOPONNESE

Introduction

The available evidence for the Peloponnese in the Dark Ages is scanty in the extreme, a deficiency which future excavations may well remedy.

The jewellery

HAIR SPIRALS

A spiral of double gold wire like those from Athens was found at Argos (Phlessas) Grave 5.

BEADS

A necklace of faience disc beads was found in Tomb 1970. 15 at Asine.

FINGER RINGS

A plain gold ring was found in Argos (Phlessas) Grave 5. Bronze rings occur in the Prison Cemetery at Tiryns in Graves 6, 13a, 13b and 28. The Mycenaean-type ring with pointed bezel also occurs in a Submycenaean tomb at Corinth; and a plain iron ring comes from Tomb 1970. 15 at Asine.

CENTRAL AND NORTHERN GREECE

Introduction

Our principal Dark Age sources for this period are three cemeteries at Lefkandi in Euboea, a cemetery at Homolion in Thessaly of about 900, a tomb at the ancient Agrinion (Sauria) in Akarnania, and rich tombs on the island of Skyros.

The jewellery

HAIR SPIRALS

Gold spirals of different forms occur at Homolion and Agrinion (Sauria). Particularly noteworthy are a pair from Agrinion with splayed circular finials decorated with raised dots.

EARRINGS

Earrings in the form of small gold hoops were found in five tombs at Lefkandi of 1100–1050.

BEADS

Biconical gold beads come from Agrinion. From two tenth-century tombs at Lefkandi come beads of glass, faience and blue compound.

FINGER RINGS

A simple finger ring of sheet gold comes from Homolion.

CLOTHING ORNAMENTS

Tombs on Skyros have yielded quantities of gold discs for attachment to shrouds, decorated with curvilinear ornaments. At first sight they seem to suggest a connection with the far earlier discs from the Shaft Graves at Mycenae (see p. 70), but Central European connections have been recognized in the associated pottery,[4] and that is perhaps the direction in which we should look for the origins of these puzzling discs.

PINS AND FIBULAE

As in Attica (see p. 90).

CRETE

Introduction

There is as yet little evidence for gold jewellery in Dark Age Crete before about 950 BC, but it is possible that Minoan traditions of craftsmanship did in fact survive in some as yet unidentified centre.

The jewellery

BEADS

Eighty flattened globular heads of solid gold were found at Knossos in Medical Faculty Grave 200 (1100–1050). Gold beads with spiral grooves come from Tomb 11 at Fortetsa (950–900).

FINGER RINGS

Plain hoops of gold were found at Knossos (Hagios Ioannis Tomb 5 and Fortetsa Tombs 6 and 11). The former tomb also contained, exceptionally, two similar rings of silver. Rings of simple bands of metal were also found at Fortetsa, in Tomb 6. A gold ring of pure Minoan type (cf. Pl. 11 B), possibly an heirloom, was found in a tenth-century tomb at Vrokastro.

CLOTHING ORNAMENTS

Two gold rosettes were found at Knossos in Medical Faculty Grave 200 (1100–1050).

PINS AND FIBULAE

In addition to the expected pins and fibulae of bronze and iron, two pairs of simple gold pins were found in tombs at Knossos of the later tenth century (Fortetsa Tomb 11 and Tekke Tomb J).

THE ISLANDS AND EASTERN GREECE

Introduction

Very little Dark Age jewellery is as yet recorded from this area, an omission which may well be fortuitous.

The jewellery

A pair of simple gold hair spirals comes from Tomb B at Assarlik, the ancient Termera. A hair spiral like the bracelets described below was found with them in a tomb at Tsikalario on Naxos.

BRACELETS

Gold bracelets of doubled wire with one end twisted come from a tenth-century tomb on Naxos (Tsikalario). They are related in form to those from the Tiryns Treasure (see p.83), and northern influence is probable.

FINGER RINGS

Gold finger rings, probably simple hoops, are recorded from tombs on Kos of the late tenth century.

THE PERIOD OF ORIENTAL
INFLUENCES 900–600 BC

General introduction

Soon after 900, contacts between Greece and the East were renewed. This period of Oriental influence on Greek art lasted until about 600, by which time the new elements had been completely absorbed into an authentic Greek idiom.

Voyages of discovery and colonization created the desire – and the means – to share in the greater prosperity of the East. The areas in which the Greeks were principally interested were Cyprus, northern Syria and Phoenicia; and it has been suggested that Phoenician crafts-men established themselves in some of the principal Greek cities, where they founded schools and took local apprentices.[1] Thus Oriental techniques were harnessed to the service of Greek art: an explanation which fits extremely well with what we know of the deve-lopment of jewellery.

Influences from Phrygia and Lydia in Asia Minor were also exerted on the Eastern Greek cities and, through them, on the rest of Greece. Direct Egyptian and Assyrian contacts were lacking, but indirect influence from both cultures reached Greece by way of Phoenician art. Forms and motifs previously found in Minoan-Mycenaean art now reappear. Most are best explained as reintroductions, ingredients of some Oriental art which had never lost them; the arts of Phoenicia and Asia Minor are the most likely sources. On the other hand, the occa-sional survival or rediscovery of Minoan-Mycenaean objects in Greek lands cannot be ruled out as a contributory factor. In addition, Central and Northern Greece were subject to influences from the Balkans.

So far as jewellery is concerned, we may divide this period into two stages: an earlier, about 900–700, and a later, about 700–600.

900–700

Soon after 900, the meagre Dark Age repertoire was greatly enriched in a few advanced centres, such as Athens, Lefkandi in Euboea, Corinth and Knossos. In these centres we suddenly find an increasing amount of jewellery in gold, electrum and silver, exhibiting new motifs and new techniques.

The jewellery is described in detail below, but the new techniques are best considered here. They include the making of chains (simple and loop-in-loop); the casting of gold; repoussé and some at least of its mechanical variants (see p. 12); filigree and granulation; inlaying with stone, amber and glass; engraving.

Some of this early jewellery has an exotic appearance, which we should probably be correct in regarding as Phoenician. Certain pieces may indeed have been imported, but most are better explained as coming from workshops founded in Greece by Phoenician craftsmen.

700–600

This somewhat exotic jewellery now gave place to a more restrained, more Hellenic style. Athens, considerably less prosperous than before, dropped back from the lead. Corinth, on the other hand, continued much as before. There is not much evidence for Cretan jewellery of this period, but what there is suggests that it formed part of an island *koine*, comprising Crete, the Cyclades and the Dodecanese.

There is evidence of another school, situated in Eastern Greece. So far, the evidence comes almost entirely from Ephesus, but future excavation will almost certainly produce further examples on the western coast of Asia Minor. This east Greek school borrowed much from Oriental sources, almost certainly Phrygian and Lydian, and produced jewellery of a distinctive kind, although related in certain respects to that from the islands.

Finally, the Greek communities in Sicily produced a little silver jewellery in the seventh century.

The techniques employed in the seventh century are much as before, but there are certain differences. Filigree is rather more common, but is still less used than granulation. Inlay is less popular. Repoussé and its mechanical variants are increasingly applied to stout sheet metal.

In view of the pronounced regional differences in the jewellery (as indeed in many of the arts) of this period, it is best treated under seven main headings: Attica; the Peloponnese; Central Greece; Crete; the Islands; Eastern Greece; and the West.

ATTICA

Introduction

Soon after 900, gold jewellery is seen again in Attica after an interval of about 150 years, limited at first to flimsy gold diadems, hoops and spirals of Cypriote inspiration.

Then, around 850, a few rich Athenian families were able to import exotic luxury objects from Phoenicia, or to commission them from Phoenician craftsmen. A generation later, it seems that Phoenician goldsmiths actually settled in Athens and set up workshops producing jewellery of superb craftsmanship, rich with filigree, granulation and inlay. Some of these objects found their way to prosperous families outside Athens, at Eleusis, Anavysos (the ancient Anaphlystos) and probably elsewhere.

From 750 to 700 gold jewellery is still found in Athens and in the Attic countryside, but the quality is not as before. Flimsy embossed diadems and gold-plated bronze hair spirals are now the order of the day. Between 700 and 600 BC no gold jewellery whatever is recorded from Attica.

The jewellery

DIADEMS

Diadems of thin sheet gold, decorated with simple linear patterns, occur in a number of Athenian graves, in the Cerameicus and elsewhere, of about 860–825. The use of such ornaments was introduced either from Cyprus or from Syria where they had a high antiquity as grave furniture. They are too flimsy ever to have been worn by the living, and were presumably made exclusively for burial with the dead.

Similar diadems, but with curvilinear patterns, occur in Athenian graves around the second quarter of the eighth century: Kynosarges Graves 3 and 9 and Kriezi Street Grave 16.

From Kriezi Street Grave 106 (800–750) comes a unique diadem with designs, impressed by hand, of warriors, horses and ships.

But the typical eighth-century Attic diadem carried embossed decoration made by pressing in a mould.[2] Two main groups can be recognized.

The first group, which may be called the Oriental Group, is represented by about twenty examples, which date between 760 and 720 (Fig. 14). Varying in length between 20 and 50 cm, they were placed round the brow of the dead or, less frequently, under his chin or round his arm. The animal friezes embossed on them are in an Oriental, perhaps a Phoenician, style; but the diadems themselves, to judge from the quantity of surviving examples, were surely local products. In fact, the moulds from which they were made were designed primarily for making gold coverings for jewel caskets, fragments of which have been found at Eleusis.

Fig. 14   Attic funerary diadem, eighth century BC.

The second group, which served the same purpose as the first, is also represented by about twenty examples. It evolved slightly later than the first, being current between 740 and 710 BC. These diadems, which we may call the Hellenizing Group, are more closely modelled on contemporary Geometric pottery in their portrayal of human and animal figures. One example was equipped, after moulding, with plates having inlaid patterns, with no relation to the embossed decoration.[3]

SPIRALS

A pair of electrum spirals was found in a girl's cremation burial of 900–875 in the Agora (D 16:2). They could have been worn equally well in her hair or as finger rings. There is, however, no evidence at this date for the use of such spirals as earrings, another theoretical possibility.

Hair spirals of gold-plated bronze, the ends somewhat splayed and decorated with incised chevron patterns, are found in Athenian graves around the middle of the eighth century: Erysichthon-Neleus Grave 6 and Kynosarges Graves 3, 9 and 12.

EARRINGS

1 A rich lady's grave on the north-west slope of the Areopagus in Athens (Agora H16:6) of about 850 has yielded a pair of gold earrings of great elaboration (Pl. 13 D and E). They are composed of an upper strap, a central plaque in the form of an isosceles trapezium, and finials

in the shape of pomegranates. The strap is made of gold strips; some plain, some twisted and set side by side. The plaque is decorated with complicated patterns in filigree and granulation, while the pomegranates, embossed from sheet gold, are set with triangular blocks of granulation.

It is difficult to see these earrings as Athenian, or even Greek work, for the methods of granulation and filigree had been forgotten in Dark Age Greece. The workmanship suggests Phoenicia (the source of other objects in this grave), but the design has no Phoenician parallels, and is most like patterns in contemporary Athenian pottery. Professor Evelyn Smithson is surely right in suggesting that the earrings were made by a Phoenician craftsman for a Greek customer.

2 From Grave A and the Isis Grave at Eleusis (around 800 BC) and from Grave 51 at Anavysos come pairs of earrings formed of a gold crescent decorated with granulation and inlay and hung with gold chains (Pl. 13F and G). The inlay has almost entirely disappeared, except on the pair from Grave A at Eleusis, where it is of glass. In the earrings from the Isis Grave, tubes with crinkled ends, originally covered by beads of amber, hang from the chains to give the appearance of pomegranates. In the other two pairs, the chains end in knobs. A fourth pair is represented by a singleton in London, from Athens.[4]

The superfine granulation and the crescent shape argue for Phoenician influence, but the numbers of surviving examples suggest local manufacture. These earrings are therefore, in all likelihood, the products of a workshop founded in Athens by immigrant Phoenician craftsmen.

3 Certain gold ornaments are known, consisting of a disc decorated with granulation and having a central inlay. The back of the disc is lightly granulated; in the centre is set a curved 'stalk', on the end of which is a double-pyramid terminal set with inlay. Two complete pairs are known, one in the Elgin Collection (Pl. 14E) and one in a private collection in Switzerland (Pl. 14D). In addition, the disc from a similar object was found at Delos, near the Artemision.

The purpose of these ornaments is disputed, but it is difficult to explain them except as earrings, worn suspended from a hook inserted in the earlobe. An Attic origin is suggested by the technical resemblance between these pieces and the Attic earrings, no. 2. A date in the first half of the eighth century is probable.

4 A pair of gold ornaments in Los Angeles County Museum (Pl. 14C) is related to no. 3. At one end of a curved wire is a detachable disc; at the other end is a fixed hollow cone, granulated on the outside and granulated and inlaid (the inlay now missing) on the inside. These must also be earrings, and of the same date and fabric as no. 3

5 A hoop earring with a pyramidal granulated pendant was found in the Erysichthon-Neleus Street Cemetery, near graves of about 740–730.

BEADS AND NECKLACES

1 Globular gold beads come from Grave A at Eleusis.

2 From Grave 2 at Anavysos (*c.* 775–750 BC) comes an exquisite gold cord with snake-head finials decorated with filigree and granulation: a finer version of the better-known snake-head cord from Knossos (Tekke). This, too, was probably made to hold a large pendant.

3 A composite necklace comes from Grave 3 at Spata of 725–700 BC (Pl. 15 A). It consists basically of five rectangular plaques decorated with cells in diamond and crescent patterns which formerly contained inlay. Below hang, some direct and some on chains, pomegranate pendants, like those on the earrings from Eleusis (Pl. 13F, G).

PECTORAL ORNAMENTS

Elements of a pectoral (?) were found at Eleusis, probably from a disturbed grave of about 750 (Pl. 15 B–F). They are decorated with geometric patterns in rather poor granulation and with amber inlay; one carries a representation of the so-called Dipylon or Boeotian shield. The complete ornament, as reconstructed by Segall,[5] consisted of a number of square plaques flanked by similar plaques in the shape of a trapezium. A set of similar plaques comes from a votive deposit at Brauron. The type of ornament has been shown by Segall to be of Syrian origin.

FINGER RINGS

1 Rings of thin sheet gold, some decorated with embossed ridges or dot repoussé, are represented in two graves in the Cerameicus, numbers 7 (900–875 BC) and 41 (850 BC) and one on the north-west slope of the Areopagus of about 850 (Agora H 16: 6) One of many examples in the Elgin Collection is shown in Pl. 13 A. The home of this form of ring is Cyprus, where examples date back to about 1000 BC.[6]

2 The Areopagus grave also contained three strip-rings decorated with zigzag patterns like the contemporary diadems.

3 Flimsy carinated rings come from Cerameicus Grave 41 (*c.* 850), Kavalotti Street Grave 5 (850–800) and Kriezi Street Grave 12 (800–750). More substantial versions come later, in Kavalotti Street Grave 4 (800–760) and Grave 3 of the Kynosarges Cemetery (760–750); and one from the Elgin Collection is shown in Pl. 13 C.

4 Finally, an elaborate ring composed of twist braids and open-work filigree comes from Erysichthon-Neleus Street Grave 6 of 735–720.

PINS

Bronze pins are very common in women's graves and need no comment here. Occasionally, however, examples are found in precious metals. A pair of gold-plated iron pins of great delicacy were found in Cerameicus Grave 41, of about 850. Nearly a century later we find gold-plated iron pins in Kynosarges Graves 18 and 19 (770–750) and Kriezi Street Grave 12 (800–750). They follow the same tradition as the ninth-century pins but the gold casing is decorated with granulated triangles and zigzags and the globe is, in some cases, made to look like a pomegranate.

What appears to be a gold quadruple-spiral bead like those from the Shaft Graves at Mycenae was found, surprisingly enough, in Grave 51 at Anavysos. Two similar objects from Skyros (p. 107), which could well be contemporary, are in fact the heads of pins, and this object could well have served the same purpose.

FIBULAE

Bronze fibulae continue in Attica throughout this period, and cannot be considered as jewellery. Occasionally, however, the standard forms were produced in precious metals.

A magnificent pair of gold fibulae in Berlin is said to come from a a tomb in Athens. They have a flat lozenge-shaped bow and a stilted triangular catchplate, and are lavishly engraved with zigzags and wave patterns. The shape of the catchplate, paralleled in bronze fibulae from Grave H16: 6 of the Athenian Agora, gives a date of about 850.

It is not for nearly a century after this that gold fibulae are again recorded from Attica. Their form is now quite different, and twelve examples are known, representing in all probability three sets of four. They are of the so-called Attico-Boeotian variety, with a leech-shaped bow and a large square engraved catch-plate.[7] They are dated about 775–750 by two tomb groups and by their place in a well-documented series of bronze fibulae.

Four examples in London from the Elgin Collection, and so probably from Athens, form two pairs, a larger (not illustrated) and a smaller (Pl. 14 A and B). The catchplates are richly engraved. Of the smaller pair, one fibula has a horse on one side and a lion on the other, while the other fibula has a horse on one side and a ship on the other. The larger fibulae have identical engravings: a grazing deer on one side and a swastika on the other. The engraving is made in two ways: ordinary work with a graver, and curving zigzags (the so-called tremolo lines) with a scorper.

Another set, also made up of two pairs of slightly different sizes, was found in Grave 2 at Anavysos, of 800–750. One pair was engraved with a swastika on one side and a bird on the other, the other pair with a scorpion on one side and a bird on the other.

Three more gold fibulae–from another set of four?–come from Grave 19 of the Kynosarges Cemetery, of about 775–750. No details are yet available, but it appears that the catchplates were not pictorially decorated.

Finally, there is a single gold fibula in Berlin, said to be from Athens. It could conceivably be the missing fibula from the Kynosarges set. The catchplate has a rudimentary star on each side.

THE PELOPONNESE

Introduction

Surviving Peloponnesian jewellery falls under three headings.

1 For the Argolid we start with a fair quantity of simple gold jewellery from Argos and Tiryns made between 900 and 840, but thereafter no gold jewellery is recorded until the end of the eighth century, when we find three finger rings in the Panoply Grave at Argos. Finally, there is an alleged tomb group from Argos in the Stathatos Collection, in the style of the late seventh century.

2 For the Corinthia the ninth century is represented only by a pair of gold spirals from Corinth and a pair of gold-plated spirals from Klenia (the ancient Tenea). The eighth and seventh centuries are better represented in a number of tombs from Corinth and two votive deposits from Perachora.

3 For Laconia, there are a few articles of jewellery, notably a wreath and a few beads, from the sanctuary of Artemis Orthia and the Menelaion at Sparta. Too little material survives for any profitable speculation about a Laconian school of jewellery, which, however, may well have existed.

The jewellery

FUNERARY BANDS

Funerary bands similar in function to those from Attica were also made in Corinth.[8] They are decorated with figured scenes and can be dated, from their relationship with Corinthian pottery, from the later eighth to the mid-seventh century. Some have continuous scenes, some isolated figures separated by ornaments, and some (the latest) are decorated with groups arranged as a series of metopes. A few funerary bands from Aegina, in eighth- and seventh-century style, have strong affinities with these, and could well be Corinthian.

A bronze mould in Oxford, evidently for the manufacture of such bands, comes from Corfu, and is illustrated in Pl. 1 B and C. The decoration can be dated, by analogy with Protocorinthian pottery, to about 650.

WREATHS

The earliest known Greek wreath comes from a deposit of the earlier seventh century at the sanctuary of Artemis Orthia at Sparta. It is made of twisted silver wires threaded with tubular gold beads; between the beads are set gold leaves and berries. Wreaths have a long history from this point. For the various purposes for which they were used, see p. 123.

SPIRALS

From Grave C at Corinth (about 900), Graves 7 and 15 at Tiryns (about 900) and Graves 37 (875–825) and 106: 1 (900–850) at Argos come pairs of gold spirals of doubled wire like those in use in Athens about 1050 (see p. 89) but with the wires at one or both ends twisted together. They were probably worn in the hair.

The more elaborate type of spiral, also found in Athens (see p. 97), is oval in shape and has splaying ends, usually decorated with herringbone patterns. Examples in gold come from Danaou Street Grave 1 at Argos (875–825) and Grave F at Corinth (about 750). A pair in gold-plated bronze comes from a grave at Klenia (the ancient Tenea) of 830–800.

EARRINGS

Two varieties, both based on the spiral, are known from the Corinthia.

1 Like the spiral of uncertain purpose from Grave F at Corinth (above), but with fewer turns, and the ends arranged symmetrically. Later representations, mainly on coins (see p. 126), show that these earrings were worn with the ends pointing upwards. They appear to have been thrust through a hole in the lobe. They occur in gilt bronze

at Perachora (Limenia). Earrings of this type occur at Sinjirli (about 700),[9] and a Syrian origin may thus be presumed. The type was very popular in Rhodes and is also found in Eastern Greece.

2 Two discs, joined by a spiral (Pl. 16 A). The type occurs at Perachora, in both the Akraia and Limenia deposits; a date in the eighth century is therefore indicated. It is also found in two alleged grave groups from Corinth, in Oxford and Berlin. Earrings of this kind were sometimes straightened out, shorn of one disc, and used as pins, of which a number were found at Perachora. This type occurs in gold and bronze.

3 A related type also occurs in bronze at Perachora (Akraia) in which the discs are replaced by solid cones.

4 An entirely different type of earring comes from an alleged grave group from Argos in the Stathatos Collection in Athens. It takes the form of a conical pendant decorated with filigree and globules of gold, and surmounted by a figure of a Mistress of Beasts, with lions. The cone earring, from this beginning, had a long life, of about four centuries. The Argive examples can be dated, by the style of the goddess's face, to the end of the seventh century.

BEADS

1 Two oval gold beads with herringbone striations are recorded from Argos: one from Grave 16 (875–850), the other from an unspecified grave in Anapauseos Street.

2 Beads in the form of a bud, either by itself or suspended from a tube, are known in gold, silver and bronze. They enjoyed a wide currency in the Peloponnese, being found at Perachora (Limenia), Sparta (Sanctuary of Artemis and Menelaion) and Argos (Stathatos Collection).

3 A biconical bead, decorated with filigree, comes from the sanctuary of Artemis Orthia at Sparta.

PENDANTS

A pendant like the Stathatos earrings comes from the same ensemble, allegedly from Argos. It has a similar cone, surmounted by a platform on which stand two confronted sphinxes.

CLOTHING ORNAMENTS

Discs of gold foil, with crude geometric patterns impressed on them, come from the Akraia deposit at Perachora.

BUTTONS

Gold-plated buttons are said to have been found in three identical examples in a tomb at Megara. They have on the face an embossed head in the Dedalic style of about 650, and on the back a metal loop (Pl. 16 B).

FINGER RINGS

1 Simple bronze rings are common, especially in the ninth century, but need no comment here.

2 A slightly convex gold strip ring, like those from Cerameicus Grave 41 at Athens, comes from Danaou Street Grave 1 at Argos (875–825).

3 Carinated strip rings like an Attic variety (p. 99) come from deposits in the Corinthia of the eighth century: Corinth, Graves D and F, and the Akraia deposit at Perachora.

4 Rings of wire come from Grave 45 at Argos of the eighth century. Three kinds are represented: one of single wire, one of twisted wires and another of twisted wires decorated with rather coarse granulation.

PINS

Two silver pins joined by a loop-in-loop chain were found in the Artemis Orthia sanctuary at Sparta, and date from the early seventh century.

CENTRAL GREECE

Introduction

For the early part of this period our only source is provided by the three cemeteries of Lefkandi in Euboea, which continue from the previous period (see p. 91). The burials are extremely rich; one grave in every two excavated contained jewellery. Unfortunately, all three cemeteries went out of use about 825.

After this there is a gap in our evidence until about 750, when gold jewellery is recorded from graves at Eretria and the island of Skyros, and bronze jewellery of outlandish forms from Thebes. These come to an end about 700, after which there is another gap.

The jewellery of central Greece is of interest in showing converging influences from the north and from the east (at first Cyprus, later Phoenicia).

The jewellery

Unless otherwise stated, the pieces described below come from Lefkandi.

DIADEMS

1 Diadems of thin sheet gold with impressed patterns of zigzags, etc., occur at Lefkandi (900–825). They are very like contemporary Athenian diadems (see p. 96) and must have a similar Cypriote inspiration.

2 Two fragments of a more elaborately decorated example were found in Grave T33 (850–825). It had embossed figures of animals in an Oriental (Phoenician?) style.

3 The second half of the eighth century is represented by embossed diadems very like the contemporary Athenian ones of the Oriental Group (see p. 97) from graves at Eretria, and by similar diadems and related objects from graves on Skyros. Both classes have a small tongue protruding from the centre of the upper edge.

4 An exceptional diadem comes from Grave 14 of the West Gate Cemetery at Eretria, of about 700. It was found round a child's head and has embossed decoration, in a Phoenician style, of leaping animals and examples of the 'tree of life'.

SPIRALS

A simple gold spiral from Grave S45 (875–850) was probably a decoration for the hair.

Certain other spirals from Lefkandi could be either hair ornaments or earrings.

1 A pair of gold-plated lead spirals, with slightly expanded ends, comes from Grave P22, of about 900, or perhaps even slightly earlier (Pl. 16H).

2 Two graves, S33 and T32 (one certainly and one probably dated 875–850), each contained one gold spiral capped at each end with a solid shallow cone (Pl. 16E). S Pyre 4 (upper), of the same date, and S59 (slightly later) contained similar spirals but with hollow cones (Pl. 16D). In view of the obvious function of a larger but similar pair from Thebes (Pl. 16j), it would be tempting to see them as earrings, but the preponderance of singletons might suggest their alternative use as hair ornaments.

3 A grave at Amphissa near Delphi of 750–700 contained, in addition to known jewellery of northern types, a pair of gold hair spirals with large hollow cylindrical finials; they, too, are surely of northern inspiration.

EARRINGS

1 A pair of small tapered hoops comes from Grave T 1 (900–875).

2 A more ornate pair of hoop earrings, from Grave T 5 (875–850), has three elongated clusters of granulation attached to their lower edge (Pl. 16 c). This is the first appearance of a variety of the mulberry earring which was to have a long life in Greece. It has been identified as the model for Homer's *hermata triglena moroenta*.[10] The form is Phoenician, but the inferior quality of the granulation suggests that it was made in Greece. If so, this is the first appearance of granulation in Greece since the twelfth century.

3 An even more elaborate type of hoop earring is represented by a pair from Grave T 13 (875–850). The upper part consists of a figure-of-eight of wire, the bottom loop being much the smaller. From it hangs a spectacle-spiral pendant (Pl. 16 k). At this date the spectacle spiral has northern connotations, and that is the direction in which we should look for the inspiration, perhaps even the manufacture, of these unique objects.

4 A pair of gold earrings in Paris, from Thebes, consists of a curved wire terminating in a hollow cone at either end (Pl. 16 j). One cone is detachable, and was secured with a pin after the wire had been pushed through the earlobe. Their date, by analogy with the Los Angeles earrings (p. 98), will be about 800.

BEADS

Most of the beads from Lefkandi are of rock crystal, amber, glass and faience. A gold-plated tin biconical bead from Grave T22 (900–875) is one of the exceptions.

BRACELETS

Children's bracelets of gold-plated bronze occur in pairs in three graves at Lefkandi, of 900–850 (T5, T22, T27). A pair of similar bracelets, but spiralled, was found in Grave 14 of the West Gate Cemetery at Eretria, of about 700.

FINGER RINGS

Finger rings are common at Lefkandi. With one exception, they are very flimsy. Many, too, are so small that they must have been made for children.

1 The commonest type, in use between 900 and 825, consists of a band of thin sheet gold, convex outside and correspondingly concave

inside; an exact counterpart of an Athenian type (see Pl 13A). It is represented by nineteen examples, from seven graves.

2 This type also occurs in ten examples from four graves of 900–850, with a slightly carinated outline.

3 Other rings occur at Lefkandi but less commonly, with two to six carinations, between 875 and 925 (Pl. 16 I); and one with six carinations is also recorded from Skyros.

4 The simplest type of ring, a plain strip, occurs in two examples from Grave T31 (850–825). In two other contemporary examples, from Graves T31 and T32, the edges are slightly flanged.

5 The only really substantial ring, from Grave T31 (850–825), has a central ridge and a double ridge at both edges. (Pl. 16 G). The type is also found at Athens and the Corinthia (see Pl. 13C), where it survived into the eighth century.

PINS

1 Gold-plated iron dress pins occurred in pairs in three graves of 875–825. The form, the shape of a long nail, is surprisingly rare. Another grave, probably contemporary (T32), contained an identical pair, with the addition of an amber bead on the shank, mounted on a gold reel with granulated edges.

2 At Skyros a pair of very different gold pins is represented by one complete and one fragmentary example. They are equipped at the head with spectacle-spiral bead related to a bead from Anavysos Grave 51, and threaded on the shank with fluted cylindrical beads. They have an exotic, probably Northern, appearance, and are most likely contemporary with the Anavysos piece (c. 800).

FIBULAE

Only one gold fibula is recorded from Lefkandi, from Grave T13, of 875–850 (Pl. 16 F). It is basically of the Mycenaean fiddle-bow type, but with a small stilted catch and a double leaf-shaped bow having a loop in the centre for a safety chain. The only known parallel is a bronze fibula from the same site, so that the type could well be a local creation.

CRETE

Introduction

In Crete, the greater part of the ninth century saw very little jewellery, and even that was of the simplest kinds. Towards the end of the century, however, as Boardman has persuasively argued, a family of Oriental (Phoenician?) goldsmiths settled at Knossos. In the workshop they started, which lasted for about a century, were produced elaborate articles of jewellery – at first Oriental in appearance, later accommodating themselves more to Cretan taste.[11]

A reused Minoan tholos tomb at Tekke, 1.5 km north of the Palace of Minos, is believed by Boardman to be the family burial place of these settlers. The earliest jewellery of this 'Tekke School' was found buried in two jars at the entrance to the tomb, put there with lumps of unworked gold to sanctify it.

By the end of the eighth century the Tekke School had either ceased to exist or had been completely Hellenized, and what little Cretan jewellery has survived from the seventh century is remarkably like that of Rhodes and the Cyclades.

The jewellery

DIADEMS

1. A simple gold diadem with a dot-repoussé border comes from Grave L at Fortetsa, Knossos (870–850).

2 A much more elaborate diadem comes from the Tholos Tomb at Tekke, of about 800. It is impressed with nine panels, all from the same mould, giving a symmetrical arrangement of two men fighting lions. Oriental (Phoenician?) influence is very strong. A better-preserved diadem, the double of this one, but without a provenance, is published by Reichel.[12]

3 Four silver-gilt roundels which originally decorated a diadem of some perishable material (cloth or leather?) were found adhering to the corpse's skull in Tomb 31 at Praisos, of the seventh century.

EARRINGS

1. An elaborately decorated open hoop earring comes from the Idaean Cave. It had been (as Levi saw) quite incorrectly attached in modern times to the plaque from the same source shown in Pl. 17 A. The hoop is decorated with wave patterns in fine granulation, and one end is bound with fine wire and tipped with a pyramid of large grains. To judge from the details, this earring must be contemporary with the earliest products of the Tekke School: early eighth century.

2. A pair of splayed spiral earrings of silver, surmounted by a gold rosette, was found in Tomb 31 at Praisos, of the seventh century. The type is commonest in Rhodes (see Pl. 18 C).

PENDANTS

1 A number of pendants, some of great elaboration, were found in the Tholos Tomb at Tekke, and so date about 800.

(*a*) A penannular pendant with a human head at each end (Pl. 17 E). Within the ring is a cross and in the four quadrants so made are figures of geese. The ring and the cross are decorated with a guilloche pattern.

(*b*) A quatrefoil rosette with a central boss, decorated with filigree and granulation (Pl. 17 D).

(*c*) A half-moon of rock crystal set in gold (Pl. 17 C). Below it hang three subsidiary ornaments of gold with amber inlay in the form of a crescent and disc, a popular Phoenician motif. Above it is a framework of inlaid gold, to which two loop-in-loop chains are attached, ending in snakes' heads. The remains of other ornaments of this nature were found in Tekke and Arkades, and similar snake-head finials are recorded from Ithaca and Grave 2 at Anavysos (p. 99).

(*d*) A simpler half-moon of gold (Pl. 17 F).

2 A pendant from the Idaean Cave in Crete (Pl. 17 A) is stylistically related to the penannular pendant from Tekke. It is in the form of a rectangular plaque, embossed and decorated with granulation and inlay. At either side and in the centre is the figure of a standing draped woman. Between the women are two identical panels decorated with an animal's (perhaps a bull's) head, surmounted by a horseshoe-shaped arch. Above and below are triangular and crescent-shaped cloisons for inlay. The crescent-and-triangle motif is a Hellenization of the Phoenician crescent-and-disc of the pendant from Tekke, no. 1(c) above. For this reason a date around 750 (contemporary with the Eleusis plaques, Pl. 15 B–F) is to be preferred.

Also from the Idaean Cave is a disc-shaped element from a necklace, with a loop at either side and granulation in triangular blocks (Fig. 15). The inspiration for this sort of ornament is Phoenician,[13] but the workmanship, as seen in the granulation, associates this piece closely with the Tekke Tholos jewellery, especially Pl. 17 C. Early eighth century.

The middle of the seventh century is represented by two pendants with a human head in the developed Dedalic style, from Fortetsa Tomb

Fig. 15 Circular pendant from the Idaean Cave, Crete, about 700 B C.

I and the Idaean Cave; and by two pendants in the shape of bees, from Fortetsa Tomb I again, and Arkades Tomb F 1.

BRACELETS

A chain from the Tholos Tomb at Tekke (early eighth century) has been interpreted, probably correctly, as a bracelet. It is a cord-like loop-in-loop chain of alternate gold and silver links. There is a snake-head finial at one end; the other end is incomplete, but would have been similarly equipped.

FINGER RINGS

Simple strip rings are common in graves at Fortetsa of the later ninth century.

From one of the jars in one Tekke Tholos Tomb comes a gold ring composed of five hoops soldered together.

From Tomb A at Praisos comes a ring with a bezel like the traditional Minoan ring, but pointed somewhat at the top, bottom and sides. (Fig. 16). There were inlays in the centre and at each angle, the area between the outer inlays being filled with zigzagging strips covered with granulation. The tomb was in use over a long period, but most of the objects appear to be eighth century. A date around 750, contemporary with the Eleusis plaques (Pl. 15 B–F), is probable for this ring.

Fig. 16   Finger ring from Praisos, Crete,
about 750 B C.

A pair of identical gold rings, recently acquired for the Metaxas Collection in Heraklion, are said to come from a burial at Fortetsa. They have bezels of the traditional Minoan pattern but pointed top and bottom. In the centre is a circular cloison, and at the sides are pear-shaped cloisons, all formerly inlaid. At the top and bottom are embossed human heads, facing in opposite directions, in the pre-Dedalic style. There is rich subsidiary decoration in lines and blocks of granulation. The rings are clearly products of the Tekke School. Their date is less easy to determine, but it could well fall about the middle of the eighth century.

PINS

1 The typical Cretan dress pins of the eighth and early seventh centuries are regularly found in pairs and occur in gold, electrum and silver. They have a disc head and, on the upper part of the shank, a delicate moulding consisting of a double cone with rings above and below it.[14] Two pairs are recorded from Fortetsa Tomb II (700–670); one pair from the chamber tomb on Gypsades (Pl. 17B); one pair from the 'Metaxas Tomb' at Fortetsa; one pair from the Idaean Cave; and a singleton from Tomb A at Praisos.

2 From the Tholos Tomb at Tekke, and datable to the early eighth century, come two pairs of the same type of pin, with silver shanks and gold tops. Figures of pelicans rest on the upper disc, and each pair is joined by a loop-in-loop safety chain.

3 The mid- and late seventh-century pin, so far recorded only in silver, is represented by two pairs, from Tombs 9 and 31 at Praisos.[15] The head is composed of a wide flanged disc with a conical projection on top, and there is a shallow moulding on the upper part of the shank.

THE ISLANDS

Introduction

The principal sources for this period are tombs at Camirus and Ialysus and, to a lesser extent, a deposit at Lindus, all in Rhodes. Jewellery has also been found on Thera, Melos and Delos. It is possible to recognize a flourishing Rhodian school, influenced in part by the Cretan school, in part by independent borrowings from Syria and Asia Minor. Gold, electrum and silver were used. The principal types are funerary bands, diadems with rosettes, spiral earrings, embossed pectoral ornaments with Greek and Asiatic motifs, and animal-head bracelets. There appears also to have been a school on Melos which specialized in rosettes for diadems, of great elaboration, and possibly also equally elaborate earrings.

The characteristic features of the Island jewellery of this period are the continued use of fine granulation; the occasional use of filigree; embossed figures in a style reminiscent of contemporary vase paintings; and human heads, animal heads and animal figures in the round as attachments to articles of jewellery. Inlay was still practised but was falling out of favour, and variety was now obtained principally by varying the surface texture of the metal.

Island jewellery has recently been exhaustively studied by Laffineur. His work, to which copious references are made in the notes, supersedes all previous publications.

The jewellery

FUNERARY BANDS

Bands with geometric patterns come almost without exception from Rhodes, and were presumably made there. Some were evidently diadems, while others were mouthpieces. They fall into two groups, dated to the eighth and seventh centuries respectively. The first group is represented at Exochi and in Chamber Tomb 82 at Camirus; the second in Grave 201 at Camirus.

DIADEMS

Rhodian and Cycladic tombs have also produced diadems, more substantial than the funerary bands, which could well have been worn by the living. These diadems, decorated principally with rosettes, belong to a type of ornament originally, it would seem, Assyrian, but copied in Syria, Cyprus and elsewhere.[16] They will have reached the Greek world from Syria. The Greek examples fall into three classes, depending upon how they were made.

1 In the simplest variety the rosettes are embossed in repoussé on the diadem, as in a piece from Grave 13 at Camirus, of the later seventh century.[17]

2 Rosettes were made separately and attached to a band of the same material, gold or electrum. One example comes from Grave 11 at Camirus, of the later seventh century; another, also from Camirus, is shown in Pl 19A.[18] An interesting variant from Kos in the Benaki Museum has sphinxes in addition to rosettes.[19]

3. Rosettes were made separately and attached by runners or by some other means to bands which no longer exist, and which were presumably of leather or textile. These rosettes vary in complexity, but for convenience may be divided into two classes, the *simple* and the *ornate*.

Simple rosettes have been found on Thera, in Grave 116, around the middle of the seventh century.[20]

Of the surviving ornate rosettes (Pl. 18 D) five in Athens come from illicit exacavations on Melos; two in the Bibliothèque Nationale and one in London are also said to come from Melos; one in Paris and one in New York are said to come from Rhodes; and one in Bologna and three in London have no known provenance.[21]

There can thus be little doubt that Melos is the home of this class. The rosettes are masterpieces of seventh-century jewellery. They are embossed and decorated with filigree and granulation and with attached figures of insects, human heads, bulls' heads, griffins' heads, birds and rosettes. The human heads, in the Dedalic style of about 650 BC, give a rough date for the whole class.

EARRINGS

Most Island earrings are variations of the spiral which has been discussed in connection with the Peloponnese (see pp. 102–3). There are several varieties.

1 Like the Corinthian variety (p. 102, no. 1), made in gold, silver, gilt bronze, and bronze (Pl. 18 B). It occurs in many Rhodian tombs throughout the seventh century; in the Votive Deposit at Camirus; in Ialysus Graves 57, 58, 98 and 107. It also occurs at Lindus, and elsewhere. In some varieties the ends are decorated with a collar of granulation and a pyramid of larger grains on top.

2 The spiral is splayed out so that the earring forms a letter W, rising higher in the centre than at the sides. The type occurs in Rhodes in the seventh century (Pl. 18 A) but is rare. It also occurs in Eastern Greece.

3 A slimmer variety of type 2 is common in Rhodes throughout the seventh century in gold, silver and bronze (Pl. 18 C). It is found at Ialysus in Graves 56 and 57, at Camirus in Grave 11, and at Lindus. In the early seventh century it occurs in its simplest form; the centre rises higher than in type 2, and the ends are finished off with horizontal discs.[22] Later in the century the apex is masked by an embossed rosette.[23] It was worn suspended from a thin wire which was threaded through the lobe.

This type lent itself to elaborate variations. Two such elaborations (in Berlin) come from Melos, and may perhaps have been made there, for they have much in common with the Melian rosettes (see Pl. 18 D). One has griffins' heads, elaborately granulated, on the discs, a type also found at Camirus (Pl. 18 E).[24] The other is decorated with twisted wires and pomegranate ornaments.[25] An even more elaborate variety comes from Grave 45 at Ialysus, of the late seventh century. The discs are turned outward and decorated with rams' heads, from each of which hang pomegranate ornaments. A framework consisting of two rams' heads topped by snakes' heads is attached to one side.[26] These rather unsuccessful creations also have a Melian look.

4 Hoops. Tapered hoops of silver and of bronze were found at Lindus in the seventh- and sixth-century 'Couches Archaïques'. This Bronze Age type lingered on through the Dark Ages in Cyprus, and these examples may well be Cypriote imports (see p. 120).

5 A silver stud, with a rosette on one face, from the seventh- and sixth-century 'Couches Archaïques' at Lindus has been plausibly identified as an earstud. It has been aptly compared with modern

earstuds from Sumatra. This object will then be an early manifestation of a form of jewellery particularly common in paintings and sculpture in the next period (see p. 127).

NECKLACES

A strap of gold with attached lions' heads is published as a sporadic find from Camirus, and there is another in London from the same source. The style of the animals' heads gives a date in the seventh century.[27]

BEADS

An attractive necklace from Camirus is composed of gold melon beads and double magic Ujat eyes of blue-green faience. The faience beads are derived from a common Egyptian motif, and are almost certainly Phoenician. The necklace may be dated in the seventh century by the faience, which was very popular in Rhodes at this period for amulets and other objects.[28]

PENDANTS

Pendant discs with geometric patterns, and sometimes a central inlay, are found in Rhodian tombs of the second half of the eighth century, at Ialysus, Grave 56, and at Exochi (Fig. 17). Examples in silver and bronze come from the 'Couches Archaïques' at Lindus. These discs, which are discussed by Reichel, show strong Cypriote or Syrian influence.[29] Similar discs were particularly common in Etruria (see p. 141).

Fig. 17 Pendant disc, Rhodian variety, eighth century BC.

A semicircular pectoral ornament comes from Delos (Hieron). It is decorated with geometric patterns in granulation, and with inlay, which has now vanished. Round the circumference are loops to hold subsidiary pendants. The date is probably somewhere in the eighth century.

Another ornament of the same general kind comes from Tralles. It is certainly Greek and, to judge from its resemblance to the Melian rosettes (Pl. 18 D), almost certainly Island Greek. A semicircular gold plaque is decorated with a Dedalic figure of a woman, griffins' heads, a bull's head, rosettes and zigzag patterns in granulation. Above it is a tube for a suspension cord, and above that are six discs, two with bulls' heads and two with rams' heads. Round the circumference are loops, as on the piece from Delos. A Boeotian terracotta of the eighth century seems to be wearing an ornament like the two mentioned above.[30]

Pendants in the shape of a bull's head and a lion's head in seventh-century style come from Rhodes.[31] From Thera, Grave 116, come pendants in the shape of a globe suspended from two tubes joined to make a T. To judge from the associated jewellery, they should be dated about the middle of the seventh century. A similar pendant comes from Tocra in Cyrenaica, from Deposit I, of the late seventh century. Human heads in the Dedalic style of the seventh century have been found on Delos (now in Berlin), and in Crete (see p. 109).

A repoussé pendant in the form of a siren with a Dedalic head, richly decorated with granulation, is said to come from Camirus.[32] From its resemblance to the Melissai (below) it is probably Cycladic work.

The Melissai take the form of bees with human heads in the Dedalic style. They have been found on Thera (Grave 116), Melos and Rhodes and probably come from the same workshop as the Melian rosettes.[33] The heads date them somewhere about the middle of the seventh century. The human-headed bee, originally a Hittite goddess by the name of Kumbaba or Kybebe, has been discussed by Barnett. It presumably reached Greece by way of Asia Minor.[34]

PECTORAL ORNAMENTS

A specialized class of ornament was very common in Rhodes in the seventh century, from 660 BC onwards. It consists of sets of rectangular (or slightly trapezoid) plaques of gold, electrum or (rarely) silver, decorated with embossed figures and generally fitted with tubes along the upper edge to take a suspension cord. Ornaments in the shape of fruit are frequently suspended from the lower edge. Numbers of identical plaques were worn by women, probably strung along the top of their dress; the plaques at the ends were fitted with hooks, masked by rosettes, to fasten the ornament to the dress at the shoulders. The method of wearing them is indicated somewhat sketchily on a bronze from Athens.[35] Some plaques have no tube along the top but are pierced at the corners; they were evidently sewn direct to the dress.

Very few of these ornaments originate from properly recorded excavations, but virtually all are belived to come from Rhodes. Two were found at Camirus, Grave 210, and six are part of a stray find from the same site. They can be firmly dated by the human heads, in the Dedalic style, which follows the classic sequence of Early, Middle and Late Dedalic, from about 660 to 620 BC.

These plaques may possibly be related to the Attic plaques from Eleusis (Pl. 15), and to the pendant from the Idaean Cave (Pl. 17A). A Syrian or Cypriote origin is, however, strongly suggested by similar plaques from Cyprus of the tenth to eighth centuries;[36] plaques from Sinjirli of about 700 are somewhat similar in form, but not in content, and may be a parallel development.[37]

The plaques are formed basically over a core or in a mould; examination of the objects themselves does not reveal which process was employed. A bronze relief from Lindus could well be a positive core over which such plaques would have been beaten, but there are other reasons for believing that they were pressed in a mould.[38] Most of the plaques were embossed from a single sheet of metal. Subsidiary ornament was stamped from the back or (less commonly) from the front, or was soldered on in the form of rosettes, filigree or granulation. Borders were frequently made by soldering a strip of ornamental wire to a punch and stamping the impression of the wire from the back.

The finest plaques were made in rather a different way. The figures were embossed separately and soldered, frequently in several sections, to a flat base. In this way a greater depth and a sharper outline were obtained.

The subjects are as follows:

1 'Astarte at the window' (Pl. 20 B). A Phoenician motif.[29] It also occurs in a plaque from Delos where three female heads are disposed side by side with a rosette above each.[40] This aberrant version could well be made not in Rhodes, but in Naxos or Thera.

2 Winged Artemis, with lions. The Mistress of Beasts.[41] A Mycenaean motif which returned to Greece by way of Syrian art in this period, and which remained a popular subject down to the fifth century. It was the most popular subject for Rhodian plaques and occurs in a number of different forms, sometimes associated with hawks (Pls 19 D and E and 20 C).

3 Winged Artemis, with birds, instead of lions.[42]

4 Winged Artemis, with no attributes (Pl. 20 E).[43]

5 Similar goddess, without wings.[44]

6 Astarte bust, and lions' heads (Pl. 19 B)[45] The motif of a woman holding her breasts as a gesture indicating fertility had a high antiquity

in Western Asia and found its way to Greece in this period, from Syria or Cyprus.

7 Melissa.[46] The significance and origins of this type are discussed on p. 115 (Pl. 20 F).

8 Sphinx.[47] A very common motif in Mycenaean art, which survived in Syria and returned thence to Greece in this period (Pl. 19 C).

9 Griffin.[48] The history of this motif is parallel to that of the sphinx. A plaque at Osborne House on the Isle of Wight (Pl. 20 D), almost certainly from Camirus, provides the only example known to the author.

10 Centaur with faun (Pl. 20 A).[49] The centaur was probably a genuine Greek creation, though inspired by Oriental composite animals. It appears as early as the second half of the eighth century on Attic funerary bands (see p. 97).

Two elaborate electrum pendants from Camirus, in Paris, have been identified as having rested on the temples, attached to diadems; but they are more likely to have served as endpieces to a pectoral ornament, for the rosettes at the top, masking hooks, are very similar to the endpieces of the ornaments just discussed. They are richly decorated with granulation and applied ornament and include heads in the Late Dedalic style, which date them about 630–620 BC.

One of them comprises a plaque with a repoussé figure of a naked standing goddess very like certain Rhodian terracottas with Syrian affinities.[50] Above the plaque is a lion's head, flanked by rosettes, from each of which hang complex pendants of pomegranates and chains. Above the lion's head is a plaque, as Pl. 20 B, and above that a rosette.

The second pendant is a plaque on which is a figure of a lion leaping on a bird.[51] Above the plaque is a rosette, flanked by smaller rosettes. The lower corners of the plaque are decorated with plastic griffins' heads, and from it hang three subsidiary pendants comprising pomegranates and Dedalic heads.

Another pair of pendants of uncertain use come from Grave 45 at Ialysus, of the late seventh century.[52] They consist of a disc, to which is soldered a griffin's head; from rings at either side hang subsidiary pendants in the form of a lion's head and pomegranates. Behind the disc are two rings to take a horizontal cord or chain. These ornaments were found in the same burial as a pair of earrings in a similar style (see p. 113) and were presumably worn with them, on the lady's temples.

BRACELETS

From Camirus comes a type of bracelet which had a long subsequent history. It is circular in section and penannular in shape, and the ends are decorated with lions' heads. The bracelets are of bronze, the hoop is silver-plated, and the lions' heads are gold-plated.[53]

A type, which occurs at Ialysus, Grave 23 (700–650), resembles Minoan-Mycenaean rings, except that the bezel is diamond-shaped. A similarly shaped bezel occurs in Crete (see p. 110).

A second type is the cartouche ring, an Egyptian type taken over by the Phoenicians and introduced by them into Greece and Etruria (see p. 145). An example in gold, a Phoenician import, comes from an alleged grave group at Camirus of the seventh century, and one in silver comes from Lindus.[54]

EASTERN GREECE

Introduction

Existing jewellery from Eastern Greece is virtually confined to discoveries at Ephesus: the foundation deposit of the earlier Artemision; related pieces from other parts of the same site; and a grave group (now in Berlin). The foundation deposit is dated by Jacobsthal in the seventh century, with the possible exception of a few outliers which may belong to the late eighth and early sixth. This dating may be taken to apply also to the rest of the jewellery from Ephesus. These pieces (of gold, electrum and silver) have much in common technically with contemporary Island jewellery, but are less elaborate. And there are further differences. The types of ornament favoured in the two groups are dissimilar, and Oriental elements and apparent Mycenaean survivals are more in evidence at Ephesus. Both the last-named features should probably, for geographical reasons, be attributed to influence from Lydian or Phrygian art, about which all too little is known.

The jewellery

Unless otherwise stated, the jewellery comes from the Artemision at Ephesus, and belongs to the seventh century.

From Tomb C at Assarlik comes a short band with impressed zigzag ornament (800–750).

EARRINGS

1 The boat-shaped type is represented in several examples (Pl. 21 E and F). First seen at Ur about 2500 BC, it had a long history in Western Asia and doubtless reached Greece from Syria, where it occurs at Sinjirli about 700. Earrings of this kind were to flourish in Greece for some four centuries.[55]

2 The simple spiral, an Island type (type 1 on p. 113), was also found at Ephesus (Pl. 21 D) and at Myndus.[56] The latter example is like the Attic and Corinthian ones (see pp. 102) and should be dated in the ninth or eighth century.

3 The variation (type 2 on p. 113) is also found at Ephesus.

4 The variation (type 3 on p. 113) is also found in Cremation Burial 6 of the West Cemetery at Samos (silver-gilt).

BEADS

Globular, melon, grain-of-wheat, biconical, segmented and triple spacers are the commonest types.

PENDANTS

A variant of the Rhodian discs mentioned on p. 114 was found at Assarlik, Tomb C (800–750), and is probably of Syrian inspiration. A number of drop pendants from necklaces of various shapes – lozenge, circular, wedge, etc. – are also found at Ephesus.

FINGER RINGS

A ring of gold wire, with overlapping ends, was found in Tomb C at Assarlik of 800–750. It was probably intended as a finger ring.

CLOTHING ORNAMENTS

Embossed discs and plaques occur with various designs. Some are paralleled in contemporary vase painting; others have a rather un-Greek appearance and probably owe much to Lydian or Phrygian models. The most popular subjects are heraldic lions attacking a man; a griffin; a sphinx; rosettes; and cup-spiral patterns (Pl. 21 A–C, G, H).

PINS

Pins are common at Ephesus, although rare in the rest of Greece at this date. The heads take various forms – spheres, egg shapes, pomegranates, drums (Pl. 22 C).

FIBULAE

1 The *arched* type, already found in Athens in the Dark Ages (see p. 90), is represented at Ephesus.

2 The *Asia Minor* type, an elaboration of the foregoing variety, is also found at Ephesus (Pl. 22 B).[57] It evidently developed in northern Syria and Asia Minor, for examples of the late eighth century come from Sinjirli and from Gordion in Phrygia.[58] After the seventh century the type is rare in Greece proper, but it migrated from Asia Minor to Thrace, where it had a subsequent history of at least three centuries (see p. 133).

3 An even more elaborate version of the arched type has a lion's head at either end, much ornament along the bow, and a large rosette in the centre.[59]

BROOCHES

Brooches were also popular. One in the shape of a disc with attached rosettes comes from Ephesus (Pl. 22 A). Several in the shape of a hawk or an owl also come from Ephesus (Pl. 22 D and E), and another comes from Samos, from a deposit dated 670 or earlier.

THE WEST

Tapered hoop earrings of silver, some plain, some with 'mulberries' at the bottom or round the sides (Fig. 18), are found in Sicilian graves of the seventh century, notably Grave 404 at Syracuse and Grave 240 at Megara Hyblaea. That is the full extent of recorded Western Greek jewellery in this period.

 Fig. 18   Type of silver earring found in Sicilian graves of the seventh and sixth centuries BC.

These earrings may well have been made locally, but the idea is not a Western Greek creation. Earrings of this kind (originally Phoenician?) were popular in Late Palatial Crete and Cyprus from about 1600 BC (see pp. 62 and 86), and continued in Cyprus and Phoenicia through the Dark Ages.[60] It is therefore presumably from one of these centres that this variety reached Sicily. The type continued into the sixth century, to enjoy a wider currency.

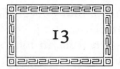

ARCHAIC AND CLASSICAL

600–330 BC

Introduction

The developments covered by this chapter may for convenience be divided into two stages, represented in the major arts by the Archaic and the Classical periods.

THE ARCHAIC PERIOD 600–475 BC

This was an age of artistic brilliance, particularly in the field of metal-work. Strangely enough, very little Archaic jewellery has survived: a deficiency all the more remarkable in view of the ample evidence for its existence in sculpture and vase painting. For example, the recently discovered statue of Phrasikleia, made about 550 and now in the National Museum, Athens, wears bracelets, earrings, a necklace and a pomegranate crown. This lack of material is best explained by a short-age of gold, especially since the only areas where Archaic jewellery was reasonably common, Cyprus, South Russia and South Italy, could draw on sources not available to the rest of Greece. Jewellery would have been chiefly of bronze and of silver, which cannot be expected to survive in large quantities. Silver earrings are in fact present in a number of Sicilian graves, where circumstances were perhaps more than usually favourable to their survival. The cause of the sudden shortage of gold in the sixth as compared to the seventh century completely eludes us; until we know the source or sources of seventh-century Greek gold, we cannot speculate on their cessation.

Though the domestic demand for their work was less, Greek gold-smiths were undoubtedly busy in the sixth century, working for foreign masters (or customers), for we find Graeco-Scythian, Graeco-Illyrian, Graeco-Etruscan, even Graeco-Celtic jewellery. Examples of the first are found in plenty in South Russian tombs; of the second at Trebenishte; of the third in Etruria (see p. 137); and of the last at Vix in Northern France. Moreover, jewellery from a tumulus burial at Gordion in Phrygia of about 560 BC could well have been made by Greeks.

The sources of the little surviving Archaic Greek jewellery are virtually restricted to graves in Rhodes, South Italy and Sicily, Olbia, and Cyprus. Valuable, though indirect, evidence comes from fragments of chryselephantine statues from Delphi, from which a certain amount of sheet gold representing the jewellery has survived.

From the scanty evidence we may make certain deductions about the nature of Archaic jewellery. It was in the main a development from that of the seventh century, particularly of the varieties popular in the Islands and Eastern Greece. So far as it reflects the sculptural arts, it shows the same advances in realism. Technically, there were two significant changes. In the first place granulation, although still used, gave place to filigree as the principal means of embellishment. Second, enamel made its first appearance towards the beginning of the sixth century, in discrete patches of colour bounded by filigree, a form possibly of Assyrian origin, which seems to have reached Greece via Ionia (see p. 25). The use of stones is restricted to engraved scarabs and scaraboids in swivel rings, and inlaying was practised rarely, if at all.

THE CLASSICAL PERIOD 475–330 BC

After the Persian wars gold evidently became rather more plentiful, but seems to have been reserved chiefly for religious uses. In the fifth century, in Greece proper, graves at Eretria of 475–400 BC have yielded quantities of jewellery, and a few pieces of very high quality have been found in the Peloponnese. Cyprus and South Russia and the rich Thracian tombs at Douvanli are fruitful sources of jewellery, some entirely, some only partly Greek. In the fourth century the chief sources are again Cyprus and South Russia, and there is an additional source in South Italy, in graves around Tarentum and in Campania. Material from the Greek mainland is now very scarce, but mention must be made of a royal tomb recently discovered at Vergina (the ancient Aegae) in Macedonia. The contents are dated 350–325 BC and the principal occupant is believed to have been King Philip II (reigned 359–336 BC).

The character of Classical jewellery follows closely from what little we know of the Archaic period. The workmanship was fine, but less fine than in the seventh century. Filigree was used in decorative patterns related to the ornaments in architecture and painting. Filigree enamel was becoming more popular. Granulation was rarely used; inlay of stone or glass even more rarely. Towards the end of the period, however, we first find engraved stones in the bezels of finger rings. In general, the sculptural forms of the gold were left to speak for themselves, diversified only by the above-mentioned processes.

The forms of Classical jewellery were very varied. Naturalistic wreaths developed in the fifth century and flourished in the fourth, and diadems continued in many forms. Earrings proliferated; the basic forms are now the boat, the spiral, the disc and the cone or pyramid. Human figures, some of great elaboration, which were to be typical of Hellenistic earrings, made their first appearance in earrings about the middle of the fourth century. Beads and pendants of types already familiar are found in this period, altered to suit the taste of the new age. Elaborate necklaces are also found with interlocking beads; and acorns, buds and human heads are popular as pendants. Bracelets take the form of spirals or penannular hoops with elaborate finials. Finger rings are found in several varieties, some containing seal stones, some purely decorative in purpose. Pins are rare, but a few elaborate examples are known. Fibulae were not generally used in Greece at this period, but a Macedonian-Thracian variety was in use in Northern Greece throughout the period and a variety, with Etruscan affinities, is found in Southern Italy.

Local schools undoubtedly existed, but can only partially be distinguished. We can, however, recognize certain regional peculiarities and preferences in North Greece, South Italy, Cyprus and South Russia. The jewellery of Greece proper and the Islands seem to have been remarkably homogeneous.

OTHER SOURCES OF INFORMATION

Apart from finds of jewellery, we have a few other sources of information for the Archaic and Classical periods. Sculptures, terracottas, vase paintings and coins all provide additional evidence, which at times supplements that of the material itself. Temple treasure records, particularly those from the Parthenon for the fifth and fourth centuries, provide confirmation on certain points. There is also a little literary evidence, but none of any value.

The jewellery

WREATHS

Wreaths were given as prizes, worn in processions, dedicated in sancturies and buried with the dead. The reason for the last-mentioned

custom was apparently to signify their victories in the battle of life.[1]
Although they are referred to in treasure records from the Parthenon of
the fifth and fourth centuries, surviving examples are few.[2] They were
made of gold, gold-plated bronze, silver, or wood covered with gold
leaf, and closely resemble wreaths made of actual leaves. Sometimes
sprays were worn in place of a wreath. A gold myrtle spray was found in
a tomb in Athens of about 450 BC, the so-called Tomb of Aspasia; a
gilt bronze myrtle wreath with gilt terracotta berries was found in
Grave 72 at Olynthus, of about 400 BC; and an olive wreath comes from
the Kekuvatsky Tomb at Kerch, of about 370 BC. Two splendid gold
wreaths, one of oak and one of myrtle, were found in the royal tomb at
Vergina (the ancient Aegae) in Macedonia; and one of equal magnificence, from Armento, is illustrated in Pl. 23. In addition to numerous
leaves, flowers, acorns, etc., it has figures of Victories and Erotes in the
round. The style of these figures would indicate a date around 350.

Illustrations of the wearing of wreaths, and of single sprays, can
be seen in gold plaques from the Priestess's Tomb of the Great Blisnitza (Taman), and on Cypriote sculptures.[3] And we learn that a goldsmith in the Agora in Athens made a wreath for Demosthenes to wear in
a procession.[4]

DIADEMS

Diadems of various kinds are found throughout this period. Some
surviving examples are clearly not the complete article, but were sewn
or otherwise attached to backgrounds of some other material such as
cloth or leather. Some, too, of the diadems were probably made, as in
the previous period, solely for funerary use; others, however, could
well have been worn by the living.

Thin strips of gold with embossed dot-rosettes from Ialysus
(Graves 35 and 42) were probably attached to diadems; they belong
to the sixth century. Rather larger strips with more lifelike rosettes come
from Eretria. One example comes from Grave 4, of the fifth century;
another, in Paris, is very similar but, surprisingly for this period, is
decorated with a large cabochon inlay of glass.[5]

Similar strips with palmettes are found at Amathus, New Tomb 10
(600–475 BC), and at Rhodes, Grave 4 (400–350 BC). The method of
wearing them can be seen in a Cypriote terracotta of the early fifth
century and in a Cyrenaic terracotta of the fourth.[6]

Diadems of more elaborate nature with figured scenes also existed.
A particularly fine example comes from a votive deposit at Thasos and
is dated stylistically in the first half of the sixth century. Another comes
from Ialysus, Marmaro Grave 10 (about 550), and a third variety with
metope-like scenes as in earlier Corinthian work (see p. 102), and

pomegranate pendants, comes from Grave 5 at Eretria, of the fifth century.

Most elaborate of all is a diadem from a tomb at Kelermes (Kuban) in South Russia, of the first half of the sixth century. It comprises a band with a griffin-head attachment in front and rosettes with filigree enamel on either side. From it hang pendants in the shape of buds and rams' heads. This remarkable object may not be entirely Greek, but Jacobsthal is probably right in relating it to Island work of the seventh century. It was perhaps made by a Greek for a Scythian customer.

Two pairs of pendant discs with patterns in relief come from tombs at Olbia of the second half of the sixth century. One pair was found on the head of the corpse, and they have consequently been identified with some probability as ornaments for diadems.

Two gold diadems belong to the very end of this period; they come from the royal tomb at Vergina (see above). One is in the form of a tied band; the other has openwork floral decoration and is decorated with blue enamel.

EARRINGS

1 The boat shape, already in use in Ionia in the seventh century, is one of the principal basic types of this period. It is most common in its simplest form. Dated examples of the fifth century come from Nymphaeum, Douvanli and the Seven Brothers burial in the Kuban; of the early fourth, from Marion, New Tomb 46, and Olynthus. The type is represented in use on coins of the late fifth and fourth centuries.[7] It spread to Thrace (Douvanli), Macedonia and Croatia.[8]

Simple elaborations are bud-like pendants on chains (Pl. 25 c);[9] an earring from Athens has a pendant plaque decorated with human figures in sixth-century style;[10] and a pair said to be from Spata has a cock-horse, in late sixth-century style, on the 'boat'.[11] A pair from Grave A at Homolion also has a cock-horse, on a 'boat' richly decorated with filigree. In Pl. 24 D the 'boat' has acquired a griffin's head.

Two pairs from graves at Eretria carry the elaboration one stage further. One pair, in London, comes from a grave of the late fifth century (Pl. 24 E). The basic boat shape is decorated with filigree and with enamelled rosettes; from it hang cockle shells on chains, and on it sits a siren. The whole complex hangs from a large enamelled rosette. The other set, published by Casson, is much the same, but the siren is replaced by a dancing-girl. A Tarentine version is the same in conception, while differing in certain details, which place it in the same school as the necklace in Pl. 28.[12] These earrings are some of the finest examples of ancient jewellery.

This form of earring was standardized in the second quarter of the fourth century, in a version which lasted till about 300 (Pl. 25 A). It is larger than the Eretrian varieties, and the pendants are buds instead of cockle shells, but it is basically the same. Examples come from many tombs in South Russia, including Kul Oba, Kerch (375–350), and the tombs of the Third Lady and the Priestess from the Great Blisnitza, Taman (350–325); and from Vratsa in Bulgaria. A pair in London is said to come from Crete,[13] and another pair comes from Grave 52 at Tarentum, of about 350 BC.

An aberrant version from Tarentum, in London, is a good example of the Graeco-Etruscan style more usually found in Campania.[14] It is decorated generously with filigree and with a repoussé gorgoneion in fourth-century style. Below it is an exaggerated cluster of globules made from sheet gold in obvious imitation of Late Etruscan models.

2 Spirals continue. The earlier types, which had remained close to their Oriental models, now split up into a number of regional varieties.

(a) An earring from Ialysus, Grave 189, of the early fifth century, develops the seventh-century Rhodian tradition as shown in Pl. 18 B. The ends are decorated with an ornamental collar and a pyramidal formation of large and small globules. A later development of this type is represented in a tomb at Douvanli of 450–425 BC and in Tomb 60 at Marion, of the early fourth century. It is also represented at Xanthus and by a pair in London (Pl. 25 E), and is clearly shown on a coin of Lycia of 450–400.[15] The finials are now tightly packed pyramids of grains; the same pattern is echoed on the lower edge of each curve, and diamond patterns of similar granulation decorated the body.

(b) A variety of this type is confined to Greek jewellery from South Russia of the fifth and fourth centuries (Pl. 24 C). The finials are similar pyramids, but they are separated from the main body by a long collar decorated with filigree; there are no pyramids underneath. Such earrings are found at Nymphaeum, in the Seven Brothers Barrows (Kuban) and in many tombs at Kerch. They occur in gold, gilt bronze and silver.

(c) The type most favoured in mainland Greece and Crete (Pl. 25 H) has a moulded collar and finials of a bud-like form. The top of the curve is frequently masked by a rosette, as in the seventh-century Rhodian example (Pl. 18 C). Examples come from graves at Halae of the later fifth century, from a mid-fourth-century grave at Tarrha in Crete, and from graves and houses at Olynthus of 425–350.

(d) A Cypriote variety, which started in the fifth century and probably continued into the fourth, has finials in the form of lions' or griffins' heads (Pl. 25 G). Many examples are known, mostly in gilt bronze and silver; enamel is common on the gilt ones. Few are stratified. One, however, comes from Amathus, Old Tomb 256, of the fifth century, another from a contemporary grave at Limassol.

(e) A variant of the foregoing variety is found at Tarentum, in graves on the Via Cagliari and elsewhere, and at Metapontum, and can be dated stylistically in the fourth century; it is apparently represented on Syracusan coins of the fourth century. The hoop is greatly enlarged in width, is heavily decorated with filigree, and terminates in human and, occasionally, animal heads.[16]

(f) The *splayed spiral* of the seventh century is represented in tombs at Olbia and Douvanli of the second half of the sixth and the fifth centuries. The spiral is so twisted out of shape as to form an omega, and the ends are pyramids. One would be tempted to regard this as a northern variety, were it not that an elaboration in the Stathatos Collection is said to come from Levidi.[17]

3 Tapered hoops, plain or with granular 'mulberries', continued from the seventh into the sixth century in Sicily. Dated examples, of silver, come from Grave 60 at Gela and from Graves 16 and 165 at Megara Hyblaea. Another silver pair comes from Grave 45 at Samos, and gold examples (undated) come from Naucratis and Daphnae. The type is represented on vases and coins.[18] (See Fig, 18, p 120.)

4 Discs. Sculpture, terracottas and vase painting leave no doubt that one of the most popular types of earring in the Archaic period was the disc, but very few actual disc earrings of this, or indeed of any, date have survived.[19] To be precise, they were probably earstuds rather than earrings.

(a) Such a stud, in silver, comes from the 'Couches Archaïques' at Lindus, and so should belong to either the seventh century or the sixth (see p. 113). Similar studs in gold, some of them enamelled, are found in Grave Y at Iasus and in Graves 153 and 155 at Ialysus, of about 400 BC, and are represented in London by examples from Rhodes (Pl. 24 A).[20] Related studs come from contemporary Cypriote tombs and are also represented in London.[21] The function of these studs has frequently been misunderstood, but there can be little doubt that the above explanation is correct.

(b) A type of earstud of a rather different kind is represented by a pair in gold from Grave 1 at Eretria, of the fifth century (Fig. 19), and

Fig. 19   Earstud from a grave at Eretria,
fifth century BC.

by an undated example in silver from Amathus, in London.[22] The studs are in two sections: the frontal piece is a disc, with a hollow tube projecting from the back; the rear piece consists of a small disc with a slightly narrower tube, which fits into the tube of the frontal disc. The two parts were joined by a safety chain (see Fig. 24). The type lasts into the late fourth century (see p. 162).

Opinions differ as to whether these studs were used as earrings or as dress fasteners. While it is true that a large hole in the ear, of about 0.5 cm in diameter, would be needed to take them, it is equally true that they are too flimsy and too insecurely attached to fasten a dress on the shoulders.

(c) Gold convex discs, decorated with embossed lions' heads and with patterns in granulation, and attached to a curved wire, have been found in many tombs at Olbia, always in pairs. One pair comes from Tomb 81, of about 550–500, and more come from other tombs of the same date. These discs have been called earrings, and it is hard to see what else they can be, but they are not the usual type of disc earring. The end of the wire was perhaps thrust through the actual cartilage of the ear. They are probably a south Russian Greek speciality.

5 Pendant earrings are another popular variety.

(a) An inverted pyramid or cone, decorated with filigree and granulation, of a kind already found at Argos in the seventh century, occurs from the sixth to the fourth century. Bronze examples are found in graves at Olynthus between 500 and 350; silver ones in graves at Halae of the late fifth century and in a grave at Isthmia. Indirect evidence for their use in the sixth century is afforded by the Berlin Standing Goddess and by the François Vase.[23] A gold example in London is shown in Pl. 25 F.

In the fourth century the type is also found hanging from a disc. It is represented in terracottas from about 400 BC and on coins of Syracuse of the same period.[24] It occurs in Grave 157 at Ialysus, of 375–350 BC. The type, suitably enriched, was popular in the later fourth century (see p. 162).

(b) Other motifs are occasionally found in this period hanging from discs or rosettes. A Mistress of Beasts, in the style of 475–450, from Corinth, recalls jewellery of the seventh century.[25] A Victory from the Pavlovsky Barrow at Kerch should probably be dated to the end of this period (about 340) rather than, with her sisters, in the next period. And a pair of earrings with female heads from Crispiano, near Tarentum (Pl. 25 B), should be mentioned, for they must come from the same workshop as the necklace shown in Pl. 28.

(c) Finally we come to a group of exceptionally fine earrings which date from the end of the Classical and the beginning of the Hellenistic period and thus cover the second half of the fourth century.[26] For convenience, the group is considered here in its entirety. These earrings are characterized by a honeysuckle palmette, from which hang pendants, frequently of great elaboration. The workmanship is superb; filigree and enamel are used in a masterly way. The finest examples are a figure of a Victory driving a chariot (in Boston) and Ganymede carried off by an eagle (Pl. 48 A). Other pendants take the form of a Victory, a siren and an Eros.

A simpler pair, from a grave at Koutsomita, near Arta, of 475–450 BC, consists of a palmette ornament, richly decorated with filigree, from which hang flower buds on chains.

NECKLACES

The sixth century is poorly represented, but the few types of bead or pendant known are developments of seventh-century varieties. Examples are a lion's head and a bull's head from Olbia, a pomegranate hanging from a bar from Eretria and Chalcidice,[27] and a bud from a grave at Tarentum by the Via Mazzini. From Tomb 131 at Marion comes a gorgoneion; and a chryselephantine statue at Delphi wore lion-head beads.

The fifth century is represented by complete necklaces. Good dated examples come from Eretria and Nymphaeum. The Eretrian necklaces include beads and pendants in the form of melons, pomegranates, acorns, eggs, bulls' heads, rams' heads and lions' heads (Pl. 26).[28] A necklace from Nymphaeum (in Oxford) is composed of ribbed discs with rosettes, and bud pendants (Pl. 27 A).

A necklace of rosettes with acorn pendants and double-palmette dividers (in Oxford) comes from Nymphaeum (Pl. 27 B); Aristophanes (*Lysistrata*, I. 407) refers to women wearing necklaces of acorns. The early fourth century is represented by a necklace of elaborate rosettes with bud pendants from Grave A at Homolion, and by an even more magnificent necklace from Tarentum (Pl. 28). Here, the pendants comprise buds, and human heads of two kinds; the larger are in the style of coins of 400–360 BC and serve to date the necklace. Necklaces of gilt terracotta, probably also Tarentine, have beads in a slightly later style, and show how the type developed in the mid-fourth century. They were undoubtedly made as cheap imitations of gold necklaces (see p. 42). Another necklace, with heads in a different style, comes from a grave at Roccanova of about 400 BC.

A cicada pendant in silver comes from the Palace at Vouni and is dated about 400; a similar one is shown in Pl. 24 F. From Grave 126 at

Cumae, of the mid-fourth century, comes a necklace of relief beads showing Etruscan influence, and comprising figures of sphinxes, heads of Heracles and Achelous and bulls' heads.

A certain type of pendant in the form of a female head was made, to judge from the style, throughout most of the fourth century. These pendants are found only in tombs in South Russia, and are apparently a South Russian Greek speciality. A good example was recently found in a tumulus burial at Velikaya Belozerka. They could be adapted to serve as earrings, but most were probably worn on necklaces (Pl. 25 D).[29]

Finally, a few other necklaces may be mentioned briefly. A cord-like chain with a raw nugget of gold as a pendant comes from Eleutherae and probably belongs to the fifth century.[30] Another chain with pendant pomegranates decorated with glass beads comes from Grave 5 at Eretria, of the fifth century. And two necklaces of cylindrical beads with spherical attachments come from Graves 153 and 155 at Ialysus, of about 400 BC. One has a rock-crystal bead as a centrepiece.

Two pairs of elaborate pendants of uncertain purpose come from tombs in South Russia, one from Kul Oba (Kerch), of about 360 B C, the other from the tomb of the Priestess of the Great Blisnitza at Taman, of about 330 BC. The style in both cases is perfectly Greek, but as nothing exactly like them has been found elsewhere we should probably regard them as a local peculiarity, possibly even made by Greeks for barbarian customers. Both sets comprise an embossed medallion, about 8 cm in diameter, from which hangs a network of chains supporting bud-like pendants and rosettes. The set from Kul Oba (Pl. 29) has the head of Athena Parthenos in three-quarter view on each disc, one being the mirror-image of the other. Those from Taman have a figure of Thetis riding a sea-monster and carrying the arms of Achilles.

The first pair was found on the corpse's pillow beside her head, the second on the corpse's breast. Minns believes that they were worn over the temples, suspended from a diadem, but this explanation does not account for the pair which were found on the breast; and, besides, the wearing of such ornaments over the temples would be uncomfortable and might even impede the wearer's vision. Possibly these medallions could serve several purposes, those from Kul Oba having been used as earrings, those from the Great Blisnitza as breast ornaments, suspended from pins like the Mycenaean ornament in Pl. 7 A. Three medallions somewhat like those from Kul Oba, with the head of Athena, were found in Grave A at Homolion; their purpose may well have been different again.

BRACELETS

The penannular tube or rod with animal-head finials continued from the previous period. A pair from Tomb 73 at Curium with rams' heads cannot be dated closely by associated finds; to judge from their style they were probably made in the first half of the fifth century (Pl. 30 A). A somewhat similar pair from Nymphaeum (in Oxford) is perhaps a little later. But the finest surviving bracelets of this period are a superb pair from Kul Oba (Kerch), of about 375–350 BC, in which the finials are formed of the foreparts of sphinxes (Pl. 30 B).

Other varieties of bracelet are known. Plain hoops of silver come from Grave 74 at Ialysus, of the early sixth century. Decorated bands are represented in the remains of a chryselephantine statue from Delphi of the early sixth century, and are found at Tomb 24 at Marion, of about 400, and at Kul Oba (Kerch). Bracelets ending in complete figures of lions come from the Tomb of the Priestess of the Great Blisnitza; and spirals come from the same tomb and from Grave 4 at Rhodes, of the fourth century.

FINGER RINGS

Finger rings in this period were used not only as seals but also for purely decorative purposes. They are mentioned in temple treasure records, notably those of the Parthenon and the Hecatompedon.[31]

1 Hoops in the form of swivels supporting engraved scarabs or scaraboids, generally of cornelian, are found in the sixth and fifth centuries, notably in Graves 10 and 254 at Ialysus, of the sixth century, at Nymphaeum, of the fifth and in Grave Y at Iasus. The type is originally Phoenician, and the earliest examples in Greek lands may well be Phoenician imports. Temple treasure records apparently refer to such rings. Occasionally the scarab or scaraboid is replaced by a gold drum, as in an example in London.[32] Two even more elaborate examples, of about 375–350, are known where the scarab is replaced by an oval plaque of blue glass or lapis lazuli on which is laid a gold cut-out which is itself covered by a sheet of clear glass or crystal. One example comes from the Pavlovsky Barrow at Kerch (Pl. 31 B). The other is from Grave B at Homolion.

2. Hoops with fixed rectangular bezels engraved in intaglio also occur in the sixth century, more often in silver than in gold. Examples come from an Archaic grave at Isthmia and from Grave C at Megara Hyblaea, of the later sixth century.

3 Hoops with an oval or pointed oval engraved bezel are first found in the sixth century, notably in Graves 41 and 42 at Ialysus, and continue down to the end of this period (Pl. 31 D and F). In the fifth century examples come from graves at Eretria and Nymphaeum. The hoop is at first slender with a pointed bezel; later the hoop becomes stouter

and the bezel a true oval. A ring of this type in London from Beirut has an engraved sard as a bezel. It is dated stylistically about 400 BC and is thus one of the earliest examples in Classical times of an engraved stone ring-bezel.[33]

4 A variation of the above variety is found in the fifth and fourth centuries, notably in Eretria, in Tomb 73 at Curium, Grave 155 at Ialysus and at Mesambria. The bezel is not engraved, but is purely decorative in function, with embossed ornament and filigree. The most frequent forms are a pointed oval and a deep oval box-shaped bezel with decoration also along the sides. The hoop is generally also of any ornate character, being made of twisted or plaited wire.[34]

5 A popular variant of the above type has a Boeotian shield as a bezel. Generally the hoop ends in animals' heads, which bite into the shield, and a gorgoneion is depicted in relief as a device on the shield. The bezels were occasionally carved from solid gold, a very rare technique.[35] The type started in the second half of the sixth century; an example comes from Grave D at Megara Hyblaea. It flourished in the fifth. Several examples come from Eretria; others from Thespiae, Perachora, Macedonia and Thessaly.[36]

6 Rings with creatures in relief as bezels – lions or beetles – come in at the very end of this period. They are found in tombs of the Great Blisnitza at Taman.

7 About 400 BC a new type of seal ring evolved with a fairly slender hoop and a circular bezel of the same metal. An example in silver comes from a mid-fourth-century grave at Tarrha in Crete. The type continued into the Hellenistic period.

8 Rings in the form of a spiralled snake come from tombs of the fourth century in South Russia and (in silver) from the same mid-fourth-century grave at Tarrha as the seal ring mentioned above (no. 7). This type also continued into the Hellenistic period and beyond.

PINS

Two very elaborate pins (in Boston) were found, joined together by a loop-in-loop chain, in a grave of the late fifth century in the north-west Peloponnese, near Aigion or Patras.[37]

One pinhead comprises a ball, rampant lions, bees and sphinxes. It is three-faced. Stylistically it is dated about 460 BC. The other comprises two balls, an Ionic capital, a pine cone, rampant lions, plants and bees. It is four-faced. Stylistically it is dated about 410 BC. Both pins are made in many sections and soldered together, with added decoration in filigree of beaded wire.

To explain the discrepancy in date between two joined pins, Jacobsthal has a pertinent suggestion: 'The sphinx pin was a family piece, perhaps the property of the buried woman's mother or grandmother, and then her father or husband gave her a modern companion piece, bespoken from the family jeweller in Corinth.'

Two pairs of silver pins come from graves at Tarrha in Crete. One pair, with conical heads, belongs to the late fifth century; the other, with melon-shaped knobs, to the mid-fourth century.

FIBULAE

Fibulae were not in general use in Greece proper during this period. Two varieties, however, are found in peripheral areas.

1 An elaborate variety of the 'Asia Minor' type evidently reached Thrace from Asia Minor, whence it spread northwards into the Balkans, and occasionally came southwards into Greece. In this period it was generally of silver. Dated examples come from tombs at Trebenishte of the late sixth century, and from graves at Halae of about 400. Examples in London (undated) are said to come from the Vale of Tempe, and Elis, and Budva in Yugoslavia (Pl. 31 E).[38] The type continued into the next period (see p. 171).

2 The second variety in its earliest form, about 500 BC, is found only at Ruvo in Apulia, and exhibits a combination of Greek and Etruscan forms (Pl. 31 A). It is basically a leech fibula (see p. 146) with a long foot ending in a ram's head. Foot and bow are decorated with fine granulation in triangular formations. In its later form, it is found in Campania (Pl. 31 C). Examples from Grave 126 at Cumae, of about 350 BC, just bring the type into this period; it continued into the next. This fibula, which is discussed in detail by Breglia, is basically Blinkenberg's 'Italic type' (no. XI), but beyond the catch is a spherical attachment. The whole surface is richly decorated with applied rosettes, filigree and a little granulation, and the general effect, although somewhat opulent, is charming.

BUTTONS

Buttons have been discussed by Elderkin.[39] They are rare *in corpore*, but have been identified with a fair degree of certainty in sculptures and vase paintings, where they fasten the peplos and himation on the shoulders, the chlamys at the throat, and the chiton down the arms.

Surviving objects of metal, bone and glass have been identified as buttons, and it has been suggested that wood was commonly used by the poor. A set of four in London is made of bronze cups with gilt terracotta fillings. The latter are decorated with gorgoneia in relief, apparently moulded from Thracian coins of about 500 BC (Pl. 24 B).

A pair of embossed gold rosettes was found on the shoulders of a corpse in a tomb at Olibia of 550–500, and similar objects have been found in pairs at Ialysus, in Marmaro Graves 5 and 10. To judge from their position, they must represent the facings of brooches or buttons which had fastened the peplos. Brooches, which would have been made of metal, are unlikely to have vanished utterly in all three instances, and the only reasonable supposition is that the rosettes covered wooden buttons, which under normal circumstances could not be expected to survive.

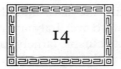

EARLY ETRUSCAN 700–400 BC

Introduction

The first traces of the Etruscan civilization of Central Italy are dated about 700 BC, and it lasted in a recognizable form until about the first century BC.

The origins of this culture are still in dispute, but the following view has the support of many scholars today and is acceptable to the author. The so-called Villanovan culture, which had flourished in Northern and Central Italy in the eighth century, was transformed in Central Italy about 720 BC by the introduction of new artefacts and new customs, many of Western Asiatic origin. The ensuing hybrid culture may best be explained, in complete accordance with the views of Herodotus, by the arrival on the western coasts of Etruria and Latium of immigrants from Western Asia Minor, who took over the Villanovan world as a ruling minority and made certain substantial modifications. The Oriental influences in Etruria are not of the same order as the contemporary Orientalizing phase in Greece. Although there are obvious resemblances, the process in Etruria was much more sudden in its inception, and far deeper-rooted in its effects.

Apart from Villanovan and Western Asiatic elements, there is a third element which may have had some influence on the development of the Etruscan civilization. On the east coast of Italy the Picene culture had much in common with that of the Thraco-Illyrian continuum across the Adriatic and must inevitably have made some impact on the Etruscans to the west. This factor may account for certain features common to Etruria and Thrace, which seem to have reached Etruria via the Faliscans (see pp. 141–2 and 148).

Throughout the seventh, the sixth and the early part of the fifth centuries the Etruscans spread over Italy and grew in power on land and sea. Their great riches, attributable largely to the mineral resources of the country, are reflected in the sumptuousness of their tombs, as rich in gold as those of Mycenaean Greece. The zenith was reached about 500 BC, but the battle of Cumae in 474 began a rapid decline in political and economic power.

Although in its earliest manifestations Etruscan art was remarkably free of Greek influences, it did not long remain so. From about 650 BC Greek pottery was imported and imitated, and before the seventh century was out Greek influence was becoming increasingly felt. Throughout the sixth century, and much of the fifth, many works of art and great quantities of pottery were imported from Greece, and all Etruscan art, although it never completely lost its identity, was heavily overlaid with Greek. So much so that in certain centres, in particular at Caere, immigrant Greek craftsmen are believed to have worked for Etruscan masters.

The period from 475 to 400 is one of decreasing prosperity, and the surviving evidence for Etruscan art is extremely scanty, except in the Po Valley, far to the north, which at this time enjoyed a brief spell of affluence. For reasons which will become clearer in the next chapter, this chapter ends about the year 400.

Although Early Etruscan jewellery developed in a gradual sequence, for the sake of simplicity we may divide it into three phases.

725–625 BC

The first phase is covered from beginning to end by tombs at Vetulonia and, around the middle of the century, by the great tombs at Praeneste and Caere and by numbers of others. One of the more important early tombs for the study of Etruscan jewellery is the so-called Artiaco Tomb at Cumae.

Characteristic forms in this phase are hair spirals; earrings; beads and pendants of various kinds, including several Phoenician varieties, and the earliest stage of the Etruscan bulla; bracelets of several kinds; clothing ornaments; pins; and, above all, fibulae. These last are mostly translations into gold and silver, with embellishments suited to the new materials, of types already established in bronze among the Villanovans.

The most important decorative technique is granulation, which was carried to greater heights of technical excellence than by any other people at any other period. Two schools have been postulated on the basis of the styles of granulation employed: a southern school, centred on Latium, which concentrated on the *outline* style; and a northern school, perhaps centred on Vetulonia, which preferred the *silhouette* style. There are indeed certain grounds for this view; but if it is accepted, it must be admitted that northern granulation found its way south and, conversely, southern granulation reached the north in fair quantities.

625–475 BC

The second stage is covered for the first fifty years by certain tombs at Populonia, by the Polledrara Tomb at Vulci and by the Pania Tomb at Chiusi. After 575 there is plenty of material of doubtful provenance, which admits only of a stylistic dating, but very little from controlled excavations which can be dated by association. A tomb group from Vulci in New York, although its antecedents are not unimpeachable, appears to be homogeneous, and can be dated, on internal evidence, about 500 BC.

The most important factor in this period is the tremendous amount of Greek influence, which transformed Etruscan art, including jewellery. Greek forms were seldom adopted, and Etruscan jewellery can seldom if ever be mistaken for Greek; but, in matters of detail and subsidiary ornament, Greek influence was paramount throughout this long period. So far as technique is concerned, granulation was gradually giving ground to the simpler process of filigree, a change which was occurring at the same time in Greece. Enamel and inlay were occasionally employed; inlay gradually became popular, but enamel was never more than a Greek innovation, which did not find lasting favour.

The characteristic forms of this period are rather different from those of the preceding period. Diadems are rare; hair spirals continue. Earrings are now extremely popular; the *a baule* variety, which evolved towards the end of the previous period, was the most popular; another variety is the disc. Beads and pendants are found in many varieties, and there are also strap necklaces with a network of pendants. Clothing ornaments, pins and fibulae continue. Finger rings are now found.

475–400 BC

The third period is poorly represented, except at such northern sites as Bologna and Spina. A tomb at Capannori (near Lucca) contained jewellery of 475–450. So far as our evidence permits, we may regard this period as transitional between Early and Late Etruscan. Characteristic forms are earrings of a new type, formed by a tubular hoop terminating in a human or an animal's head; a few *a baule* earrings; beads of various kinds; and pins and fibulae of the Certosa type.

The jewellery

DIADEMS

Diadems are rare in Etruria. A gold-plated bronze example in London comes from the Polledrara Tomb at Vulci and so should date about 600. It is in the form of an oblong strip, 51 cm long, with semicircular spaces cut out to fit over the ears, and is decorated in low relief with stamped figures of lions and lotus flowers.

Also from Vulci are four diadems in London, composed of strips of sheet gold tapering towards each end and terminating in a hook at one end, and a loop at the other.[1] Such diadems bear a striking likeness to two from the Aegina Treasure (see p. 62). They do not seem to be in the Villanovan or Etruscan tradition, and may be Oriental.

HAIR SPIRALS

Spirals and rings of wire are common, especially in seventh-century tombs, and are generally believed to have been used in the hair (Pl. 32 D). They are found in Tre Fontanili Tomb 2 at Veii, at Marsigliana, Vetulonia and Populonia.[2] A sixth-century antefix from Capua (in London) illustrates the wearing of such ornaments.[3]

EARRINGS

Earrings are not common in the first half of the seventh century, if indeed they occur at all, and it is not till about 625 that they were in general use. A few examples, however, may be placed slightly earlier.

1 A boat-shaped earring in London has no known provenance, but the granulated decoration is so like Etruscan granulation of the mid-seventh century, and the shape of the 'boat' is so like Etruscan fibulae, that we should have no hesitation in calling it Etruscan of the mid-seventh century.[4]

2 A hoop earring like a bugle but curled right round so that the mouthpiece runs near or actually into the flaring end is first found at Vetulonia and Narce, and should perhaps be dated from the third quarter of the seventh century. The type had a long life in Etruria (Pl. 43 B).

3 Another pair of earrings in London come from Vulci (Pl. 32 E). They consist of a chiselled openwork disc in the technique later to become popular with the Romans as *opus interrasile*, with a crescent-shaped nick cut out of the top, and central inlay of stone, amber or glass (now missing). They were evidently suspended by a short wire from

a stud inserted through the lobe. Coche de la Ferté traces the type
back to Lydia, thence to Syria and the Hyksos peoples of the Bronze
Age.[5] These earrings probably constitute one of the few concrete links
between Lydia and Etruria to support the views of Herodotus. The type
did not find favour in its new home.

4 Another early type of earring consists of a metal band bent round
into a circle and attached to the ear by a wire, which also joins the ends.
A pair of such earrings comes from Vetulonia (Fig. 20). It is composed

Fig. 20   The earliest stage of the *a baule* earring, later
seventh century BC.

of three strips of openwork filigree side by side, each strip being topped
at one end by a human head in low relief. The earrings themselves are
very like the filigree bracelets so popular at Vetulonia, and the style of
the heads shows them to be contemporary with the latest of these
bracelets, which we may date about 640–620 BC (see p. 144). Earrings
of this nature are represented on two terracotta statuettes in London of
about the same date (Fig. 21). In essence they are merely hoop earrings
made from a strip of metal instead of a wire or a tube.

Later types are as follows:

5 The characteristic earring of the later seventh, the sixth and the
earlier fifth centuries is the *a baule* variety, so called by the Italians because of its resemblance to a small bag or valise (Pl. 32 c).[6] It is an
original Etruscan creation, which evolved from the bent strips of metal
discussed under no. 4 above. This earring is composed of a strip of metal
bent round to form the greater part of a cylinder, the two ends being
joined by a wire, which also passed through the lobe of the ear. The
wire was often masked from a frontal view by a plate of decorative
metalwork, and one end of the cylinder was sometimes closed by a
similar plate. The chief means of decoration is very fine filigree, frequently of the openwork variety, and attached ornaments such as
berries, rosettes, etc. Granulation was also used to a small extent,
and enamel is sometimes found. Motifs borrowed from Archaic Greek
art abound and help to date individual examples. Pieces from controlled excavations are not numerous, but the earliest examples, from tombs

Fig. 21   Terracotta, about 650 B C.

at Populonia of the late seventh and early sixth centuries, serve to date the evolution of the type; its latest appearance may be dated from a tomb at Capannori of 475–450 BC. A slightly aberrant form comes from Tomb 86 of the Certosa Cemetery at Bologna, of about the same date, and from Tomb 26 at Orvieto.

6 The disc earring was also worn in Etruria over the same period as the *a baule* (Pl. 32 A and B). The type is represented by a number in London and by a pair in New York from a tomb at Vulci of about 500 B C.[7] They are richly decorated in front with granulation, filigree and, occasionally, inlay; a hollow tube ending in a loop is attached to the centre of the back. The discs vary in diameter from 2 to 6 cm, and the tubes project for about 1 cm. The evidence of the New York tomb group and the subsidiary decoration, which recalls the *a baule* earrings, indicate a date in the sixth and the early fifth centuries. The counterparts of these discs in Greek jewellery have been identified as earrings (see pp. 127–8) and there is no reason to doubt that these served the same purpose. Further confirmation of their use is given by the representation of similar objects worn in this way in paintings and terracottas of the sixth century. The disc was attached by thrusting the projection through the lobe and securing it by the insertion of a ring through the loop. A safety chain ran from a loop in the side of the disc to this ring.

7 A tubular hoop with a pattern of large globules hanging from the

base originated in the later sixth or the fifth century.[8] It is evidently derived from the Cypriote-inspired hoop earrings so common in Greece and Sicily in the seventh and sixth centuries (see pp. 120 and 127). This type of earring is interesting not so much for itself as for what became of it in the fourth and third centuries.

8 In the fifth century the northern sites of Spina and Bologna (Certosa) can produce virtually only one type of earring: a tubular hoop equipped at one end with the head of a woman, a river god, a ram or a lion (Pl. 43C).[9] This type was also the basis of a popular variety of earring in the fourth and third centuries.

BEADS, PENDANTS AND NECKLACES

A circular pendant with a central boss has already been mentioned (on p. 114) as a Syrian or Cypriote type which found its way in the early seventh century to Greece and Etruria. Etruscan examples of the early and middle seventh century are numerous, some having the central boss composed of an amber inlay. They come from Tre Fontanili Tomb 2 at Veii, from Bisenzio and Narce, and from the Artiaco Tomb at Cumae. There are also some particularly fine examples in a necklace in New York, together with other, stylistically related pendants with marked Phoenician affinities.[10]

A variant type has an inverted crescent over the boss, a Phoenician motif indicating the sun and the moon in association. An example from Vulci is covered with fine granulation (Pl. 33 B); one from Bisenzio, Tomb 10, is inlaid with amber. A third example comes from Marsigliana.

Another Phoenician type of pendant, which achieved a certain popularity in Etruria in the seventh century, is a large scarab or scaraboid of gold, amber or faience pivoting on a swivel. It occurs in Tre Fontanili Tomb 2 at Veii, at Vulci (now in Munich), and at Vetulonia, and is represented in London by an amber scaraboid, with a silver swivel (Fig. 22). It was originally a seal holder, but was appreciated in Etruria more for its decorative than for its utilitarian characteristics, and the scarab or scaraboid is seldom engraved. The type is, not surprisingly, also found in Cyprus.[11]

The bulla, originally a lentoid pendant hanging from a broad loop, was to become the typical Etruscan ornament, the *Etruscum aurum* of the Romans. In later days it was worn as an amulet, especially by generals at triumphs, by freeborn boys and by domestic animals, but it does not seem to have been in general use before the fifth century.

The earliest recorded examples are in bronze and come from Faliscan tombs at Narce of the mid-seventh century (Tombs 42 M and 102 F in Philadelphia). Pendants from Douvanli in Thrace of some two centuries

Fig. 22   Silver and amber pendant,
seventh century BC.

later are remarkably like the bulla, and it is possible that this ornament had an earlier history in Thraco-Illyria, and reached Etruria from
the east, via the Faliscans. The same explanation is suggested for the
'needles' discussed below (see p. 148).

The necklace (in London) illustrated in Pl. 35 B exhibits an unusually
fine form of the bulla. It is said to come from Atri in the Abruzzi and
can be dated stylistically about 500 BC. It is probably not complete.
In its present state it is composed of eight bullae, two finials and six
filling beads (one of which is modern). The finials are decorated with
lions' masks in relief. The bullae are identical, decorated in low relief
on one side with a gorgoneion and on the other with a lion's mask with
eyes of enamel. At the top are two rings for suspension and between
them a hollow cylinder which serves as the lid of a stopper fitting into
a hole in the top of the bulla. The suspension cord passed through the
rings and the cylinder and kept the stopper secure. The combined use of
granulation (on the filling beads) and filigree (on the stopper) is typical
of the period. These bullae were evidently intended to contain some
fluid, possibly scent.

We may now consider the most popular types of beads and pendants
of the seventh century, a period in which they are particularly common.

Melon beads come from Vetulonia and Marsigliana; flanged beads
from Vetulonia, Bisenzio and Narce; lemon-shaped beads with granulation from Narce (see also Pl. 33 A). Double-cylindrical spacers come
from Vetulonia and Vulci (Pl. 33 B).

Flask-shaped pendants come from Tre Fontanili Tomb 2 at Veii and
from the Regolini-Galassi Tomb at Caere. Acorn beads are found at
Populonia; such beads were long popular, for one not dissimilar
comes from a tomb at Capannori of 475–450 BC. The type is represented

in London by an example from Tarquinii.[12] Anchor-shaped pendants come from Marsigliana and from Vulci (Pl. 33 B).

Relief beads depicting a human bust are found at Vetulonia, in La Pietreria (640–620 BC), and are represented in London (Pl. 33 A). A human half-figure, the arms crossed on the breast, in a related style, is found at Narce and at Vulci (now in Munich).

Mention should also be made of grotesque beads of multicoloured glass, which were used as pendants in the later seventh century (Pl. 33 A). They are found throughout the Mediterranean, and are generally believed to be of Phoenician origin.

The sixth century is poorly represented by beads, but there is more material in the fifth.

A silver necklace in Paris, which can be dated stylistically about 500 BC, is composed of four-winged human-headed creatures decorated with filigree spirals and hung with amphora pendants, and globular beads, some of which are also hung with amphora pendants.[13] Relief beads in a related style come from a tomb at Capannori of 475–450 BC. It is composed of frontal figures of sirens, winged female busts and acorns.

A cord chain with a satyr-head pendant (in London) comes from Caere.[14] The head is evidently modelled on some Greek original of the later sixth century, and is decorated with unusually fine granulation for this late date. Heads very similar in style are found on Campanian terracotta plaques.[15] Another satyr-head pendant in Paris, to judge from its style, must have been made about the same time, but in its coarser execution is more typical of the period.[16]

Strap necklaces with a complicated system of pendants are represented in two fine examples, one in London (Pl. 34) and one in Naples, from Ruvo.[17] The pendants include satyr heads, sirens, rosettes, flowers, acorns and scarabs. The style of the heads dates these necklaces about 500 B C.

CLASPS

Clasps, possibly for narrow belts, in the form of pairs of acorns are found in tombs at Populonia of about 600 BC, and are represented in London.[18] Similar clasps composed of spectacle spirals come from Marsigliana and Vetulonia and are also represented in London.[19]

BRACELETS

Bracelets are particularly common in the seventh century. They fall into six main groups.

1 Hoops decorated with animals' heads, the ends overlapping. They are particularly common at Vetulonia, where they are found in the Tomb of the Foreigner, the Circle of Oleasters, and the First Circle of Pellicie. A pair in London is said to come from Tarquinii.[20]

2 Strips of openwork filigree running side by side and frequently topped by human heads in relief (Pl. 37 B). These bracelets are particularly common at Vetulonia, where they are found in the Circle of Bracelets, the Bes Circle, the Migliarini Tomb and the Pietreria. The type is also found at Marsigliana. A slightly different version in London is decorated in addition with figures of sphinxes in the round.[21]

3 Bracelets similar in shape to the foregoing, but of solid sheet gold, decorated with embossed figures and outline granulation (Pl. 36).

4 Large rectangular strips, richly decorated in the same way as the foregoing. A pair comes from the Regolini-Galassi Tomb at Caere; another in London, said to be from Praeneste, is illustrated in Pl. 37 A.

5 An articulated openwork bracelet, probably of the seventh century, comes from Vulci (in Munich). Another, in Paris, of uncertain provenance, is decorated very much in the style of the *a baule* earrings and should probably be dated somewhat later, in the early sixth century.[22]

6 A spiral of openwork filigree, somewhat like the individual strips of no. 2 above. Bracelets of this kind are recorded from Bisenzio.

PLAQUES

A number of gold relief plaques are found among Early Etruscan jewellery. Some served as clothing ornaments, some as clasps, and the purpose of others is not clear. They may for convenience be considered together.

1 Plaques depicting draped women in the East Greek style of the later sixth century, and decorated with touches of enamel. A pair in London is said to come from Caere; there are two finer examples in Paris, of unknown provenance.[23]

2 Plaques comprising a figure of a goddess of Oriental appearance, merged in an elaborate floral pattern. One such plaque comes from Tomb 10 at Caere (the 'Chamber of the Firedogs'); and a pair in London is also said to come from Caere (Pl. 32 F).

3 A clasp in London composed of two plaques is said to come from Chiusi. A siren is represented, in the style of about 500 B C.[24]

4 Another clasp in London with a reclining satyr in relief on one plaque, and a reclining maenad on the other. To judge from the style, this piece should be dated about 500 B C.[25]

FINGER RINGS

Finger rings are not common in Early Etruscan jewellery, but one class achieved a certain popularity in the late seventh and the sixth centuries (Pl. 35 A).[26] It is a type of ring which reached Greece from Phoenicia, and Etruria from Greece. The ring is ultimately of Egyptian type, with a slender hoop and a cartouche-shaped bezel of gold or gilt bronze. The bezel is decorated with designs in relief or in intaglio in a markedly East Greek style. Were it not for the Etruscan provenance of these rings, one would be inclined to call them Greek; possibly they were made in Etruria by Greek craftsmen.

In addition, a swivel ring with an engraved scarab was adopted from Greece at some point in the fifth century, but is rare before the fourth.[27]

PINS

Pins are fairly common in Early Etruscan jewellery.[28] The heads are as a rule spherical, or in the shape of an inverted pear; in a few instances they are composed of a pyramidal arrangement of spheres. Pins of the seventh century from Vetulonia are often richly granulated; a particularly impressive example comes from the Lictor's Tomb. Pins are also found at Populonia, about 600 BC; at Vulci (in New York), about 500 BC; and at Capannori, 475–450 BC.

FIBULAE

The fibula had a continuous history in Italy from the Late Bronze Age into Etruscan times, and the basic Etruscan varieties were taken over, fully developed, from the Villanovans.[29] But the Etruscans, in addition to the everyday varieties of bronze, produced luxury versions in gold and, to a lesser extent, silver. Their goldsmiths and silversmiths not only reproduced forms already known in bronze, but also (the goldsmiths especially) employed all the resources of their craft to diversify these basic forms. Of these forms the two principal are the *serpentine* and the *leech*, and these will be considered first.

1 Serpentine. This is a Villanovan type, in which the bow is twisted into a variety of shapes, and is sometimes also fitted with knobs and swellings. Even more ornate examples exist, decorated to a fantastic extent with applied figures and patterns in granulation. Many fibulae of this form were made in gold and silver from earliest Etruscan times until the end of the sixth century. Select examples of about the seventh century come from the Artiaco Tomb at Cumae, the Barberini and Bernardini tombs at Praeneste, from Marsigliana and from Vetulonia. A silver-gilt

one from Tomb 312 of the Certosa Cemetery at Bologna brings the type down to about 500 BC.

Two of the ornate examples are worthy of special mention. The first is the famous gold fibula in Paris decorated in granulation with geometric patterns and with the name of the owner.[30] The second (in London) comes from Vulci and is illustrated in Pl. 38 A. The fibula itself is richly decorated with granulation; in addition, the entire upper surface is encrusted with figures in the round, also richly granulated: lions, lions' heads, horses' heads and sphinxes.

2 A curious type, represented in London by three examples, appears to be related to the serpentine type. It has a broad flat bow, with the spring at one side. The bow in one example is quite flat, and of trapezoid form.[31]

3 The leech (or boat) shape was also taken over from the Villanovans. It was made in a surprisingly large number of variant forms, especially in the seventh century. The shape is essentially that of the earlier arched form, but the bow is thickened in various ways to resemble a leech or a boat. It may be solid, or hollow and closed, or hollow and open underneath. Sometimes it is drawn out in the middle into points, occasionally knobbed. The particular varieties are sometimes given different names—leech, boat or kite—but it is simpler, in view of their basic unity, to give them all the same name; the leech is suitable for the simplest form and will serve for all.

The foot, too, takes different forms; it may be short, with a bent-up catchplate, or long, like an open sheath, with perhaps a knob on the end. Many examples are richly granulated. That in Pl. 38 B is one of the very finest to have survived.

In the sixth century the typical leech fibula had a long foot, with a small knob. Granulation is still found, but was not practised as lavishly.

A different variety is found in tombs at Populonia of about 600 BC. It has a slender bow and a small rectagular catchplate. Towards the end of the sixth century an even simpler type evolved, the so-called Certosa type (Fig. 23). As its name implies, it is found in abundance in the Certosa Cemetery at Bologna between 525 and 400 BC, in silver and bronze. It is also represented in gold (in New York) by two examples from a tomb at Vulci of the late sixth century. These fibulae are small

Fig. 23   Type of Certosa fibula, lifesize.

in size, with a sharply arched bow and an upturned foot. This is about the last manifestation in Etruria of a form which had a long and exuberant life, and can only be regarded as something of an anticlimax.

A variety of the leech fibula, itself of Villanovan origin, is composed of segments of various materials threaded on the bow of an arched fibula. The segments were sometimes entirely of amber, sometimes of amber alternating with a substance which has disappeared and which may be presumed to have been wood; this vanished substance was frequently covered with gold foil, which has survived. The type occurs with a long foot and with a short foot. Examples are common; they come from Bisenzio, the Artiaco Tomb at Cumae, Tre Fontanili Tomb 2 at Veii, and elsewhere. All seem to be of the seventh century.

In another seventh-century variety, of Villanovan origin, the foot terminates in a large metal plate, approximately oval in shape and set at right-angles to the bow. Frequently one or more transverse members are interpolated between the bow and the plate. The type is represented in gold by a fairly simple variety, in London;[33] much more elaborate examples, with granulation and embossed ornament, come from Vulci (in Munich) and from the Regolini-Galassi tomb at Caere (Pl. 40).

4 In another type of fibula, the bow takes the form of an animal modelled in the round, a lion or a chimaera. The rendering of the animals dates these fibulae in the sixth century.[34]

Two other forms of clothes fasteners, although they functioned on a different principle, are generally known as fibulae.

5 The comb fibula.[35] A type found in the Bernardini and Barberini tombs at Praeneste, at Marsigliana and Falerii, in the Artiaco Tomb at Cumae and represented in London by an example illustrated in Pl. 39 B. They are as a rule of silver, parcel gilt. The central element is a richly decorated tube, with a wire running down either side. There are also two comb-like elements. The 'combs' were sewn to opposing corners of a garment, and were joined at the shoulder by means of the tube, being hooked over the side wires. The wearing of such a fibula is illustrated on a terracotta figure (in London) from Caere (Fig. 21). The origins of this fibula are unknown. It belongs to the seventh century BC.

6 The bolt fibula, with much the same distribution and date as the comb fibula, and serving the same purpose.[36] An example from Caere is shown in Pl. 39 A. Like the comb fibula, its origins are unknown. It consists of two principal elements. The first comprises three or four horizontal tubes, curving downwards at one end; long pins protrude from the straight ends of the outer tubes. The tubes are joined to each other by a transverse plate, to which is hinged another, similar plate. The second element is identical with the first, except that the pins are absent,

and the tubes are bent up instead of down. The two pins of the first element are pushed through the garment and into the ends of the outer tubes of the other element. The clasp is then locked by fastening the two secondary plates, with hooks and eyes, or by some other means. All four plates are encrusted with figures of animals in the round, richly granulated.

'NEEDLES'

It remains to consider a class of object whose purpose is completely unknown. It is a needle-like object, equipped with an eyelet hole at one end, and richly decorated at the other with openwork filigree. In Italy, the type occurs only at Narce, and is therefore in all probability not truly Etruscan. Similar objects in the Stathatos Collection in Athens are said to come from the neighbourhood of Salonika.[37] It is possible that we have here, as with the bulla (p. 141), an example of related objects coming from the eastern and the western ends of a Thraco-Illyrian cultural continuum. The absence of similar 'needles' in the intervening area is certainly surprising, but is perhaps attributable to the chances of survival and discovery.

These objects are unlikely to be bracelets, in spite of the superficial resemblance to certain Etruscan openwork bracelets; for the eyelet at one end was clearly never intended to join the other end, and the examples from Salonika were apparently found straightened out. The most likely explanation is that they served as decorations for clothing.

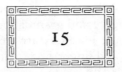
LATE ETRUSCAN 400–250 BC

Introduction

About 400 BC, for reasons which are not entirely clear, there occurred something like a renaissance in Etruscan art, which continued to exist in a recognizable form until the first century BC. For the purposes, however, of a history of jewellery, the Late Etruscan period may be deemed to end about 250 BC. By the middle of the third century, the Etruscan cities were finally defeated and absorbed in the Roman Confederation; and their minor arts were drawn into the Hellenistic orbit, of which Rome, in many respects, now formed a part. The jewellery of Etruria after 250 BC may be regarded as Hellenistic, and will be mentioned in the following chapter, to which it clearly belongs.

The date when jewellery of specifically Etruscan type ceased to be made cannot be fixed with any exactitude; it continued into the third century, but is hardly plentiful enough to have lasted till the end of the century.

Etruscan jewellery again becomes plentiful about 400 BC. It now has a character entirely its own, in many ways very unlike Early Etruscan, and is remarkable in that, once developed, it remained without any significant changes for some one and a half centuries. It is clear that the forms of Late Etruscan jewellery developed from Early Etruscan, but the intervening stages cannot always be traced, for our evidence for the transitional period, 474–400, is slight, and is confined to the far north, which was probably apart from the main current. Moreover, although the forms of jewellery of the two periods are related, the feeling behind them is entirely different.

149

The new style consists of large convex surfaces of sheet metal, with embossed decoration. Filigree and granulation are seldom, and enamel never, found. The articles of jewellery are almost confined to wreaths, earrings, bullae, bracelets and finger rings. Although Greek influence is evident in details, such as the scenes embossed on wreath ends and bullae and engraved on rings, the jewellery itself has practically no counterparts in Greece.

When this style was succeeded by Hellenistic, a little of the genuine Etruscan spirit remained. In particular, bullae continued in use in Etruria and lasted until early Roman Imperial times.

From the beginning of the Hellenistic period in Greece, about 330, jewellery of the Hellenistic pattern was imported from the South Italian Greek communities and similar pieces were made in Etruria itself, for Hellenistic and Late Etruscan pieces appear side by side in Etruscan tombs of that date, at Todi, for example. This chapter, however, will deal only with genuine Etruscan creations, and will leave the purely Hellenistic jewellery (whether imported or indigenous) for later consideration.

Our sources are tombs at a number of sites, especially Praeneste, Vulci, Populonia, Todi and Perugia. Representations of jewellery in paintings and on terracottas also provide useful information.

The jewellery

WREATHS

The commonest variety of Late Etruscan wreath is a flat, stylized and extremely flimsy arrangement of leaves (Pl. 41 B). This wreath is probably the *corona sutilis* mentioned by Roman writers, in which the leaves were sewn to a background. The ends are decorated with embossed scenes frequently borrowed from Greek mythology. An example from the Sperandio Tomb at Perugia can be dated, by associated finds, to the fourth century. Other examples, of which there are a fair number in the Vatican from Vulci and in London from various sites, can be dated by the style of the embossed designs to the fourth or third century.[1]

Two other varieties of wreath, no less stylized but more robust, and capable of being worn without additional support, may be mentioned. One is composed of ivy or vine leaves gracefully arranged on a central stalk. An example comes from the Marini Cemetery at Praeneste, of the third century; one in London has no known provenance.[2] The type is represented on a terracotta head in London which belongs to the late fourth or the third century.[3]

The second type is a myrtle wreath, illustrated in Pl. 41 A, which should probably belong to the same period as the foregoing.

EARRINGS

1 (a) A simple tubular hoop, a debased version of the bugle type (see p. 138), continued into this period, and is found in the Sperandio Tomb at Perugia, and in a tomb at Volterra (Monteriggioni).

(b) The basic type is enlarged and elaborated with the form of a bead or a lion's head at one end, and, occasionally, with superficial decoration.[4] An example comes from Peschiera Tomb 1 at Todi.

(c) The next elaboration is the addition of a ring, sometimes accompanied by a pendant representing a jar (Pl. 43 D).[5] An example comes from Peschiera Tomb 20 at Todi.

(d) The most extreme variety of this type of earring is represented by a pair from Peschiera Tomb 1 at Todi; a pair from Perugia, of which one member is in London (Pl. 42 C), the other in Perugia; and a pair in New York said to come from Rome.[6] The hoop is now completely masked in front by a decorated plate of gold in the shape of a long thin shield, from which hang pendants in the shape of a human head, and a number of jars. The heads are strongly influenced by Greek art; they particularly recall terracottas of the Tanagra style.

2 (a) The tubular hoop with a pattern of large globules at the base continued from the previous period.[7] Good examples come from Praeneste and Capena. An example in London is shown in Pl. 43 A.

(b) The hoop is decorated with a small plate of embossed gold shaped like an inverted horseshoe.[8] The type is found in Peschiera Tomb 16 *bis* at Todi, and at Praeneste.

(c) The hoop shrinks in size until in some cases it disappears. The horseshoe-shaped plate is greatly enlarged, and extended at its lower end to include the pendant globules, which are now simply embossed decoration from the same sheet of metal (Pl. 42 D).[9] The type is found at Civitavecchia and Capena. Earrings of this type are frequently represented in Etruscan wall paintings and terracottas.

3 A pair of earrings from Chiusi in London (Pl. 42 A) is a rare example of a Hellenistic earring of the disc-and-pendant class translated into the Late Etruscan idiom.[10]

BEADS, PENDANTS AND NECKLACES

The bulla is the typical Late Etruscan ornament. Bullae are now as a rule richly decorated with patterns, figures or scenes in low relief, frequently borrowed from Greek mythology (Pl. 42 B). The two principal types are shown in Pl. 44: the globular (the original type) and the heart-shaped. The Achelous head on the same plate is an unusual variation. Examples come from tombs at Vulci, Todi, Filottrano and elsewhere. The type continues through the Hellenistic period and even beyond.

A few other types of necklace ornament may be considered. An agate mounted in gold and pendants representing buds or flasks accompany bullae in a necklace from Peschiera Tomb 1 at Todi.

BRACELETS

Bracelets are extremely rare in Late Etruscan jewellery, but a pair in London has embossed designs in the style of fourth- and third-century bullae, and can only be Late Etruscan.[11] The type is also represented in the semi-Etruscan cemetery at Montefortino.

FINGER RINGS

Finger rings were more popular in the Late Etruscan period than before. Several varieties were current.

1 The swivel with an engraved scarab, first used in the fifth century, was very popular in the fourth and third. Examples are found at Volterra (Monteriggioni), in Peschiera Tombs 1, 9 and 20 at Todi, and elsewhere (Pl. 43 E). In some examples the ends of the swivel are decorated with large discs or cylinders somewhat in the style of the contemporary earrings.[12]

2 A peculiarly Etruscan type was in use in this period; it can be dated, by the style of the engraving, to the fourth and third centuries.[13] It has a large fixed convex bezel, set sometimes at right-angles to the line of the hoop, sometimes along its axis. In the centre is a stone, sometimes engraved and sometimes plain, framed by embossed gold-work (Pl. 43 F and G).

3 Purely Greek shapes with a round or a pointed oval bezel were also in use in this period. Dated examples are found in Peschiera Tombs 1 and 20 at Todi, but should probably not be included here, as being more Greek than Etruscan (see p. 169).

HELLENISTIC 330–27 BC

Introduction

The conquests of Alexander the Great between 333 and 322 transformed the Greek world. Vast new territories of the former Persian Empire were Hellenized by settlements of Greeks, and Greece in return was exposed to influences from the newly conquered territories of Egypt and Western Asia.

From about 300, when the chaos following Alexander's death was at last halted, the Greek-speaking world is seen to be made up politically of a number of self-contained groups. The most important were Old Greece, precariously independent; the Antigonid kingdom of Macedonia; the Ptolemaic kingdom of Egypt; the Seleucid kingdom of Syria; the Greek cities of South Italy and Sicily; and the Greek or semi-Greek communities of South Russia. From about 250 Roman Italy, which now included Etruria, may be reckoned for our purposes as yet another section of the Hellenistic world. By the end of the first century BC all of these communities, with the exception of the South Russian Greeks, had been swallowed up by the growing power of Rome. But the arts of this period, especially the minor arts, were not greatly affected by political considerations, and, although local preferences and peculiarities undoubtedly existed, there was much cross-fertilization, and we may safely regard Hellenistic jewellery as basically homogeneous throughout this large area. This chapter ends, somewhat arbitrarily, with the end of the Roman Republic.

So far as jewellery is concerned, the most important fact is the far greater quantity of surviving material, attributable without doubt to the greater availability of gold. For the first time since the Bronze Age, gold was plentiful in Greece; thanks partly to the intensive mining operations in Thrace initiated by Philip II, but mostly to the dissemination of the captured Persian treasures. The general appearance of the jewellery was at first much as before, but by the early second century there were new forms beside the old, and the system of decoration had radically changed. Then, for about two centuries, there was little change.

Many forms of jewellery and systems of decoration in this period follow the traditions established in the fifth and fourth centuries. As examples we may cite many of the wreaths, diadems, earrings, finger rings and bracelets. Similarly, filigree enamel and plain filigree occupy about the same place in Hellenistic jewellery as they did in Classical. Granulation, too, was occasionally employed.

The principal changes which took place between 330 and 200 BC may be classed under three headings: new decorative motifs; new forms of jewellery; and new systems of decoration.

1 *New motifs*. The so-called Heracles knot (the reef knot) was introduced at the beginning of this period and retained its popularity as an ornament for jewellery into Roman times. It may be presumed to have come from Egypt, where its history as an amulet goes back to the beginning of the second millennium.[1] To the Greeks also it had an amuletic as well as a decorative purpose; it was believed particularly efficacious in assisting the healing of wounds.[2]

Another Egyptian motif, whose use was more restricted, is the disc, feather and cow-horn crown of Isis-Hathor, which is found on earrings of the second and first centuries BC.

The crescent is another foreign import. It was introduced from Western Asia, where it had a high antiquity, and whence it had already reached Greece in the eighth and seventh centuries. In its homeland it was sacred to the Moon God. It is found in Hellenistic necklaces as a pendant; although its purpose was doubtless primarily decorative, it had a certain amuletic value.

Of purely Greek motifs, figures of Eros are among the most popular, as in all Hellenistic art.

2 *New forms*. The animal- or human-headed hoop earring, introduced from Persia about 330, became very popular and retained its popularity in certain regions till the Roman period.

Elaborate diadems, frequently with a Heracles knot as a centrepiece, are first found about 300 and lasted for about two centuries. Bracelets in the same general style were also made, doubtless to accompany the diadems.

New types of necklaces are also found from about 330 of which chains with animal-head finials and straps with pendants of buds or spearheads are the most important. Beads not threaded but linked together are typical of the second and first centuries. Medallions with heads in high relief are found in the second century and served various purposes. Finally, new types of finger rings evolved.

3 *New techniques*. The most important innovation, which transformed the appearance of Greek jewellery, is the polychromy provided by the inlay, or attachment by other means, of stones and coloured glass. Archaic and Classical jewellery relied for its effect primarily on the sculptural forms of the metal itself, and on such surface decoration as granulation and filigree could provide. The decorative use of stones or glass was extremely rare, and the only other colours generally tolerated were those obtained by a very discreet use of filigree enamel. But in Hellenistic jewellery inlaying was lavishly practised. Of the stones, chalcedonies, cornelians, the clear quartzes and, above all, garnets were in use from 330 onwards. In the second and first centuries emeralds and pearls are occasionally also found.

Where did the polychrome style originate? Not surely in South Russia, an area which has been suggested on the basis of the numerous examples of this technique found there. It had in fact been practised throughout the old Persian Empire–in Egypt, in Asia Minor, in Syria, in Mesopotamia and in Persia itself–and it could have reached Greece from any of these quarters after Alexander's conquests.

Another new technique, also designed to give a multicoloured effect, is *dipped enamel*, which was used principally for earring pendants in the shape of birds or other creatures.

Openwork filigree also makes a brief appearance in this period, in diadems and bracelets. It is chiefly found in the late fourth and early third centuries.

We can no longer speak of local styles, but regional preferences lingered on. For example, a certain type of fibula, and medallions of a particular kind, apparently the tops of hairnets, are peculiar to North Greece; hoop earrings after about 100 BC are found only in Egypt and the East; another type of fibula is restricted to Campania; and the bulla is peculiar to Etruria. Cyprus and South Russia exhibit further peculiarities; but this is not surprising, since both areas were only marginally Greek, and would naturally include other elements in their repertoire.

Most of the recorded material comes from tombs of the late fourth or early third century BC, and it comes from every quarter of the Hellenistic world, as a direct result of the sudden abundance of gold in Greece. Frequently, whole sets were buried with the dead. There are such sets in New York, one from Madytus in the Troad and one from near Salonika; and a set in Pforzheim, said to be from Sardis. Jewellery (in London) said to come from Kyme in Aeolis probably represents several such ensembles from related tombs. It includes earrings and necklaces decorated with the same motif and clearly intended to be worn together.

Our evidence for the later periods is less plentiful. After about 250, except in certain favoured quarters, gold was evidently scarcer than before. Tombs in South Russia, particularly at Kerch, cover the third century. The early second is represented by the rich tomb from Taman, Artjukhov's Barrow, and the full second century by two graves at Pelinna in Thessaly. We should probably also place in the second century the treasure, now divided between the National Museum (Stathatos Collection) and the Benaki Museum in Athens, which comes from Thessaly (probably Karpenisi), and a small but very choice collection now in Chicago, from an unidentified site in Syria. To the second–first century belongs a set of jewellery found in the House of Ambrosia at Delos, the so-called Family Tombs at Eretria, and an alleged tomb group from Palaiokastro in Thessaly.

Jewellery was undoubtedly made in many places, frequently by itinerant craftsmen, but it would be safe to say that among the most important centres were Alexandria and Antioch. We cannot, however, in the present state of our knowledge, attribute any particular style to either centre.

Apart from the finds of actual jewellery, there are a few other sources of information for this period.

1 *Archaeological.* A goldsmith's stock-in-trade, dating from about the second century, was discovered at Galjub in Egypt. This hoard of bronze objects consists of punches of various kinds, very similar to those in use today, cores for hammering sheet gold, prototypes for the making of moulds, and various composite figures whose precise function is by no means clear.[3]

Sculptures, bronzes, terracottas, paintings and coins may also illuminate questions connected with jewellery.

2 *Literary.* The few extant literary references to Hellenistic jewellery are mostly given under the articles to which they refer. We may, however, mention here Athenaeus, who describes the gorgeous displays of goldwork in Alexandria, and the goldsmiths and sil ersmiths of Antioch.

3 *Epigraphic.* Temple treasure records frequently list articles of jewellery deposited as votives. The most useful are those from Delos for 279 and subsequent years, in which reference is made to wreaths,

diadems, necklaces with pendants, bracelets, finger rings, pins and but-tons.[5] Further mention will be found under the articles to which they refer.

The jewellery

WREATHS

1 Temple inventories from Delos for 279 BC and subsequent years mention gold wreaths of laurel, myrtle, ivy, olive, oak and vine.[6] Num-bers of such wreaths have been found, occasionally of silver or gilt bronze, generally of gold foil. They are mostly naturalistic, like the wreaths of the previous period (see p. 124). Surviving examples come for the most part from South Russian tombs from the late fourth to the early second century. The tombs on the Quarantine Road at Kerch, and Artjukhov's Barrow at Taman, are especially prolific. Like most of the Classical examples, the vast majority of these wreaths are too flimsy to have been worn by the living, and must have been made especially for funerary use, to secure the maximum effect for the minimum outlay of gold.

2 Another type of wreath, stout enough to have been worn by the living and too elaborate to have been made solely for the dead, is found in the Tomb of the Gold Ornaments at Canosa (Pl. 45 B) The type is represented by other examples in London and Paris.[7] It consists of a solid framework to which is attached a vast quantity of leaves and flowers, many of them decorated with filigree and filigree enamel. Numbers of beads of coloured stones and glass to indicate berries are attached by means of wires. The total effect is one of brilliant, but some-what overwhelming, magnificence.

3 About the second century BC a new type of wreath, probably al-ways funerary, makes its appearance; it was to achieve greater popu-larity under the Roman Empire (see p. 176). It is made up of stylized leaves of gold foil in groups of three or four on a backing of some other material. A fine example comes from a cremation in the Athenian Cerameicus; and leaves from a similar wreath are recorded from a grave in Lenormant Street, Athens.

DIADEMS

1 Strips of gold with embossed designs of various kinds continued in use, and do not differ radically from those of the previous period; they lasted well into the first century BC. Examples come from a third-century tomb at Eretria and from the 'Family Tombs' of about the second or first century, also at Eretria.

2 An elaborate type of diadem, stout enough to have been worn on festive occasions by the living, was found in a tomb of the early third century at Santa Eufemia, the ancient Terina. It is roughly triangular in shape and when worn would rise to a point over the brow. It is richly decorated in a pictorial style by means of low relief and filigree. A less elaborate version of this type, probably worn with a backing of some other material, is represented in a tomb group from Madytus, of the late fourth century (Pl. 45 c), and (in many examples) from Kyme in Aeolis, of the same date.

3 An even more elaborate type is found in tombs of the third and second centuries (Pl. 46). The centre is a richly decorated Heracles knot, frequently inlaid with garnets, set with gold figures, and enamelled at the edges. The diadems themselves vary in their composition. They may consist of one or more chains or straps, or of an unbroken framework of gold. From the diadems hang pendants of great complexity, usually set with quantities of garnets and other materials. The diadems have been fully discussed by Segall and Amandry.[8] The earliest securely dated example is a fragment from the Gela Hoard, of the early third century. Pendants from such a diadem are included in the group from Kyme, and may put the start of this type slightly earlier. A complete and extremely elaborate example comes from Artjukhov's Barrow at Taman, of the early second century. Other examples come from Thessaly (Karpenisi?), Ithaca, Kerch and elsewhere. As might be expected, they are particularly common in the rich tombs of South Russia and North Greece.

4 A simpler, and perhaps all the more pleasing, version of this type of diadem is said to come from Melos (Pl. 45 A). The diadem itself is composed of three parallel strands of twisted gold bands, the central one decorated with applied rosettes. In the middle of the diadem is an ornate Heracles knot of gold wire richly enamelled and finished off with a large cabochon garnet in the centre. A matching pair of bracelets evidently comes from the same or a similar set (see p. 167).

5 An incomplete diadem from Abdera is closely related to the group described above, in particular to the example from Artjukhov's Barrow, by the very similar pendants attached to it, and should be dated round about the early second century. The main body, however, is quite different, and is composed of a number of linked rectangular plaques, divided vertically into two sections. One side is decorated either with a filigree rosette or an inlaid cabochon garnet; the other with a head in relief, a dramatic mask, a satyr, a nymph or a maenad. A poorer version of this diadem, with similar designs on a single embossed strip, comes from one of the Family Tombs at Eretria, of the second to first century.

6 Another variety comes from Sedes Tomb Gamma at Salonika, of

the later fourth century. It has a central plaque with a figure of Eros, and on either side four lyre-shaped members, terminating in a lion's head. The curves and coils of wire from which the diadem is made give an effect of lightness which distinguishes it from usual Hellenistic diadems. A similar diadem comes from an alleged tomb group from Demetrias in Thessaly in the Stathatos Collection in Athens.

EARRINGS

1 The boat type is not a favourite Hellenistic earring, but the North Greek variety continues down to the end of the fourth century at Madytus (Pl. 25 A) and Derveni Grave 5. The type makes a belated final appearance in Artjukhov's Barrow at Taman, of the early second century BC.

2 Tapering hoops, generally with animal-head finials, less frequently ending in a human head or some other motif, originated in Greece about 330 and continued in certain areas into the first century AD. A much higher antiquity has been claimed for these earrings in Greece, and indeed somewhat similar hoops do go back in Etruria into the fifth century and in North Greece and Thrace perhaps even earlier; but in Greek jewellery there is only one tomb (Kerch, Quarantine Road, Tomb E) which appears to offer any evidence earlier than 330 BC; and the evidence of that tomb cannot at the moment be accepted at its face value in view of so much evidence to the contrary. The markedly Achaemenid character of some of these animal heads would suggest a Persian origin, and recent research has indeed identified Persian proto-types for these popular Hellenistic earrings.[9]

Several varieties are known.

(a) The hoop is formed of coiled wires or, less commonly, a twisted metal band; it tapers to a point at one end and at the other is equipped with an ornamental collar, from which springs the head of an animal or a human being, generally in gold, but occasionally in stone.[10] The point of the tapering end is thrust through the lobe of the ear and into a loop in the other end. Some earrings are so made that the human or animal head is worn upside down; in others it is the right way up. Earrings of this nature are extremely common in Hellenistic tombs of the later fourth and third centuries and probably lasted into the second. They are represented in use in works of art, especially in Etruscan mirrors and terracottas. Many different forms of finial are known and are listed below. Most varieties are so common that it is not reasonable or neces-sary to note more than a selection of the sites on which they have been found.

(i) The head of a lion (Pl. 47 F).[11] The commonest, and probably the original type, which flourished in the later fourth and early third centuries. Select examples come from tombs at Salonika (Sedes, Tomb Gamma), Kozani, Amphipolis, Curium (Old Tomb 80), Syracuse and Todi (Peschiera Tomb 9); an example from Rheneia has a bead in the collar.

(ii) The head of a horned lion.[12] This is in fact the head of the Persian lion-griffin. The type is not as widespread as the true lion-headed variety, and is almost restricted to Cyprus and South Russia; it may well be a Cypriote creation. Dated examples are rare, but the type probably ran parallel with the foregoing. It occurs at Curium (Old Tomb 69), frequently at Amathus, and at Olbia.

(iii) The head of a bull or a calf (Pl. 47 K).[13] Another popular type, found at Marion (New Tomb 60), Aphendrika (Tomb 33) and Rheneia.

(iv) The head of a goat or a gazelle (Pl. 47 D).[14] Many have inlaid eyes. Examples come from a grave in the Athenian Cerameicus and other graves at Rheneia, Tresilico and Marion (New Tomb 58).

(v) The head of a lynx or a tiger.[15] A rare type. Examples come from Ithaca and Vulci.

(vi) The head of a dog.[16] Another rare type. Examples come from Pergamon, a third-century tomb at Eretria, and Aegina.

(vii) The head of a woman (Pl. 47 H).[17] A number in London are said to come from Crete. To judge from the style of the heads, these earrings were made in the third and second centuries.

(viii) Negro heads. An earring in London has a negress's head of garnet, set in gold (Pl. 47 J). It is said to come from a group from Kyme in Aeolis, which dates for the most part rather before 300 BC, but the resemblance to finials from second-century necklaces suggests that this piece may be intrusive to the group (perhaps added by a dealer) and should really be dated in the second century. A somewhat similar earring, with an amber head, comes from a tomb at Bettona of the second century; a third comes from a tomb at Tarentum.

(b) At some time in the second century the hoop earrings described above fell out of use. In the West they were succeeded by other types of earring, in the East by a more elaborate version of the same type, which seems to have been restricted to Egypt, Syria and Cyprus, and which in these areas lasted well into the Roman period. The hoop is now threaded generously with beads of stone, glass or, less commonly, gold, which cover about half the circumference. Generally, two or three globular beads are employed; but in some examples a single barrel-shaped bead is found. Thin washer-shaped disc beads of gold with granulated edges frequently separate the beads from each other and from the hoop. The finials are composed, as before, of animal and human heads, but are seldom identical with those of the earlier variety. Although this type is as much Roman as Hellenistic, it will be treated, for the sake of convenience, in its entirety in this chapter.

(i) The head of a dolphin is by far the commonest type of finial, but disappointingly few come from dated deposits (Pl. 47 E).[18] One example comes from a house at Tanis (Egypt) of the first century BC, and one from a tomb at Vasa in Cyprus of the first century AD or later. Many others are reported from Egypt and Cyprus, and the type is represented on mummy cases from Akhmin and on wooden Egyptian coffins of the first and second centuries. AD.[19]

(ii) The next commonest type of finial is the head of a tiger or a lynx.[20] Examples are said to come from Rheneia, Delos (the House of Ambrosia), Rhodes, Egyptian Thebes and Syria.

(iii) Other animal heads were also used for finials, but less commonly. We find the heads of a bull;[21] a ram;[22] a goat, from Samsun and Salamis in Cyprus;[23] and a cock.[24]

(iv) The head of a woman, probably a maenad, is found on earrings from Syria and Salamis in Cyprus, and there are many examples of the type with no known provenance.[25] Of two examples from Syria, one is combined with an Eros pendant, the other with an amphora pendant.[26]

(c) There are a few examples of earrings ending in the complete forepart of an animal. We may take as typical a pair from Montefortino, of the third century, with the forepart of a horse; and a pair from Mesambria has the forepart of a Pegasus on the hoop and an amphora pendant.

(d) Hoop earrings comprising complete figures are also known but are less common. One type has a figure of Eros bent backwards and forming part of the hoop (Pl. 47 I). Sometimes there is a garnet above his head.[27] Examples, of the later third and early second centuries, come from Quarantine Road Tomb B at Kerch, Artjukhov's Barrow at Taman, and Morgantina. A pair in London, from near Damascus, has amphora pendants in addition.[28] Another type has a dove, with a garnet above its head.[29] It is evidently contemporary with the Eros hoop earrings. A fine pair from Pelinna is composed of a figure of Eros driving a chariot; the front part of the hoop is set with inlaid stones.

(e) A by-form of the lion-headed hoop has an incomplete hoop and a smaller lion's head at the other end. The same type seems to be a Western speciality; it occurs in a tomb group from Cumae, and is also found at Capua, Tarentum and Ithaca.[30] It cannot be closely dated, but probably belongs to the late fourth or early third century, to judge from the style of the lion's heads.

(f) The hoop has no finial, but tapers at both ends; a rare form, and not closely datable, found at Rheneıa and Volterra (Monteriggioni) and in South Russia.[31]

(g) The hoop ends in a floral pattern, with filigree and granulation.[32] Another rare form, dated to the early second century by its occurrence in Artjukhov's Barrow at Taman.

3 A hoop earring of an entirely different kind is occasionally found.[33] It consists of a wire ring of uniform thickness threaded with a globular bead, very like those in Pl. 28. It is represented in a group from Kyme in Aeolis, most of which is dated in the late fourth century.

4 Two-piece earstuds like those described on p. 127 continued into the beginning of the Hellenistic period (Fig. 24). Examples are found at Kyme, in Marmaro Tomb 32 at Ialysus, and in Galata Tumulus 6 near Varna in Bulgaria. These studs are, from the front, almost identical with the discs of contemporary disc-and-pendant earrings as illustrated in Pl. 48 D.

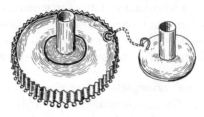

Fig. 24   Back of earstud, late fourth century B C

5 Pendant earrings were extremely popular throughout this period.

(a) A cone or pyramid suspended from a disc continues from the previous period (see p. 128), now suitably enriched for Hellenistic taste. It is particularly common in the late fourth century. Between the disc and the pendant we frequently find an intermediate member in the form of a minute figure of a Victory or a similar motif, and subsidiary pendants in the form of Victories, spearheads or buds hang from the sides of the disc. One such pair comes from the Dammusi Tomb at Syracuse, of the late fourth century, and another, identical pair from the Karagodeuashkh Tomb in the Kuban. A slightly different form is represented in several examples from Kyme in Aeolis, and in a pair from Kalymnos (Pl. 48 D). Variants of the type also occur at Montefortino (third century) and Ancona (about 200).

(b) In the second century, type 5 (a) was succeeded by a polychrome variety, in which the cone or pyramid is replaced by a pendant of stone or glass of roughly the same shape set in gold. This type is found in second-century tombs at Bettona and Morgantina and is worn by the figure on the sarcophagus of Seianti Hanunia, of the same date.[34] It probably continued into the first century BC and perhaps beyond, for one example comes from Herculaneum.[35]

There is an Etrusco-Hellenistic variety of this type from a late third-century cremation at Volterra (Monteriggioni, Urn 16), also found in the François Tomb at Vulci. A pyramid or a cone hangs from a crescent-shaped shield of the kind known as a *pelta*, or Amazon shield.

(c) Another popular form of pendant earring is a figure of an amphora hanging from a disc or a semicircular plate (Pl. 48 c).[36] The type may have evolved by equipping a conical pendant with the few attachments necessary to convert it into an amphora, but an amphora is in itself a suitable motif for jewellery because of its amuletic properties. Both the amphora and the support from which it hangs are frequently inlaid with stones or enamelled, and subsidiary decoration in filigree and granulation is also found. Additional pendants frequently hang from either sides of the support, sometimes threaded with garnets, emeralds or pearls.

The type, which seems to belong to the second and first centuries BC, is found in the François Tomb at Vulci, in tombs at Bettona and Perugia of the second century, in a tomb in Samothrace said to be of the Augustan period (in silver) and in a house at Delos of about 100 BC. In a particularly fine pair a long chain, attached to the lower ends of the amphorae, runs from one earring to the other.[37] Similar amphorae also hang from hoop earrings. The type is represented in London by a lynx-head hoop and an Eros hoop.[38]

(d) One of the most popular types of pendant on Hellenistic earrings is a figure of Eros, frequently cast solid, with details soldered on.[39]

(i) The earliest variety is suspended from a gold rosette-like disc (Pl. 47 B). Representative examples come from Kyme, a tomb at Thebes, and Tomb A at Quarantine Road, Kerch (late fourth century); from Tombs C and D at Kerch (third century); and from the Family Tombs at Eretria (second–first century).

(ii) A more ornate variety, with a garnet in the centre of the disc, was introduced in the second century. It is found in Artjukhov's Barrow at Taman, and in a second-century tomb at Salonika. In the Family Tombs at Eretria and in the tomb at Palaiokastro, of the second–first century BC, the disc is inlaid with two stones, one set about the other (Pl. 48 E).

(iii) Another form, where the figure of Eros hangs directly from a hook, comes from the Antikythera shipwreck, of the first century BC, and is also found at Herculaneum.[40]

(e) A companion to the Eros earring is the Victory earring, in which a figure of Victory replaces that of Eros (Pl. 47 A). The type had its roots in the mid-fourth century, and existed in this period side by side with the Eros earrings, but was never so popular. It is found in a tomb near Mount Pangaeus, of the third century, and in a group from Thessaly (Karpenisi?) of the second.

(f) The superb pair of earrings in New York, from near Salonika, with a pendant figure of Ganymede, have been discussed above (see p. 129, Pl. 48 A).

(g) The earring illustrated in Pl. 47 G from Leukas, is composed of a figure of a siren hanging directly from a hook. Although it is frequently a late characteristic to dispense with the disc, the modelling of this figure is very much in the Early Hellenistic tradition.

(h) Occasionally, as in Pl. 47 C, a female head hangs from a disc, but that form also is rare. The one illustrated probably dates from the third century, according to the resemblance of the head to those on terracottas of the Tanagra style.

(i) Figures of birds form another type of pendant, either suspended from a disc or, less commonly, attached direct to the hook. The former variety occurs in the François Tomb at Vulci, the latter in Thessaly (Karpenisi?). The dove is the most popular bird to be portrayed, doubtless because of its association with Aphrodite, but the eagle is also represented.

(j) A model of a shrine, suspended from a disc, occurs in a tomb of Hellenistic date at Ancona.

6 A special variety of pendant earring consists of a bird or other figure of dipped enamel hanging, like the amphorae mentioned above, from a disc or a semicircular plate of metal and equipped, like them, with subsidiary pendants at the sides.[41] Many examples are known, especially from South Russia and Italy, but only one recorded example can be dated with any degree of exactitude; it comes from Artjukhov's Barrow at Taman, and is of the early second century (Pl. 48 B). We should probably date most of these earrings, with the amphora earrings which they so much resemble, in the second and first centuries BC (but see type (f) below). The following varieties of pendant are known:

(a) Swan. From a Family Tomb at Eretria, Grave 86 at Tarentum, the François Tomb at Vulci, and South Russian tombs.

(b) Cock. From various Etruscan sites, Vulci, Chiusi, Bolsena, and Tomb A at Volterra.

(c) Dove. From Artjukhov's Barrow (Pl. 48 B). The bird hangs from a rosette, above which are the disc and feathers of the Egyptian goddess Isis. The disc and the two subsidiary pendants are encrusted with garnets.

(d) Peacock. From an unidentified site in Etruria.

(e) Centaur. From Vulci. Presumably the *kentauridion* earring mentioned by Pollux.[42]

(f) Bunch of grapes. From the François Tomb at Vulci, and from the Tomb of the Gold Ornaments at Canosa, of the third century. Presumably the *botrydia* earrings mentioned by Pollux.[43] This type would appear to be rather earlier than the preceding varieties.

NECKLACES

1 Straps reappear about 330 BC, after a gap of some three centuries since their use in Rhodian jewellery of the seventh century (Pl. 49 B). The gap is probably more apparent than real, since they are found in Etruscan jewellery in the intervening period (see Pl. 34).

The Hellenistic strap necklace rapidly became popular, and remained so for some two centuries. The straps are hung, either directly or from chains, with many small pendants in the form of flasks or spearheads. Joins are masked by rosettes or other devices of great delicacy, decorated with filigree and enamel. The finials are similarly decorated. At a late stage, probably not before 200, inlaid garnets were also used.

The pattern of the spearheads remained constant throughout. The flasks, however, vary. At first flower bud, popular in earlier jewellery, is equipped with a neck and forms a bud-like jar not unlike the pottery amphoriscs of the late fifth century. Later, in the second half of the third century, the flask takes a more recognizable form. The necklace illustrated in Pl. 49 B exhibits both forms side by side. Temple inscriptions from Delos of 279 and subsequent years mention necklaces with spears and amphorae; they evidently refer to this type.[44]

The first recorded appearance of these necklaces is in the Priestess's Tomb of the Great Blisnitza (350–325 BC); at Corinth and at Kyme in Aeolis (late fourth century); and in a number of Macedonian and South Russian tombs of the late fourth and third centuries. Their latest appearance *in corpore* is in the Karpenisi(?) group from Thessaly, of about the second century; their continued use in the early second century is further attested by their representation on the sarcophagus of Seianti Hanunia.[45]

2 Chain necklaces were also popular.

(a) Simple chains, loose-linked or corded, are found as necklaces at Kyme, Santa Eufemia, Karpenisi (?), the François Tomb at Vulci, and Peschiera Tomb 9 at Todi. They were undoubtedly in use throughout the Hellenistic period. Two corded chains with tassel pendants come from Kyme and are thus probably of the late fourth century. The pendants are composed of elaborate beads and figures of flowers or pomegranates threaded on the chain.

(b) A popular type of necklace throughout this period is the chain, loose-linked or corded, terminating in animal heads. As with the hoop earrings, the commonest finial is the lion's head. Necklaces of this kind are found in many south Russians tombs between 330 and 175, and elsewhere. A particularly fine variety, from Pelinna, is composed of a corded chain with lynx-head finials. From it hang gold pendants in the shape of a crescent, star, amphora, Eros, Victory, eagle and two medallions with busts of Artemis and Helios.

(c) A variant, with complete dolphins as finials, comes from a Family Tomb at Eretria, of the second–first century.

3 Linked globular, or occasionally spool-shaped, beads of various materials ending like the chain necklaces with animal heads were equally popular in Hellenistic jewellery. Examples occur in Artjukhov's Barrow at Taman, at Karpenisi(?) and in the François Tomb at Vulci. A variant, also from the François Tomb, has complete dolphins as finials. Another variant has negro heads of garnet as finials.

4 Another popular type, first in Artjukhov's Barrow (Pl. 50 A) and later at Palaiokastro, and destined to last well into the Roman period, is a necklace composed of linked bezel-set stones, frequently terminating in animals' heads.

5 A necklace of the second–first century from Palaiokastro anticipates the developed Roman style. It is composed of linked long beads of jet, with pendants in the form of heads and dramatic masks.

6 A typical cross-section of the individual beads popular in Hellenistic jewellery can be found in Artjukhov's Barrow, and in the Family Tombs at Eretria. They include a Heracles knot; globular, segmented, heart-shaped, star-shaped and cage beads; crescents and mushroom-shaped pendants. See also Pl. 49 A.

7 The Etruscan bulla lived on in Etruscan-Hellenistic jewellery; it is found in the François Tomb at Vulci.

MEDALLIONS

1 Four medallions, all very similar in appearance, constitute an important part of the Karpenisi(?) group of jewellery from Thessaly, and so probably date from the second century (Pl. 52 B). They consist of a central roundel with a bust of a goddess in high relief, framed by a circle of ornamental goldwork, richly decorated with filigree, granulation, enamel and inlaid garnets. Round the circumference are loops, to which is attached a network of loop-in-loop chains, decorated in a similar manner. The outer ends of the chains are equipped with rings, apparently to take a cord or a drawstring. A fifth medallion, now in Providence, is similar, but somewhat earlier in style.[46] A sixth, in Costanza, was found at Kallatis.

The purpose of these articles has been disputed. Benton's attractive suggestion of hairnets with ornamental tops[47] is confirmed by the recent publication of a rigid gold hairnet, said to be from Tarentum, encrusted with garnets and fitted with a somewhat similar medallion.

2 Two medallions in Princeton are decorated respectively with a bust of Athena and a bust of Artemis (Pl. 52 A). They are closely related, stylistically and technically, to the hairnets (?) mentioned above, but differ in the absence of nets, and in the relative proportions, the central roundel being smaller and the surrounding framework correspondingly larger. A salient feature of the surround is a thick circle of garnets, reminiscent of the Heracles knot of the diadem in Pl. 46. Round the circumference are double loops in four places, arranged so as to suggest a *periamma*, a circular breast ornament kept in place by crossed straps.[48] Other medallions (breast ornaments) come from Delos (House of Ambrosia).

3 A third variety of medallion is in a private collection in Paris.[49] In the central roundel is a bust of Eros. The proportions are closer to the hairnets than to the *periammas*, but there is no net; and the loops, placed in groups of three on either side, near the top, suggest a breast ornament, held by a triple cord passing round the neck.

Bronze cores for the hammering of similar busts form part of the Galjub hoard from Egypt.[50] The relief is so high that the bust was hammered in two sections over different cores, one for the face and one for the rest, the two parts being subsequently soldered together.

There are other somewhat similar medallions whose authenticity is open to considerable doubt (see p. 4).

Other examples of the *periamma* are known, circular in form, with openwork filigree and inlay. One comes from a Family Tomb at Eretria (second or first century).

BRACELETS

1 Penannular bracelets, circular in section, with animal-headed or human-headed finials, continue from the previous period and last into the second century. A magnificent pair in New York, of crystal, with gold rams' heads, comes from a tomb near Salonika of the late fourth century (Pl. 51 A). Sometimes the hoop is decorated with one or more wires twisted round a central core. Examples of the late fourth or early third century come from Kyme in Aeolis, Cumae and Toukh-el-Quarmous (Egypt). The second century is represented by pairs from Mount Pangaeus and Salonika.

2 A pair of bracelets in London is composed of three twisted ribbons of gold with animal-head finials. They match exactly the diadem shown in Pl. 45 A, and must surely come from the same or a related set.

3 A rare variant of the penannular bracelet is represented in three examples from Karpenisi (?) and one, from Asia Minor, in a private collection in Paris.[51] The three Thessalian pieces are each composed of two tubular sections, covered with a network of filigree and hinged together; the other ends terminate in bulls' or lynxes' heads. The piece in Paris represents only half a bracelet. It differs from the others in having an animal's head at either end, a lynx's at one end and a goat's at the other, both like those on contemporary hoop earrings. A date in the second century is suggested by the Karpenisi(?) group.

4 Another rare type of bracelet is made of a circlet of gold (either a solid band or of openwork filigree) with a central ornament, as on the diadem shown in Pl. 46, in the form of a Heracles knot. One such pair comes from a tomb at Toukh-el-Quarmous of the early third century, and another from a tomb near Mount Pangaeus. A variant without the Heracles knot occurs in a group from Western Syria, of about the second century (Pl. 50 B). A tomb (?) at Palaiokastro in Thessaly of the first century BC yielded a more elaborate version of this type. A wire circlet is decorated with cut-out leaves inlaid with garnets, turquoise and malachite. At the centre, where the two ends meet, is a cloisonne inlay of glass in a wave pattern with emeralds at the sides. The actual join is masked by a large amethyst in a deep bezel setting.

5 Spiral bracelets, mostly in the form of snakes, continue from the Classical period and were apparently popular throughout this period. Examples come from Western Syria (Pl. 51 c), from Demetrias (?), Toukh-el-Quarmous, Artjukhov's Barrow at Taman, a grave at Pelinna, and Abdera; and the effigy of the Etruscan lady Seianti Hanunia, of the second century, wears one.[52] A magnificent pair of bracelets of the same general type is now in New York, representing, instead of snakes, a triton and a tritoness respectively (Pl. 51B).

BELTS

Belts are seldom sufficiently elaborate to be classed as jewellery, but two gold ornaments from Karpenisi (?), credibly identified as such, more than fulfil the necessary conditions. They are decorated with massed floral ornament, somewhat like the wreaths mentioned on p. 124 above, with plentiful use of filigree, granulation, and inlaid stones and glass. One has a central member formed by an elaborate Heracles knot like those on contemporary diadems (see Pl. 46); in the other, the central member is missing, but was probably similar.

BUTTONS

Buttons, too, seldom merit inclusion in a survey of jewellery. In Greece proper, although they are represented in sculptures and terracottas as fastening the chiton on the shoulders, no actual examples have been recognized from this period. In the North, however, and in South Russian Greek settlements, gold buttons or button tops have survived. In Tumulus 2 at Odessus (the modern Varna), of about 300, two gold button tops were found on the shoulders of a corpse, leaving no doubt of their purpose. Buttons of plain gold were found in a tomb at Kazanlak in Bulgaria about the same date; as there were 140 of them, most will have been for ornament rather than for use. Gilt terracotta buttons were found in Sedes Tomb Gamma at Salonika, of the later fourth century. And gold buttons were found in Tomb D at Quarantine Road, Kerch, of 250–225.

FINGER RINGS

A number of Classical types continued into the Hellenistic period virtually unchanged, and new types evolved. Stones were now extremely popular as bezels, both plain and engraved. A Delian treasure record for 279 mentions a gold ring set with a garnet.[53] The Roman custom of engraving portraits of royalty on ring bezels has its origins in the Ptolemaic kingdom, where rings engraved with the likeness of the reigning sovereign were evidently not uncommon and were perhaps used for sealing official documents.

1 Solid gold signet rings with a circular bezel continue into this period and last, to judge from the style of the engravings, into the third century. A dated example comes from the Gela Hoard of the early third century.

2 A decorative ring with a circular bezel is found in the second century, in Artjukhov's Barrow (Pl. 53 D) and in the Family Tombs at Eretria. The example from Artjukhov's Barrow has a bezel decorated with a floral pattern in cloisonné enamel. A pin from the same tomb (Pl. 53 F) has a pendant made to match, and the pattern occurs for a third time in a pendant on a necklace from Samsun.[54] Does this suggest an origin in Asia Minor for this sort of jewellery?

3 Hoops of the Classical type with an oval bezel continued (see p. 131). An example comes from Sedes Tomb Gamma at Salonika of the later fourth century. An ornate ring with a box-shaped pointed oval bezel comes from Tomb 157 at Cumae, of the same date, and a somewhat similar ring, with a large chalcedony bezel, comes from Artjukhov's Barrow, of the early second century.

4 A typical ring of the period 330–150 BC has an oval bezel and a massive hoop, rounded outside and flat inside, and frequently meeting the bezel at a sharp angle (Pl. 53 A). The bezel may be in high relief in metal; it may be a stone cut *en cabochon*; or it may be a stone engraved

or cut as a cameo. The type, which has many varieties, was made in gold, bronze and (surprisingly) glass. Examples come from tombs at Kerch of the late fourth and the third centuries; from Santa Eufemia, of the early third century; from Western Syria (now in Chicago) and from Karpenisi(?).

5 Rings, generally of a slender type, with an oval bezel, and vertical or in-sloping shoulders (Pl. 53 C), are first found in the second century.[55] They occur in a Family Tomb at Eretria, in Artjukhov's Barrow, in Tomb 3 at Ancona and in the House of Ambrosia at Delos.

6 Other rings, of the second century, have a very thin bezel, little wider than the hoop, with a small stone in the centre; a dated example comes from Artjukhov's Barrow. This type is also found in a doubled form, notably at Karpenisi(?) and in the Family Tombs at Eretria.

7 A type of ring with a large projecting bezel, overlapping the setting (Pl. 53 B), occurs in a Family Tomb at Eretria of the second–first century, in Tomb 3 at Ancona and a grave at Pelinna of the second century. This type is very like the bracelet from Palaiokastro discussed above (see p. 168).

8 A ring from Artjukhov's Barrow, of the early second century, has a bezel in the shape of a sandalled foot inscribed in Greek with the words 'Hestiaios to his mother' in gold letters against a background of black enamel. It also has a Heracles knot at the back, inlaid with a garnet (Fig. 25).

Fig. 25   Finger ring from Artjukhov's Barrow, second century B C.

9 A gold ring with a bezel of wire and large grains in the form of the magical Heracles knot is first found in the third century, in Tomb B at Quarantine Road, Kerch. Another example is shown in Pl. 53 E. In some, the bezel is inlaid with garnets.

10 Rings in the form of a spiralled snake—smaller versions of the bracelet in Pl. 51 C— started in the preceding period and were extremely popular in Hellenistic times.[56] Examples come from Madytus (late fourth century); the Gela Hoard (early third century); Karpenisi (?) (second century); and the Family Tombs at Eretria (second–first

century). An elaborate variation, probably of the second century, in the form of a coiled sea monster, with inlaid stones, comes from a grave at Mesambria.

PINS

Pins are not normally considered part of Hellenistic jewellery, but two exceptional types are worthy of mention.

1 An elegant pin from Artjukhov's Barrow at Taman, of the early second century, has hanging from it a gold disc with a floral pattern of cloisonne enamel; from it hang pendants set with garnets (Pl. 53 F). The ring from the same tomb (Pl. 53 D) has a bezel with a similar pattern, and the two were evidently meant to be worn together.

2 The other exception is a gold pin from Karpenisi (?) of roughly the same date. The head is composed of a figure of a draped woman standing on a capital. A similar pin (in London) comes from Syria (Pl. 53 G).

FIBULAE

1 The North Greek type discussed on p. 133 and illustrated in Pl. 31 E continued until about 300. Examples in gold occur in Sedes Tomb Gamma at Salonika and (six examples) in Grave 5 at Derveni, both of the later fourth century, and in a collection in New York said to come from near Salonika, of about the same date.

2 The Campanian type of leech fibula discussed on p. 133 and illustrated in Pl. 31 C also continued until about the end of the fourth century. Examples occur at Cumae (Tomb 157) and Teano (Tomb 79).

3 Another type of fibula was very popular in Campania in the Early Hellenistic period. It occurs in some thirteen tombs at Teano of the late fourth and early third centuries. It is of silver, with a semicircular gold-plated bow and a rectangular, almost square catchplate with a long projection, on one example threaded with coral. The bow is decorated with rosettes and filigree spirals.[57]

BROOCHES

1 A circular brooch comes from a tomb at Taman (1913) of the late fourth century. It has a central garnet carved in the shape of a satyr's head with a gold wreath. Round it is a palmette frieze of filigree inlaid with blue glass (enamel?) and red stones. Such polychromy is rare in Greek jewellery at this early date, but is a foretaste of what was to come in the course of a century or so. Possibly the brooch was made to the special requirements of a Scythian customer.

2 Another circular brooch, from Artjukhov's Barrow at Taman, is inlaid in a floral pattern with five garnets.

SCEPTRES

Sceptres were last encountered as articles of jewellery in the eleventh century in Cyprus (see p. 25). They are found again in two examples from Apulia of the third century. The first (in London) is said to come from Tarentum.[58] It consists of a hollow gold tube covered with a network of gold wire, partially enamelled. The tube ends in a Corinthian capital, on which is a large sphere of green glass, surrounded by acanthus leaves. The early character of the Corinthian capital gives a date in or near the third century.

The second sceptre comes from the Tomb of the Gold Ornaments at Canosa, of the third century. It is stopped by a bone knob, from which project two figures of Victory. Compared with the sceptre from Tarentum, it has a provincial appearance.

ROMAN 27 BC–AD 400

Introduction

For the sake of convenience it is proposed in this survey to end the Hellenistic and to start the Roman period with the inauguration of the Empire in 27 BC. So far as jewellery is concerned, this date has little significance, but it is as good a point as any for a convenient break in what is really a continuous development. Similarly, the end of the fourth century AD is a reasonable date for the end of the Roman period.

Before reviewing the jewellery of the Empire, it may perhaps be helpful to consider that of Republican and Pre-Republican Rome. There is very little material in gold or silver at our disposal, but from what has survived, and from the rather more plentiful ornaments of bronze and other materials in Roman tombs, it appears that from 700 to 250 BC Roman jewellery was for all practical purposes Etruscan. Between 250 and 27 BC our material is even scarcer, but we may assume that Roman jewellery, together with Etruscan, was now basically Hellenistic, but was leavened with a few genuine Etruscan survivals, of which the bulla is the most important example.

The meagre archaeological evidence for Roman jewellery before the the Empire may be supplemented to a certain extent from literary sources. We know, for example, that jewellery was for long under official disapproval. The Law of the Twelve Tables, in the fifth century BC, limited the amount of gold which might be buried with the dead; and the Lex Oppia, of the third century BC, fixed at half an ounce the amount of gold which a Roman lady might wear. An exception was the gold bulla, the *Etruscum aurum*, which was worn as an amulet, especially

173

by children. Under the Republic, the wearing of rings of gold was reserved for certain classes of persons or for certain occasions. In the late third century senators and knights *equo publico* apparently had this privilege, which could also be bestowed on knights and others as a military distinction. Towards the end of the Republic, the gold ring was also bestowed on civilians.[1]

By the date at which this chapter begins, Rome had finally swallowed up the last remnants of the Hellenistic world with the annexation of Egypt in 30 BC. Although the changes consequent on the inauguration of the Empire had little immediate effect on Roman minor arts in general, yet in the realm of jewellery new and intrusive elements begin to appear; some at once, others later on. The result is that the beginning of the fourth century sees a completely different style, which was to dominate Late Antique and Byzantine jewellery.

The sources of Roman jewellery vary at different times. For the first century, Pompeii and Herculaneum are paramount. In particular, the jewellery from the House of Menander at Pompeii gives a unique idea of the personal jewellery of a well-to-do Roman lady.[2] Additional material is recorded from the Peiraeus, South Russia and Cyprus.

The second century is represented particularly well by finds from British sites. In the third century we draw on Britain again; also on Gaul in the West; and Tarsus, Aleppo and Doura Europos in the East.

Finally, the fourth century is represented in such diverse quarters as Britain, Gaul, Asia Minor and Algeria.

Apart from the jewellery itself, further information is provided by Roman mummy portraits from Egypt and funerary sculptures from Palmyra in the Syrian desert. The former cover the entire period of this chapter. The latter run approximately from AD 100 to 250 and would appear to be rather ahead of Roman fashions.

Because of the uneven nature of the evidence, the development of Roman jewellery is not easy to trace, but the following outline cannot be too wide of the truth.

In the first century a few new elements were grafted on to the Hellenistic stock. An emphasis on large dome-like surfaces was probably derived from a Late Etruscan fashion (see p. 150). It is found in earrings and bracelets from Pompeii.

Other earrings and a necklace from Pompeii demonstrate a new interest in polychromy which was to dominate Byzantine jewellery. Pearls and uncut emerald crystals are threaded on wires and massed in formal profusion, in marked contrast with the more formal Hellenistic bezel settings, which, however, were not forgotten. Raw emeralds were also threaded on loosely linked chains.

In addition to emeralds and pearls, harder stones such as the sapphire, aquamarine and topaz become increasingly popular. Even uncut diamonds were sometimes used, set in rings.

Filigree and granulation are occasionally found. Enamel disappears, except in the Celtic west, where we find remnants of filigree enamel and (more commonly) champlevé in ornaments of bronze.

Of the forms and motifs of Roman jewellery, the bulla continues into the first century AD as a purely Italian feature. The fibula, imported from the Celtic lands, was popular in the West but rare in the East. The East continued to use the human- and animal-headed hoop earrings which had fallen into disuse in Greece and Italy as early as the second century BC. A few new motifs make their appearance: the wheel, which had magical properties (Pl. 56), and a new type of crescent with knobs on the ends, frequently worn inverted (Pl. 56). This new crescent was, like the Hellenistic moon crescent, of Syrian origin; but it belonged not to the Moon God but to Baal Rekub, the charioteer god.[3]

About the middle of the first century a new type of earring was introduced from Western Asia, consisting of a horizontal bar with two or three vertical pendants (Pl. 54 B). It did not, however, become at all popular until the second century.

The principal innovation of the second century, the piercing of gold in a kind of fretwork technique, became very popular and completely transformed the unbroken surfaces of Early Imperial work. This process, known to the Romans as *opus interrasile*, is discussed on p. 138 and illustrated in Pls 59 and 63 A.

A new custom, which was introduced in the second century and quickly became popular, was the use of Imperial gold coins or medallions as bezels for finger rings, as pendants on necklaces or as fronts of brooches. It is possible that rings with Imperial coins were awarded as military distinctions, but the necklaces are best explained as a form of flattery not uncommon in court circles at any period.

The third century sees the introduction of massive gold bracelets and crossbow fibulae.

About AD 300 niello (a process described on p. 26), which had been used in gold and silver plate from the second century BC, was first applied to jewellery.

Technically, Roman jewellery sees some falling off in the standards of workmanship, although good work could still be produced.

OTHER CONSIDERATIONS

The chief centres of production of Roman Imperial jewellery were probably in the first place the old Hellenistic centres of Alexandria and Antioch; in the second place Rome itself, where we have evidence for the existence of goldsmiths' guilds, and where many epitaphs of goldsmiths and silversmiths have been found.[4] Roman craftsmen, as in other arts and crafts, were doubtless to a large extent immigrants from the East. In this connection we may mention the often-illustrated goldsmith's sign in Rome, inscribed 'aurifex brattiarius', which shows a Roman goldsmith at work,[5] and the fresco from the House of the Vettii at Pompeii (Pl. I A), which shows Cupids at work making jewellery.

Inscriptions from Spain record the jewels which decorated certain statues. They refer to diadems, earrings, necklaces and bracelets and mention the presence of pearls, emeralds, garnets and cylinders; the latter are generally taken to be beads of emerald crystals.[6]

We also know from inscriptions that there were guilds of goldsmiths and silversmiths at Palmyra, who doubtless made the jewellery so lavishly depicted in the Palmyrene funerary statues.[7]

It remains to consider the literary evidence for the jewellery of this period. Pagan and Christian critics unite in condemning the love of luxury exhibited by Roman ladies. St Paul urged women to adorn themselves with good works instead of 'broided hair, or gold, or pearls, or costly array'.[8]

Pliny tells us that Lollia Paulina, Caligula's wife, at an ordinary function, wore emeralds and pearls on her head, hair, ears, neck, arms and fingers. He also tells us that women wore two or three pearls in their ears, so that they rattled. He attributes the origins for this love of jewellery to Pompey's victories in the East.[9]

THE SEQUEL

The two most characteristic aspects of Later Imperial jewellery survived well into Late Antique and Byzantine times. In the first place, the lace-like effect of much Byzantine jewellery is a logical development of the *opus interrasile* of the third and fourth centuries. Second, the wholesale use of coloured stones as inlay merely continues a trend which is first seen at Pompeii in the first century AD.

The jewellery

Dates in this section are all AD.

WREATHS

Roman Imperial wreaths are a development of a Late Hellenistic variety (see p. 157). They are made up of stylized leaves, frequently in groups of three, sewn to a background of some other material. Such wreaths are common in South Russian tombs, especially at Kerch, of the first and second centuries AD. They can sometimes be dated by impressions of coins placed in the centre. Such wreaths are represented in funerary statues from Palmyra and in a mummy portrait in London.[10]

DIADEMS

Diadems are not common, but the Hellenistic repoussé variety continued, in the East at least. One in London from Naucratis can be dated from its inscription to the first century AD.[11]

HAIR ORNAMENTS

1 Roman ladies wore pins, sometimes of gold, in their hair, as can be seen in mummy portraits. A few pins in London, of gold, of silver and of gold and ivory, may have served this purpose.[12]

2 A complicated hair ornament in London comes from Tunis and is closely paralleled on Palmyrene statues of the second and third centuries (Pl. 54 F). It is composed of a row of oval and rectangular bezel settings, some filled with emeralds, some now empty, surrounded by a row of pearls in bezel settings. Below hangs a horizontal rod, from which are suspended three vertical rods, threaded with two pearls and a sapphire. It closely matches the bracelet illustrated in Pl. 61 B, with which it was found.

EARRINGS

1 The plain hoop continues in the East from the Hellenistic period, slightly modified. The ends are now hooked together.[13] Examples come from a tomb at Eleutheropolis in Palestine of the second century, a Roman tomb at Salonika and many Cypriote tombs. This hoop is also at times fitted with a pendant club (Pl. 54 A),[14] or (at Nea Anchialos) with a bezel-set conical stone.

2 Another hoop incorporates a round shield-like member. It commonly has a club as a pendant, in which form it occurs in Tombs 87 and 95 at Amathus, of the second century (Pl. 54 C).[15] A variant form from Eleutheropolis, of the second century, has a large decorated plaque as a pendant.

3 The hoop with animal or human head and beads continued in Egypt and the east from the Hellenistic period into the first or perhaps the second century AD; it is discussed on p. 159. It also survives in a degenerate version with a vestigial animal head,[16] or with no head at all.

The latter type is represented at Pompeii and Thebes[17] and at a burial at Curium (Hagios Hermogenis) of the Augustan period. It is also represented in mummy portraits.[18]

4 Some examples of the foregoing types, mostly of the first century AD, are equipped with a long S-shaped hook for insertion in the ear (Pl. 54 G). The type occurs at Zara and at Salonika, and is represented in Egypt in mummy portraits and on the baseboards of sarcophagi of the first and second centuries AD.[19] In a pair in London, from Episkopi in Cyprus, the beads are replaced by an engraved gem.[20]

5 An earring composed basically of a pendant club and an S-shaped hook was common in the first and second centuries AD. It is found at Pompeii, Zara and Eleutheropolis, and at Rome in the sarcophagus of Crepereia Tryphaena. In a pair from Bubastis in Egypt the club is replaced by a lotus flower.[21]

6 The ball type appears suddenly in the first century AD and lasts into the second (Pl. 54 H). It consists basically of a hemisphere of gold with an S-shaped hook at the back. Subsidiary decoration is sometimes found in the shape of a smaller boss above the main element.[22] The type is represented in mummy portraits and found at Pompeii, Herculaneum and Boscoreale, on Siphnos, in Cyprus and at Eleutheropolis in Palestine. In one example from Pompeii the hemisphere is doubled.[23] It is tempting to derive this type from Late Etruscan earrings, with their similarly curved surfaces and similar small bosses; but the intermediate stages, if they ever existed, no longer survive, and the origins of this widespread type must for the present remain a puzzle.

7 Closely related to the foregoing type is an earring made up of a cluster of emeralds or pearls (Pl. 54 E). Many examples come from Pompeii and Boscoreale, and the type is represented in mummy portraits.[24]

8 An elaboration of the ball type, with subsidiary bosses and imitation pendants in sheet metal, is found in Egypt and Syria, and is generally dated in the third century. There is a pair in Hamburg said to be from Jaffa (Pl. 54 D), two pairs in London from Samsun in Asia Minor,[25] and many in Beirut and Damascus from local sites.

9 In the course of the second century there arose a new class of pendant earring, completely unrelated to the Hellenistic pendants, which rapidly replaced the ball type in popularity. One type consists basically of a drop pendant hanging from a bezel-set stone. It is secured in the ear by a hook, frequently S-shaped. Typical dated examples come from a tomb at Lyon of the early third century (Fig. 26), and from a tomb at Vasa in Cyprus of the third century.

10 Another type of pendant earring consists basically of a stone or glass in a bezel setting above a horizontal bar, from which hang two or

Fig. 26   Earring from a tomb at Lyon,
about AD 200.

three pendants, with stones threaded at their lower end (Pl. 54 B). These earrings are secured in the ear in the same way as the foregoing variety. This very popular type, which lent itself to countless minor variations, reached the Roman world from the East (Palmyra?), was in use from the first to the fourth century, and continued in a modified form into the Byzantine period. It is represented at Pompeii and Herculaneum in the first century, and in tombs at Lyon and Villardu of the third century. It is depicted in mummy portraits and Palmyrene sculptures.[26]

NECKLACES

1 A necklace composed either wholly or in part of linked stones in bezel settings was taken over direct from Hellenistic jewellery. The stones are usually amethysts, garnets, topazes or sapphires. Pl. 55 B shows a singularly attractive example, where bezel-set stones are used in combination with a chain to form a necklace, and more bezel-set stones form a butterfly-shaped pendant. It can be dated by comparison with a similar one from Kerch of the first century. The necklace of bezel-set stones continued in a simpler form into the early third century; it is represented in a tomb at Lyon of that date.

2 A later version of this type, which first appeared about 200, is represented by some four examples from the above-mentioned tomb at Lyon, of the early third century, and by an example in London.[27] Stones in bezel settings are now associated with patterns pierced in stout sheet gold, in the so-called *opus interrasile* technique (see p. 29).

3 Chains and straps, of all known varieties, continued in popularity from the Hellenistic period, but usually with different adjuncts (Pls. 55B, 56, 57B, 58B).

(a) They were worn without pendants throughout this period.

(b) An extremely popular type incorporated a wheel either as a pendant or as a finial (Pl. 56). It occurs at Pompeii and Boscoreale in the first century, at Backworth, Carlisle and Eleutheropolis in the second, and at New Grange about 200.

(c) A crescent (generally of the knobbed kind mentioned on p. 175) is also a popular pendant to a chain (Pls 56 and 57 B). Examples come from Pompeii, Herculaneum and Boscoreale in the first century, and at Eleutheropolis in the second. The type is represented in mummy portraits.[28]

(d) A third popular form of pendant is a gold coin or medallion, sometimes by itself, sometimes in a decorative setting.[29] These necklaces can be dated by the coins; they are commonest in the second and third centuries. An unusually elaborate example (dated to the year 321) is shown in Pl. 59 B. A gold coin of Constantine the Great is surrounded by a band of elaborate scrollwork in *opus interrasile* in which six relief medallions of deities are set (one is now missing).

(e) Another type of pendant, which died out in the first century after a very long history in Italy, is the bulla (cf. p. 141). It is found at Pompeii and Herculaneum and at Ostia.[30]

(f) Stones or glass in ornate bezel settings achieved popularity as pendants in the third and fourth centuries. The type is represented by several examples from a tomb at Beaurains of about 300, where topaz, amethyst, cornelian and glass were used.

(g) Another type of necklace is composed of a chain with very loose links, terminating in cylindrical finials, which frequently clip on either side of a relief medallion. That illustrated in Pl. 58 B has a Medusa head which may be compared with heads from the Forum Novum at Lepcis Magna, of the early third century.[31] The type is represented in mummy portraits.[32]

(h) Some very elaborate chains and pendants are recorded from the third and fourth centuries. An example in Paris is shown in Pl. 59 A. The chain is composed of openwork gold cages, gold beads and emerald crystals. The pendant consists of a black stone scarab in a wide *interrasile* setting, to which are threaded pearls, sapphires and emeralds. The style is completely alien to the Classical spirit and leads the way to the Byzantine fashion.

4 Beads in the form of natural hexagonal crystals of emerald, imitations of them in glass or cornelians cut to the same shape were popular throughout this period, often threaded on chains (Pl. 57 A). A number of such necklaces, with emerald beads, were found at Pompeii. The type is commonly represented in mummy portraits.[33] An example from Syria (Pl. 58 A) has beads of this type alternating with cut-out Heracles

knots, and one from Lyon of the early third century includes pierced-work elements and spool beads.

5 A necklace of gold beads representing vases in the Benaki Museum in Athens is said to come from a woman's grave in the Peiraeus of the early first century AD. The beads, in the shape of a kantharos, a kalathos and a flask, are made of embossed sheet gold, with details in filigree, and are inlaid with large pieces of glass. A bracelet in London in exactly the same style is shown in Pl. 60 A.

6 An unusual necklace from Pompeii is composed of a substantial chain of gold set with emeralds and pearls (Pl. 55 A).

BRACELETS

1 A popular bracelet of the first century, well represented at Pompeii, is the counterpart of the ball earrings mentioned above (Pl. 61 A).

2 A chain-and-wheel bracelet from a tomb at Backworth of the second century is the counterpart of the chain-and-wheel necklaces mentioned above.

3 A rare hoop bracelet of the later first century is illustrated by the pair in Pl. 62 C. The ends of the stout wire forming the hoop are thinned out and wrapped round it. The date is assured by a similar pair from Tekiya in Yugoslavia.

4 The snake bracelet continued, in a rather more substantial form, from Hellenistic times (Pl. 62 A). It is found at Pompeii, but does not seem to have outlived the first century AD.

5 Another Hellenistic survival is a two-part bracelet, the upper section ending in lions' heads. This type, represented by one example from Pompeii, is clearly derived from the Hellenistic variety described on p. 168.[34]

6 A slender type of bracelet, found in a tomb at Lyon of the early third century, is made of twisted wires, arranged at one point to form a large Heracles knot (Fig. 27).

7 The typical bracelet of the second half of this period is a stout hoop,

Fig. 27   Bracelet from the same tomb as Fig. 26.

generally of twisted wires, the ends of which are secured by a large bezel setting with a projecting stone (Pl. 62 B). The type is represented at Lyon (about 200), and at Villardu and Doura Europos in the third century.

8 The bracelet illustrated in Pl. 61 B is a less common type, but the technique is typical of jewellery of about the third century. It consists of a central disc inlaid with emerald and sapphire and threaded with pearls. On either side is an openwork band cut to represent a row of ivy leaves and threaded with pearls. It was found at Tunis with the hair ornament shown in Pl. 54 F, and evidently formed part of the same ensemble.

9 The bracelet illustrated in Pl. 60 A is composed of a centrepiece in the form of a gold kantharos, with wings below the handles. In the centre of the kantharos, and on all four sides, are squares of glass; on top, flanking the inlay, are an ear of corn and a poppy. An ornamental band of gold is shown attached to the left side; it was originally bent round in a circle so that the far end joined the right side of the kantharos. It is decorated with a plaited band and with openwork leaves and berries. The decoration of the band recalls the bracelet from Palaiokastro of the second to first century B C (see p. 168), but the treatment of the kantharos and the inlay are more to Roman taste. Beads very like the kantharos come from a tomb at Peiraeus of the early first century A D (see p. 181) and serve to date the bracelet.

10 A pair of somewhat similar bracelets, but without the centrepiece, comes from a tomb at Rhayader in Wales, of uncertain date.

11 The bracelet illustrated in Pl. 60 B consists of nine square bezel-set emeralds; one, in the centre, is rather larger than the others. The inlays are connected together by means of four Heracles knots of thin wire. The appearance of the inlays and the employment of the wires suggests that this bracelet is contemporary with the kantharos bracelet, no. 9 above.

12 A new variety of bracelet is found in the fourth century, consisting of a broad band with intricate openwork patterns (*interrasile*). It is represented in the Tenès Treasure, of the fourth century, and there is an example, in the Bibliothèque Nationale in Paris, from Pont Aude-mer.[35] A third example, in Berlin, from Tartus, is illustrated in Pl. 63 A. The lace-like effect was to become typical of Byzantine jewellery.

FINGER RINGS

Under the Empire the gold ring, although still regarded as a privilege and awarded as a military distinction, was very freely bestowed on all and sundry.

Apart from their uses as marks of dignity, as ornaments and as seal rings, finger rings had other purposes. Unlike the Greeks, the Romans used them as tokens of betrothal; and they also wore special rings with keys attached.[36]

Although in the first century BC it was unusual in the Roman world for a man to wear more than one ring, the habit of gem collecting, which started about this time, soon caused a change. Crassus was one of the first men to be seen wearing two rings. In Horace's time three on one hand was considered excessive; but Martial (although he should not be taken too literally) speaks of a man who wore six rings on every finger day and night.[37]

Pliny says that the Emperor Claudius gave permission for people to wear his portrait engraved on a gold ring, and numbers of imperial portraits engraved on rings have survived.[38] The use of gold coins or medallions with the imperial portrait as the bezels of rings has been mentioned above.

So many different kinds of ring were in use in this period that it is only possible to select certain prominent types, and to suggest dates for them.

1 Snake rings of the Hellenistic type continued into the first century AD: they are found at Pompeii and Herculaneum.[39] A new type, also found at Pompeii and Herculaneum, consists of a hoop with a snake's head at either end (Pl. 64 I).

2 A seal ring with a thick hoop, expanding slightly at the bezel (Pl. 64 K and L), was popular in the first and second centuries, and is found at Pompeii and Herculaneum, Slay Hill Saltings and Backworth.[40] The engraving in Pl. 64 L shows a charming group of an old shepherd and his dog. In the third century the ring becomes more elliptical in shape, as in an example in London from the Tarsus Treasure.

3 A seal ring with bevelled shoulders, widening towards the bezel, which is sometimes an engraved stone and sometimes a coin (Pl. 64 D and G), was current from the late second century into the fourth.[41] It is found in the tomb of Crepereia Tryphaena in Rome, at Beaurains, and at Ilchester, Grovely Woods and Cardiff.

4 A ring with humped shoulders was roughly contemporary with the foregoing (Pl. 54 H). The bezel is sometimes an engraved stone, sometimes a gold coin.[42] The type is represented in a tomb at Lyon of the early third century. The example here illustrated contains a coin of the second century.

5 Another Roman ring is very massive, with strongly projecting shoulders and an eye-shaped bezel.[43] The type is found in the Tarsus Treasure, of the third century (Pl. 64 J).

6 Rings with a thin hoop and a circular bezel from Pompeii represent a Hellenistic survival.[44]

7 A ring with a thick hoop spreading to a circular bezel also comes from Pompeii. This type, like the foregoing, is a Hellenistic survival.[45]

8 A seal ring with an oval bezel and a pair of globules at each junction of hoop and bezel (Fig. 28) belongs to the first and second centuries; it is found at Pompeii and Backworth.

Fig. 28   Finger ring from Backworth, second century AD.

9 Ornamental rings with one or more stones standing out from them were extremely popular in the later part of this period (Pl. 64A, E, F). The type, very like modern rings, is found in a rudimentary form as early as the first century of our era, for it occurs at Pompeii; but it is not common till the second century. It is represented in a tomb at Lyon of the early third century and in a tomb at Beaurains of about 300. The rings are of various forms, sometimes flimsy, sometimes robust. The stones are of many kinds; sapphires and amethysts are fairly common, and uncut diamonds are not unknown. The ring from Beaurains (Pl. 64 F) has a cabochon aquamarine and an inscription in niello.

10 A circular ring with patterns in pierced work is illustrated in Pl. 64 B. The type is very like the bracelets discussed above and illustrated in Pl. 63 A. Like those, it should be dated about the fourth century.

11 An octagonal ring. One variety has a hoop with a pierced openwork decoration and an engraved stone on one face. Another variety is made of solid metal, and frequently inscribed. The technique of the first variety, and the Gnostic and Early Christian associations of the second, combine to give a fourth-century date for these rings.[46]

12 A ring with stones set all round the hoop is a late type, of the third and fourth centuries, to judge from the extent of the polychromy (Pl. 64C). The stones used in the ring illustrated comprise garnets, cornelians, sapphires and emeralds.

13 Rings composed of two, three or four superimposed hoops are said to be Romano-Egyptian, and were probably made throughout this period.[47] There are Hellenistic precedents (see p. 170).

14 Double and triple rings are occasionally found. They were made, to judge from their style, in the third and fourth centuries. It is

possible, as Segall believes, that such rings were made only for funerary use.[48]

FIBULAE

Roman fibulae do not derive from Etruscan fibulae, which probably fell out of use about the fourth century BC, but are an innovation of Celtic origin. As their antecedents would suggest, they were not much used in Italy itself or further east, but are found in quantity in the former Celtic territories on the northern and western fringes of the Empire. They were chiefly made of bronze, and it is with bronze fibulae that the typology is established. The exceptional gold and silver fibulae are, however, the only ones with which we are concerned.

In Pl. 63 C is a fibula in London of La Tène affinities, which is dated about the first century AD. It comes from Ravenna.

The commonest Roman fibula, the crossbow type, developed from the foregoing variety in the second and third centuries and flourished in the fourth.[49] A fully developed example is shown in Pl. 64 B. It is inscribed 'HERCULI AUGUSTE SEMPER VINCAS' ('Hercules Augustus, may you always conquer'). It probably refers to Constantine the Great and was made between 307 and 310.[50] Other gold fibulae of this kind come from Odiham and Colchester, and a number from a fourth-century treasure at Tenès in Algeria. The example from Odiham is decorated with niello.

BROOCHES

Gold coins and medallions in ornate settings, like the pendants mentioned on p. 180, were also worn as brooches.

Bronze brooches, richly decorated with champlevé enamel, are also found in the former Celtic areas of the Empire.[51] It may be objected that such articles have no place in a survey of this nature, since, being of bronze, they are not truly jewellery, and, being predominantly Celtic, they are not truly Roman. They do, however, merit a passing mention, if only for their attractive and novel appearance.

NOTES

Chapter 1

1 Pliny, XXXIII, 80.
2 Forbes, *Metallurgy*, p. 155.

Chapter 2

1 Lucas, *Materials and Industries*, p. 231.
2 This was very kindly established for me by Andrew Oddy of the British Museum Research Laboratory.
3 For example, in *BMCJ*, no. 141. Report by British Museum Research Laboratory, 4 January 1978.

Chapter 3

1 Coche de la Ferté, pl. 36.
2 British Patent no. 415181 (1933).
3 Woolley, *Ur Excavations*, II, pl. 138.
4 Troy: Schmidt, Beil. 1 and 2. Byblos: (1) P. Montet, *Byblos et l'Egypte* (Paris, 1929), pl. 63; (2) M. Dunand, *Fouilles de Byblos*, II (Paris, 1950), pls 131–7.
5 Evans, *Palace*, IV, p. 423; fig. 349. *AJA*, XLIX (1945), p. 16.
6 Wilkinson, *Ancient Egyptian Jewellery*, p. 52.
7 Coche de la Ferté, pl. IX.
8 Von Luschan, *Sendschirli*, V.
9 J. R. Melida, *Tesoro de Aliseda* (Madrid, 1921), Becatti, nos 228–31. *BMCJ*, pls 23–5. Becatti, nos 221, 223–4, 226–7.

10 Segall, nos 286 ff. (Byzantine, tenth century). *Antiquity*, XXXII (1958), pl. 19 (Czechoslovakian, ninth–tenth century). J. R. Kirk, *The Alfred and Minster Lovell Jewels* (Oxford, 1948) (Anglo-Saxon, ninth century). M. Stenberger, *Die Schatzfunde Gotlands der Wikingerzeit* (Lund, 1947), figs 140, 141 (Scandinavian, tenth century).
11 R. Rosenthal, *Jewellery in Ancient Times* (London, 1973), col. pls 6 (Arabian, 969–1171) and 8 (Uzbekistan, *c*. AD 1800).
12 In the Nilgiri Hills, South India (information kindly given me by Dr Henry Hodges). In addition, I am informed by Miss Sipra Bhattacharya that granulated gold jewellery is made and sold in the bazaars of Calcutta to this day.
13 Sutherland, *Gold*, p. 38.
14 *BCH*, XCII (1968), p. 162.
15 *AJA*, LVIII (1954), p. 140.
16 It is recorded at Mycenae in Tombs 88 and 103 (unpublished, but see Rosenberg, *Zellenschmelz*, p. 22, figs 1–10, and p. 24, fig. 25), and on the Acropolis (*AE* (1887), pl. 13: 27); in Tomb 10 at Dendra (see p. 209) and at Volo (see p. 209).
17 Coche de la Ferté, p. 32, pl. 4: 2. A. Godard, *Le Trésor de Ziwiyé* (Haarlem, 1950), fig. 90.

18 Rosenberg, *Zellenschmelz*, p. 38, figs 54–8.
19 *BSA*, XXXVII (1936–7), p. 112. Karo, *Schachtgräber*, pp. 312–13.
20 Maxwell-Hyslop, *Western Asiatic Jewellery*, p. 14.
21 Wilkinson, *Ancient Egyptian Jewellery*, p. 27, etc.
22 Maxwell-Hyslop, *Western Asiatic Jewellery*, pl. 69.
23 Jacobsthal, *Pins*, p. 209.
24 Coche de la Ferté, p. 60; pl. 17:2 and 3.

Chapter 4

1 Pliny, XXXIII, 29 and 30.
2 Theophilus, III, 31.
3 Theophilus, III, 73.
4 *History of Technology*, I, p. 652.
5 Persson, *New Tombs*, p. 198. Wace, *Chamber Tombs*, p. 27.
6 Observed by the writer.
7 *BMCJ*, p. xxxvii. *BCH*, VI (1882), p. 120.

Chapter 5

1 V. E. G. Kenna, *Cretan Seals* (Oxford, 1960), p. 46, n. 8. G. M. A. Richter, *Catalogue of Engraved Gems in the Metropolitan Museum* (New York, 1956), p. xix.
2 Pliny, XXXVII, 91 and 92.
3 Information from Miss Mavis Bimson, British Museum Research Laboratory.
4 Analyses conducted by British Museum Research Laboratory.
5 Corning Museum of Glass, *Glass from the Ancient-World: R. W. Smith Collection* (New York, 1957), pp. 16 and 31, no. 25. A. J. Forbes, *Studies in Ancient Technology*, V (Leiden, 1957), p. 144. *History of Technology*, II, p. 319; fig. 296.
6 *BMC Terracottas* (1903), E 100 ff.
7 W. M. F. Petrie, *Nebesheh and Defenneh* (London, 1888), p. 42.
8 Richter, *Etruscan Coll.*, fig. 15. *JRGZM*, VI (1959), p. 57.
9 Evans, *Palace*, I, p. 486.
10 *Naukratis*, I, p. 36.
11 T. J. Dunbabin, *The Greeks and their Eastern Neighbours* (London, 1957), p. 49.
12 Persson, *Royal Tombs*, p. 56.

Chapter 6

1 Maxwell-Hyslop, *Western Asiatic Jewellery*, p. 82.
2 Ibid. pls 6, 7–10, 30. Schmidt, Beil. I, nos 6014–15.
3 Maxwell-Hyslop, *Western Asiatic Jewellery*, pl. 32b.
4 Schmidt, p. 236, no. 5952.
5 Schmidt, Beil. II, nos 5941, 6044. *Iraq*, IX (1947), pls 33 and 36.
6 Schmidt, Beil. II, nos 5942, 6131.
7 *Troy*, I, fig. 357, no. 37–522. *Troy*, II, fig. 47.
8 Maxwell-Hyslop, *Western Asiatic Jewellery*, p. 43; fig. 25.
9 Schmidt, p. 252. *Troy*, I, fig. 358. *Troy*, II, figs 47 and 234.
10 Schmidt, p. 254, nos 6399–402. *Aegean and Near East*, pl. 2, no. 14a. H. Goldman, *Tarsus*, II (Princeton, NJ, 1956); fig. 431, no. 207. R. W. Ehrich (ed.), *Relative Chronologies* (Chicago, Ill., 1954), p. 91. *Liverpool Annals*, XXIII (1936), p. 118. Jacobsthal, *Pins*, p. 126.
11 *Troy*, II, p. 91; fig. 47, no. 37–739.
12 Schmidt, Beil. II, no. 6133.
13 A. J. Evans, *Shaft Graves and Beehive Tombs of Mycenae* (London, 1929), p. 43.
14 *Iraq*, IX (1947), pl. 42:8.
15 See Jacobsthal, *Pins*, p. 63.

Chapter 7

1 Maxwell-Hyslop, *Western Asiatic Jewellery*, p. 33.
2 Ibid. p. 27.
3 Ibid. p. 230.
4 Woolley, *Ur Excavations*, II, pl. 139.

Chapter 8

1 *BSA*, IX (1902–3), pl. 13, no. 74.

Chapter 9

1 S. Marinatos, *Excavations at Thera*, V–VII (Athens, 1972–6), colour plates.
2 Maxwell-Hyslop, *Western Asiatic Jewellery*, p. 71; fig. 46a.
3 C. Schaeffer, *Ugaritica*, I (1939), p. 42; fig. 31. L. Woolley, *Alalakh* (Oxford, 1955), pl. LXIX:9.
4 (1) Heraklion no. 1303 (unpublished). (2) *A. Delt.*, XVII (1961–2), B, pl. 348.

5 *Excavations at Thera*, VII (1976), pls B and J.
6 *Excavations at Thera*, V (1972), pl. K.
7 Wilkinson, *Ancient Egyptian Jewellery*, pl. 17 and col. pl. 2.
8 J. M. Coles and A. F. Harding, *The Bronze Age in Europe* (London, 1979), p. 151, fig. 52.
9 In Heraklion; unpublished.
10 *CMS*, II, Pt V, no. 255.
11 Cf. Marinatos and Hirmer, pl. 69.
12 See Maxwell-Hyslop, *Western Asiatic Jewellery*, passim. Especially p. 31, fig. 22; p. 34, pl. 34; p. 35; p. 44, fig. 29a; p. 53, fig. 37b and pl. 39; p. 71, fig. 46c; p. 267.
13 Ibid. p. 189, fig. 113 and pl. 136; p. 192, pl. 145; p. 193, fig. 114; p. 207, pl. 165.
14 Ibid. p. 44, fig. 29b.
15 *BMCR*, no. 14.

Chapter 10

1 Evans, *Palace*, II, p. 427, fig. 248, and IV, p. 286, fig. 220. H. Reusch, *Die zeichnerische Rekonstruktion des Frauenfrieses im Böotischen Theben* (Berlin, 1956). Hood, *APG*, p. 79, fig. 62.
2 Maxwell-Hyslop, *Western Asiatic Jewellery*, pl. 115 (from Shechem).
3 Wace, *Chamber Tombs*, p. 205. *BSA*, LII (1957), p. 199. Beck, *Beads and Pendants*, p. 19, fig. 18, no. A 2.8. *Syria*, XIII (1932), pl. 9:2 (Ras Shamra). *AJ*, XIX (1939), p. 28 (Atchana).
4 *BSA*, XXV (1921–3), p. 399. Wace, *Chamber Tombs*, p. 192.
5 *Theoria: Festschrift für W.-H. Schuchardt* (Baden-Baden, 1960), p. 151.
6 Boardman, *GGFR*, p. 56.
7 Ibid. p. 102, caption to pl. 110.
8 Buchholz and Karageorghis, no. 1356.
9 *BMCJ*, nos 818–19.

Chapter 11

1 Theoria: *Festschrift für W.-H. Schuchardt* (Baden-Baden, 1960), p. 156.
2 *Kerameikos*, I, p. 85. *BSA*, XXIII (1918–19), p. 17.
3 *Kerameikos*, I, p. 82.
4 Desborough, *GDA*, p. 202.

Chapter 12

1 T. J. Dunbabin, *The Greeks and their Eastern Neighbours* (London, 1957), p. 37.
2 Ohly, *passim*. Reichel, nos 1–31. J. M. Cook, *BSA*, XLVI (1951), p. 45. *Gnomon*, XXI (1949), p. I.
3 *BSA*, LXIV (1969), Pl. 37c.
4 *BMCJ*, no. 1240.
5 *Boston Bull.*, LXVIII (1943), p. 44. *BSA*, LXIV (1969), pl. 38.
6 *SCE*, I, pl. 105: 16, 20.
7 C. Blinkenberg, *Fibules grecques et orientales* (Copenhagen, 1926), type VIII.
8 Reichel, nos 37–43.
9 Von Luschan, *Sendschirli*, V, pls 44–5.
10 'Triple-gleaming mulberry-like earrings'. See *AJA*, LXV (1961), p. 62; pls 35–6.
11 *BSA*, LXII (1967), p. 57.
12 Reichel, no. 23.
13 Cf. von Luschan, *Sendschirli*, V, pl. 44.
14 Jacobsthal, *Pins*, p. 17; figs 55a, 57.
15 Ibid. p. 24; figs 96, 97.
16 Frankfort, pls 96–7 (Assyria). S. Lloyd, *Early Anatolia* (Harmondsworth, 1956), pl. 15 (Syria). Barnett, *Nimrud Ivories*, pls 70–1 (Phoenician?). Ibid. pl. 129 (Urartu). A. Godard, *Le Trésor de Ziwiyé* (Haarlem, 1950), p. 104, fig. 90 = Coche de la Ferté, pl. 4: 2 (North Persia). *SCE*, IV, Pt 2: pl. 10: 1.
17 Laffineur, nos 163–6.
18 Laffineur, nos 160, 161, 168, 179, 180, etc.
19 Laffineur, no. 159.
20 Laffineur, nos 122, 127–9, 135–51.
21 Laffineur, nos 117–21, 123–6, 130–4, 152–8.
22 Laffineur, no. 212.
23 Laffineur, nos 207, 208, 214.
24 Laffineur, nos 203, 205.
25 Laffineur, no. 204.
26 Laffineur, no. 202.
27 Laffineur, nos 218, 229.
28 Laffineur, no. 219.
29 Reichel, nos 57–61. Frankfort, pl. 167. Von Luschan, *Sendschirli*, V, pl. 44. Becatti, no. 216. *SCE*, IV, Pt 2, p. 394.
30 R. A. Higgins, *Greek Terracottas* (London, 1967), pl. 9 D.
31 *BMCJ*, nos 1198, 1208.

32 Laffineur, no. 193.

33 Laffineur, nos 191, 192, 194, 195.

34 *Aegean and Near East*, p. 218.

35 *Boston Bull.*, LXVIII (1943), p. 44.

36 *SCE*, I, pls 44, 51 and 155. Becatti, nos 213–15.

37 Von Luschan, *Sendschirli*, V, pls 46–7.

38 *Lindos*, no. 472. Laffineur, p. 24.

39 Barnett, *Nimrud Ivories*, p. 145. Laffineur, nos 1, 29–34, 106, 115.

40 Laffineur, no. 2.

41 Barnett, *Nimrud Ivories*, p. 82. Laffineur, nos 3–4, 8–11, 18–22, 35, 48–58, 86–9, 91, 97, 98, 100, 108, 116.

42 Laffineur, nos 59, 60, 102.

43 Laffineur, nos 61–74, 92–5.

44 Laffineur, nos 26–8, 75–82, 105.

45 Laffineur, nos 83, 84.

46 Laffineur, nos 6, 7, 23–5, 46, 47, 90.

47 Laffineur, nos 36–42. Barnett, *Nimrud Ivories*, p. 83.

48 Laffineur, no. 107.

49 Laffineur, nos 5, 12–17, 43–5, 99, 101.

50 Laffineur, no. 198. Cf. *BMC Terracottas*, I (1954), nos 16–18.

51 Laffineur, no. 199.

52 Laffineur, no. 201.

53 *BMCJ*, no. 1205.

54 *BMCR*, no. 15. *Lindos*, no. 280.

55 Woolley, *Ur Excavations*, II, pl. 138. Schmidt, Beil. I, nos 5929–32 and 5986–7. Coche de la Ferté, p. 36. Von Luschan, *Sendschirli*, V, pl. 45.

56 *BMCJ*, no. 1245.

57 C. Blinkenberg, op. cit., type XII

58 Von Luschan, *Sendschirli*, V, pl. 43. *Archaeology*, XI (1958), p. 230.

59 Hogarth, *Ephesus*, pls 3: 2 and 4: 35. *JHS*, LXXI (1951), pl. 31c.

60 *SCE*, I, pl. 155. Becatti, nos 289–91. For Phoenicia, see p. 106.

Chapter 13

1 *Olynthus*, X (1941), p. 158, no. 318. *BMCJ*, p. xxxi.

2 Michel, *Recueil*, p. 644.

3 *BMC Sculpture*, I, Pt 2 (1931), p. 48.

4 Demosthenes, *Contra Meidiam*, 522.

5 Coche de la Ferté, pl. 11: 3.

6 *SCE*, IV, Pt 2, pl. 15. Coche de la Ferté, pl. 3: 2.

7 *BMCJ*, p. 178. C.M. Kraay, *Greek Coins* (London, 1966), pls 27–30.

8 *Jahrbuch für Kleinasiatische Forschungen*, I (1950–1), pl. 8.

9 Becatti, no. 382. Hadaczek, p. 25, fig. 47.

10 Hadaczek, p. 24, fig. 45. *JHS*, II (1881), p. 324.

11 *Collection Stathatos*, I, nos 282–3.

12 U. Zanotti-Bianco, *La Magna Grecia* (Genoa, 1964), fig. 209.

13 *BMCJ*, nos 1655–6.

14 *BMCJ*, nos 1657–8.

15 *BMC Coins of Lycia, etc.* (1897), pl. 5: 8.

16 Coche de la Ferté, pl. 16: 1 (coin). Becatti, no. 380. *BMCJ*, no. 1652.

17 *Collection Stathatos*, I, no. 278.

18 Kraay, op. cit. no. 80 (pl. 27). *Naukratis*, II, pl. 19: 10. *BMCJ*, no. 1593* (Smyrna).

19 Hadaczek, p. 10.

20 *BMCJ*, nos 2067–9.

21 Ohnefalsch-Richter, *Kypros*, pl. 33: 10 and 11. *BMCJ*, nos 2065–6.

22 *BMCJ*, nos 1605–6

23 R. Lullies and M. Hirmer, *Greek Sculpture* (London, 1957), pl. 20. A. Furtwängler and K. Reichhold, *Griechische Vasenmalerei*, I (Munich, 1904), pl. 13.

24 Kraay, op. cit. nos 127, 129 (pls 46 and VI). Hadaczek, p. 31, fig. 51.

25 Jacobsthal, *Pins*, fig. 284. Greifenhagen, *Schmuckarbeiten*, II, p. 46; pl. 38: 12 and 13.

26 *Boston Bull.*, XI (1913), p. 50. Jacobsthal, *Pins*, pls 286–9. Becatti, pl. 105. Segall, p. 64.

27 Greifenhagen, *Schmuckarbeiten*, II, p. 15; pl. 4: 1. *Collection Stathatos*, I, nos 82 and 83.

28 To refs in Bibliography add Greifenhagen, *Schmuckarbeiten*, II, p. 15, pl. 4: 2.

29 Hadaczek, p. 44, fig. 82. Minns, fig. 29 (= *ABC*, pl. 7). *AA*, XXVIII (1913), p. 197.

30 *Collection Stathatos*, I, no. 215.

31 *BMCR*, p. xxx.

32 *BMCR*, no. 41.

33 *BMCR*, no. 350. Ibid. p. xli, type C xii, for this general type.

34 Ibid. p. xli, type C xviii.

35 Coche de la Ferté, pl. 17: 2 and 3, from Thespiae.

36 *Collection Stathatos*, I, no. 214. For other refs see Bibliography.

37 *Boston Bull.*, XXXIX (1941), p. 54. Jacobsthal, *Pins*, p. 65, figs 274–9.

38 *BMCJ*, nos 2841–8. See also Jacobsthal, *Pins*, pp. 204 ff.

39 *AJA*, XXXII (1928), p. 333. Jacobsthal, *Pins*, p. 111.

Chapter 14

1 *BMCJ*, nos 1258–61.
2 See also *BMCJ*, nos 1311–44.
3 *BMC Terracottas* (1903), D 591
(= *BMCJ*, p. 118, fig. 28).
4 *BMCJ*, no. 1308.
5 Coche de la Ferté, p. 45.
6 Hadaczek, pp. 56 ff. *BMCJ*, nos
1286–1306.
7 Hadaczek, p. 68. *BMCJ*, nos 1414–26.
8 Hadaczek, pp. 59 ff.
9 *BMCJ*, nos 2196–210.
10 Alexander, *Jewellery*, fig. 3
11 *SCE*, IV, Pt 2, p. 165, fig. 35: 1.
12 *BMCJ*, no. 1458.
13 Coche de la Ferté, pl. 38.
14 *BMCJ*, no. 1463.
15 *BMC Terracottas* (1903), nos B 522–43.
16 Coche de la Ferté, pl. 37.
17 Becatti, no. 273. Breglia, no. 22.
18 *BMCJ*, nos 2322–3.
19 *BMCJ*, no. 1413.
20 *BMCJ*, nos 1368–9.
21 *BMCJ*, nos 1362–3.
22 Coche de la Ferté, pl. 29: 3.
23 *BMCJ*, no. 1267. Coche de la Ferté,
pl. 32: 1 and 2.
24 *BMCJ*, no. 1269.
25 *BMCJ*, no. 1270.
26 See Coche de la Ferté, p. 79. *BMCR*,
p. xxxix, types B vii and C ii.
27 *BMCR*, p. xliii, type D i.
28 *BMCJ*, nos 1347–53.
29 Montelius, *Civ. Prim. It.*, I, series A,
pls 1–21. G. M. A. Richter, *Greek,
Etruscan and Roman Bronzes* (New York,
1915), pp. 314–30.
30 Coche de la Ferté, pl. 28: 2. *MEFRA*
(1971), p. 9.
31 BMCJ, nos 1376 a–c.
32 *BMCJ*, nos 1397–1401.
33 *BMCJ*, no. 1373.
34 See *BMCJ*, nos 1390–2. Coche de la
Ferté, pl. 38: 1.
35 *St. Etr.*, XXXVI (1968), p. 277.
36 See preceding note.
37 *Collection Stathatos*, I, nos 53–77.

Chapter 15

1 *BMCJ*, nos 2293, 2296–303.
2 BMCJ, no. 2294.
3 *BMC Terracottas* (1903), D 196 (=
BMCJ, p. 265, fig. 78).

4 Hadaczek, p. 65, figs 126–8. *BMCJ*,
nos 2211–27.
5 Hadaczek, p. 65, figs 129–32. *BMCJ*,
nos 2228–36.
6 Alexander, *Jewellery*, pl. 74.
7 Hadaczek, p. 60, fig. 114. *BMCJ*,
nos 2243–8.
8 Hadaczek, p. 60, fig. 116. *BMCJ*,
nos 2250–1.
9 Hadaczek, pp. 61 ff., figs 118–21.
BMCJ, nos 2252–9.
10 *BMCJ*, nos 2263–4.
11 *BMCJ* nos 2287–8
12 *BMCR*, p. xliv, types D ii–vii.
13 Ibid. type D viii.

Chapter 16

1 Aldred, *Jewels of the Pharaohs*, pls 34
and 44.
2 *DA*, s.v. 'Nodus'.
3 Ippel, *Galjub, passim.*
4 Athenaeus, V, 193 and 196.
5 *BCH*, VI (1882), pp 1–167. Michel,
Recueil, p. 681.
6 See preceding note.
7 *BMCJ*, no. 1631. Coche de la Ferté,
pl. 23: 2.
8 Segall, pp. 32 ff. *Collection Stathatos*, I,
p. 118.
9 Maxwell-Hyslop, *Western Asiatic
Jewellery* p. 213.
10 Hadaczek, p 46.
11 *BMCJ*, nos 1721–67.
12 *BMCJ*, nos 1782–5.
13 *BMCJ*, nos 1808–19.
14 *BMCJ*, nos 1786–1804.
15 *BMCJ*, nos 1805–7.
16 *BMCJ*, nos 1830–7.
17 *BMCJ*, nos 1684–1705.
18 *BMCJ*, nos 2426–32.
19 Schäfer, p. 78, fig. 79. Edgar, *Gr. Eg.
Coffins*, pl. 44. Also unpublished sarcophagi in London: nos 29586 (from
Akhmin), 6705, 6950.
20 *BMCJ*, nos 2436–43.
21 *BMCJ*, no. 2433.
22 *Collection Stathatos*, I, nos 304–5.
Segall, nos 117–18.
23 Pollak, *Samml. Nelidow*, no. 160.
Cesnola, *Salaminia*, p. 34, fig. 26.
There is an unpublished pair in
London: 1960. 4–11. 1.
24 Cesnola, *Salaminia*, p. 33, fig. 23.
25 Hadaczek, p. 49, fig. 89. Segall, no.
123. Cesnola, *Salaminia*, p. 35, fig. 28.
26 Fontenay, pp. 105 and 107.
27 *BMCJ*, nos 1714–17.

28   *BMCJ*, nos 2324–5.
29   Hadaczek, p. 50, fig. 91. *BMCJ*, nos
     1840–1.
30   *BMCJ*, nos 1768–71. Breglia, p. 123.
31   Hadaczek, p. 51, fig. 95.
32   *BMCJ*, nos 1842–3.
33   *BMCJ*, no. 1844.
34   *BMC Terracottas* (1903), D 786.
35   Breglia, no. 121.
36   Hadaczek, p. 33. *BMCJ*, nos 2326–71.
37   *BMCJ*, no. 2331.
38   *BMCJ*, nos 2442–3 and 2324–5.
39   Hadaczek, p. 42. *BMCJ*, nos 1858–
     1916.
40   Siviero, nos 148–9.
41   Hadaczek, pp. 44 and 72. *BMCJ*,
     nos 1675–82.
42   Pollux, V, 97.
43   Ibid.
44   Michel, *Recueil*, p. 682.
45   *BMC Terracottas* (1903), D 786.
46   *AJA*, LIX (1955), p. 219. Said to come
     from Pagasae.
47   *JHS*, LXXV (1955), p. 174.
48   See *BMC Terracottas*, I (1954), no.
     1172.
49   Coche de la Ferté, pl. 25: 2.
50   Ippel, *Galjub*, pls 6–9.
51   Coche de la Ferté, pl. 25: 1.
52   *BMC Terracottas* (1903), D 786.
53   Michel, *Recueil*, p. 833.
54   Rosenberg, *Zellenschmelz*, p. 37, fig.
     53.
55   *BMCR*, p. xliii, types C xxiii–xxv.
56   Ibid. p. xlvi, type E ix.
57   *MA*, XX (1910), p. 39. *BMCJ*, no.
     1382.
58   *BMCJ*, no. 2070.

Chapter 17

1   *BMCR*, pp. xviii ff.
2   A. Maiuri, *La Casa del Menandro*
     (Rome, 1933), p. 14.
3   Information given by Dr R. D.
     Barnett.
4   *BMCJ*, p. xliii.
5   Coche de la Ferté, pl. 1.
6   BMCJ, p. xlviii.
7   *BMCJ*, p. xliii.
8   1 Tim. 2: 9.
9   Pliny, *Historia naturalis*, IX, 58; IX,
     56; XXXVII, 6. See G. M. A. Richter,
     *Catalogue of the Engraved Gems in the
     Metropolitan Museum* (New York,
     1956), p. xviii.
10   Egyptian Dept, no. 21810.

11   *BMCJ*, no. 3045.
12   *BMCJ*, nos 3029–33 and 3035–41.
13   *BMCJ*, nos 2464–79
14   *BMCJ*, nos 2412–24.
15   *BMCJ*, nos 2509–34.
16   *BMCJ*, no. 2432. Segall, no. 121.
17   Breglia, no. 470. *BMCJ*, no. 2565.
18   W.M.F. Petrie, *Hawara, etc.* (London,
     1889), pl. 11.
19   Edgar, *Gr. Eg. Coffins*, pls 10 and 16.
     Also no. 6705 in London (Egyptian
     Dept). *JHS*, XXV (1905), p. 230,
     fig. 1c.
20   *BMCJ*, nos 2677–8.
21   *BMCJ*, nos 2399–2400
22   *BMCJ*, nos 2616–21. Shore, *Portrait
     Painting*, pls 2, 11 and 17.
23   Siviero, no. 252.
24   *BMCJ*, nos 2622–3. Schäfer, p. 87,
     fig. 84.
25   1914. 10–14. 1–4. See *Roman Crafts*,
     p. 60; fig. 71.
26   *BMCJ*, nos 2643–73. Shore, *Portrait
     Painting*, pls 3 and 18. *BMCJ*, p. 320,
     fig. 88.
27   *BMCJ*, no. 2824
28   *BMCJ*, nos 2719–23, 2918–35. Shore,
     Portrait Painting, pls 2 and 11.
29   *BMCJ*, nos 2727, 2735, 2936–43.
30   Becatti, nos 506–7. Breglia, nos 916–18
31   E. Buschor, *Medusa Rondanini* (Stutt-
     gart, 1958), pls 40 and 41.
32   Shore, *Portrait Painting*, pl. 3.
33   Shore, *Portrait Painting*, pls 12–14.
34   Breglia, no. 348.
35   Coche de la Ferté, pl. 44: 2.
36   *BMCR*, p. xv.
37   Ibid. p. xxv.
38   Pliny, *Historia naturalis*, XXXIII, 12.
39   Breglia, nos 669–75. *BMCR*, p. xlvi,
     types E ix and x.
40   Ibid. type E xvi.
41   Ibid. p. xlviii, type E xxxii.
42   Ibid. type E xxix.
43   Ibid. type E xxxv.
44   Breglia, nos 594 and 599.
45   Breglia, no. 668. *BMCR*, p. xlv, type
     E v.
46   Ibid. p. xlix, type E xl.
47   Ibid. p. xlv, type E vii. Becatti, no. 518.
     Breglia, nos 734–45, 990, 991.
48   *BMCR*, p. xlix, type E xxxvii. Segall,
     no. 169.
49   See *BMCJ*, nos 2853–9. Brailsford,
     Antiqs of Roman Britain, p. 21, fig. 10.
50   *B. Met. Mus.*, XXIV (1966), p. 284.
51   *BMC Bronzes*, nos 2162–222. *Roman
     Crafts*, p. 43.

BIBLIOGRAPHY AND SITE LISTS

The following lists are designed to indicate the framework on which this survey is based and also to be a guide to further reading. For the abbreviations used, see p. xxxv. Dates are BC except in the Roman section.

General works

Becatti.
Beck, *Beads and Pendants*.
Boardman, *GGFR*.
Coarelli, F. *Greek and Roman Jewellery* (London, 1966).
Coche de la Ferté.
DA, s.v. 'Annulus', 'Armilla', 'Aurifex', 'Aurum', 'Brattea', 'Bulla', 'Caelatura', 'Catena', 'Inauris', 'Monile'.
Ebert, *Reallexikon*, s.v. 'Gold', 'Goldfunde', 'Goldschmiedekunst', 'Granulation'.
Hadaczek.
Jacobsthal, *Pins*. (Deals with much besides pins.)
Richter, G. M. A. *A Handbook of Greek Arts* (London, 1959), pp. 251–60
Sutherland, *Gold*.

Collections: catalogues, etc.

Those publications marked with an asterisk(*) are valuable not only as catalogues but also as general studies.

ATHENS, NATIONAL MUSEUM

Stais.
*Collection Stathatos, I, III, IV.

ATHENS, BENAKI MUSEUM

*Segall.

BASLE, SPECIAL EXHIBITION, 1960

Schefold, Meisterwerke, nos 551–609.

BERLIN, STAATLICHE MUSEEN

*Greifenhagen, Schmuckarbeiten, I and II. (A superb catalogue of the jewellery in West Berlin.)
Greifenhagen, A. Schmuck der alten Welt (Berlin, 1974, 1975) (A picture book with excellent coloured illustrations.)

BERLIN, PRIVATE COLLECTIONS

*Zahn, R. Galerie Bachstitz, II (Berlin 1921).
*Zahn, R. Sammlung Baurat Schiller (Berlin, 1929), pp. 23–74.

BOLOGNA, SPECIAL EXHIBITION, 1958

Alfieri, N., and others. Ori e argenti dell'Emilia antica (Bologna, 1958).

CAIRO, ARCHAEOLOGICAL MUSEUM

Vernier, E. Catalogue général . . . Bijoux et orfèvreries (Cairo, 1927).

HAMBURG, MUSEUM FÜR KUNST UND GEWERBE

Hoffman, H., and Claer, V. von. Antiker Gold und Silberschmuck (Mainz, 1968).

LENINGRAD, HERMITAGE MUSEUM

*Artamonov, Treasures.

LONDON, BRITISH MUSEUM

*BMCJ.
*BMCR.
Higgins, R. *Jewellery from Classical Lands* (London, 1965).
Jewellery Through 7000 Years.

NAPLES, MUSEO NAZIONALE ARCHEOLOGICO

*Breglia.
Siviero.

NEW YORK, METROPOLITAN MUSEUM

*Alexander, *Jewellery*.
Oliver, A. *B. Met. Mus.*, XXIV (1966), p. 269.
Richter, *Met. Mus. Gk. Coll.* (A general guidebook to the Greek antiquities.)
Cesnola, L. P. di. *Atlas of the Cesnola Collection of Cypriote Antiquites in the Metropolitan Museum*, III (New York, 1913).

NEW YORK, HISTORICAL SOCIETY

*Williams, *Gold and Silver Jewelry*.

NICOSIA, THE CYPRUS MUSEUM

Pierides, *Jewellery in Cyprus Mus.*

PARIS, LOUVRE MUSEUM

Ridder, A. de. *Catalogue sommaire des bijoux antiques du Musée du Louvre* (Paris, 1924).
Lenormant, F. 'Collection Campana: Les bijoux', *Gazette des Beaux-Arts*, XIV (1863), pp. 152–63, 307–24.

PARIS, PRIVATE COLLECTION

Ridder, A. de. *Collection de Clercq : Catalogue*, VII (Paris, 1911).

RHODE ISLAND SCHOOL OF DESIGN, MUSEUM OF ART

*Hackens, T. *Catalogue of the Classical Collections : Classical Jewellery* (Providence, Rhode Island, 1976).

ROME, VATICAN MUSEUM

Museo Etrusco Vaticano, I (Rome, 1842).

ROME, PRIVATE COLLECTION

Pollak, *Samml. Nelidow.*

TARANTO, NATIONAL MUSEUM

Breglia, L. *Iapigia*, X (1939), pp. 5–54.

TURIN, SPECIAL EXHIBITION, 1961

⋆Ori e argenti dell'Italia antica (Turin, 1961).

Forgeries

THISBE GEMS

JHS, XLV (1925), p. 1. (Published in good faith.)
Biesantz, H. *Kretisch-Mykenische Siegelbilder* (Marburg, 1954) p. 84.
Nilsson, M. P. *The Minoan-Mycenaean Religion* (2nd ed. Lund, 1950),
    pp. 40, 267.

TIARA OF SAITAPHERNES

Kurz, O. *Fakes* (London, 1948).
Furtwängler, A. *Intermezzi* (Leipzig and Berlin, 1896), p. 81.

MEDALLIONS, BRACELETS AND OTHER HELLENISTIC
FORGERIES

AJA, LVII (1953), p. 5. (Published in good faith.)
Collection Stathatos, I, p. 104.
JHS, LXXV (1955), p. 174.
AJA, LIX (1955), p. 221.
AJA, LXXIII (1969), p. 448.

OTHER FORGERIES

Furtwängler, A. *Intermezzi* (Leipzig and Berlin, 1896), p. 81.
Coche de la Ferté, pl. 28.

CASTELLANI'S GRANULATION

BMCJ, p. liv, n. 4.
Rosenberg, *Granulation*, p. 5, figs 9 and 10.

LITTLEDALE'S REPRODUCTIONS

Emerson, A. R. *Hand-Made Jewellery.* (Leicester, 1953), Pl. 9.

Other civilizations

Maxwell-Hyslop, *Western Asiatic Jewellery.*
Wilkinson, *Ancient Egyptian Jewellery.*
Aldred, *Jewels of the Pharaohs.*
Coles, J. N., and Harding, A. F. *The Bronze Age in Europe* (London, 1979).

1–5 Technical

GENERAL TECHNICAL STUDIES

Blümner, *Technologie*, III and IV.
BMCJ, pp. li-lxii.
BMCR, pp. xxx-xxxvii
Coche de la Ferté, pp. 3–24.
Forbes, *Metallurgy.*
Kluge, K., and Lehmann-Hartleben, K. *Die antiken Grossbronzen* (Berlin and Leipzig, 1927), p. 32.
Lucas, *Materials and Industries.*
Maryon, H. *Metalwork and Enamelling* (London, 1954).
Maryon, H. *AJA*, LIII (1949), p. 93.
Vernier, E. *Catalogue général* ... *Bijoux et orfèvreries* (Cairo, 1927).
Williams, *Gold and Silver Jewelry.*
Hoffman and Davidson, *Greek Gold*, p. 18.
Roman Crafts, p. 53.
Sutherland, *Gold.*
Aldred, *Jewels of the Pharaohs.*

ANCIENT LITERARY SOURCES

Homer, *Odyssey*, Book III, 425.
Agatharchides. Late second century BC. Incorporated in Diodorus, Book III. (Goldmining in Egypt.)

Pliny the Elder, *Historia naturalis*, Books XXXIII–XXXVII. First century AD. (Goldsmiths' techniques. Stones.)

Strabo. First century BC–AD. (Mining processes.)

Theophilus, *De diversis artibus*. Ed. and trans. C. R. Dodwell (London, 1961).

Theophrastus, *De lapidibus*. Fourth–third century BC. (The use of precious stones.)

'Leyden Papyrus X', *Gold Bulletin*, IX (1976), p. 24.

ADDITIONAL WORKS ON SPECIAL SUBJECTS

Mines

AJ, XLIX (1970), p. 244. (Wales.)

Davies, O. *Roman Mines in Europe* (Oxford, 1935).

Bonner Jahrbücher, CLXXII (1972), p. 36. (Spain.)

JRS, XVIII (1928), p. 129, and LX (1970), p. 169. (Spain.)

Mining Magazine (1929), p. 3. (Siphnos and Skyros.)

AJA, XLVI (1942), p. 400 (Balkans.)

AJA, LXXXI (1977), p. 107. (Greece: sixth and fifth centuries BC.)

Nature, CXXX (1932), p. 985. (Aegean Bronze Age.)

Guide de Thasos (Paris, 1967) p. 3.

Sutherland, *Gold*, p. 26. (Egypt.)

Refining

Forbes, *Metallurgy*, p. 155.

AJA, LXXIV (1970), p. 172. (Sardis, sixth century BC.)

Coche de la Ferté, p. 47.

Ancient workshops, etc.

Thebes:

Workshop 1: *AE* (1930), p. 29. (1400–1350 BC.)

Workshop 2: 5: Symeonoglou, S. *Kadmeia. Studies in Mediterranean Archaeology*, XXXV (1973). (1300–1250 BC.)

Workshop 3: *AAA*, VII (1974), p. 162. (1300–1200 BC.)

Roman Egypt:
Ippel, *Galjub*.

Raw materials:
BSA, LXII (1967), p. 61. (Tekke.)

Minoan gold analysis:
Boston Bull., LVII (1959), p. 19.

Paintings, etc., showing workshops

Aldred, *Jewels of the Pharaohs*, p. 46. (Egyptian.)
Wilkinson, *Ancient Egyptian Jewellery*, p. 1. (Egyptian.)
Roman Crafts, p. 54. (Roman.)
Coche de la Ferté, pl. I. (Roman.)

Repoussé

Aldred, *Jewels of the Pharaohs*, p. 72. ('Pitchblock' from Amarna.)
Excavations at Tell el-Amarna 1913–14 (Smithsonian Institution. Washington, DC, 1916), p. 453, pls 7 and 8. ('Pitchblock' from Amarna.) *AJA*, XLV (1941), p. 375. (Experiments in embossing.)
Ippel, *Galjub*, pl. 10. (Punches.)

Stamps

Roman Crafts, pp. 54–5, fig. 54.
Oxford, no. 1966. 1155. (Unpublished.)

Wooden cores

AA (1913), p. 220.
AA (1914), p. 257, fig. 81.

Bronze cores

Ippel, *Galjub*, pls 5–9.
Lindos, I, pl. 17, no. 472.

Experiments in working over a core

AM, I (1925), p. 182.

Moulds for rubbing or beating

JHS, XVI (1896), p. 323. (Corfu.)
Furtwängler, A. *Olympia*, IV. Berlin, 1890. p. 27, pl. 7, no. 88.
Corinth, XII, pl. 126, no. 2661.
Richter, G. M. A. *Greek, Etruscan and Roman Bronzes* (Metropolitan Museum. New York, 1915), p. 444, no. 1710.

Wires and chains

Petrie, W. M. F. *Arts and Crafts of Ancient Egypt* (London, 1910), p. 86.
DA, s.v. 'Catena'.
Williams, *Gold and Silver Jewelry*, p. 133.
Oddy, A. *Gold Bulletin*, X (1977), p. 79.
AJA, LXXVI (1972), p. 321. (Arguments for primitive draw-plates.)

Moulds for casting metal: Minoan and Mycenaean

BMCJ, p. 40, no. 609. (For a ring. Steatite.)
BM, no. 1924. 11–14. 1. (Unpublished. For a ring. Steatite.)
Arch. Rep. (1974–5), p. 17, fig. 27. (For a ring.)
Mylonas, *To dytikon nekrotapheion*, I, p. 306; II, p. 254; pls 64–5.
   (For a ring.)
Études Crétoises, XI, p. 137. (For a ring.)
BCH, XCV (1971), p. 1049, fig. 540. (For pins.)
Asine, p. 250. (For pins.)
Boardman, *Cretan Collection*, no. 546. (For an earring.)
A. Delt., XVII (1961–2), B, p. 283, pl. 348. (For an earring.)
Heraklion Museum, no. 1303. (Unpublished. From Mochlos. For an
   earring.)

Moulds for casting metal: Roman

Schreiber, p. 277.

Experiments in casting

ÖJH, VII (1904), p. 154.
Roman Crafts, p. 59.

Filigree, granulation and colloid hard soldering

Curtis, C. D. *MAAR*, I (1915–16), pp. 63–85.
Ebert, *Reallexikon*, s.v. 'Granulation'.
Goldsmith's Journal (December 1957), p. 564.
Maryon, H. *Technical Studies*, V (Harvard, 1936), pp. 75 ff.
Rosenberg, *Granulation*.
Treskow, E. *Kunst and Leben der Etrusker* (Cologne, 1956) p. 41.
Treskow, E. 'Kunst and Technik der Granulation', *Gold und Silber*,
   X–XI (1953).
Carroll, D. L. *AJA*, LXXVIII (1974), p. 33.

Enamelling

Rosenberg, *Zellenschmelz*.
Garner, H. *Chinese and Japanese Cloisonné Enamels* (London, 1962), p. 18.
Roman Crafts, p. 43.

Niello

Moss, A. A. *Studies in Conservation*, II (1953), p. 49.

Inlaying

Aldred, *Jewels of the Pharaohs*, p. 127.

Plating and gilding

Campbell, W. *Greek and Roman Plated Coins* (New York, 1933).
Thompson, H. *Athenian Studies Presented to W. S. Ferguson* (Harvard, 1940), p. 183.
Gold Bulletin, XII (1979), p. 35.

Soldering

Gold Bulletin, VI (1973), p. 112.
Hoffmann and Davidson, *Greek Gold*, p. 41.

Stones

Pliny the Elder, *Historia naturalis*, Bk XXXVII.
McLintock, W. F. P., and Sabine, P. A. *Guide to the Collection of Gem-Stones in the Geological Museum* (London, 1951).
Richter, G. M. A. *Catalogue of Engraved Gems in the Metropolitan Museum* (New York, 1956), pp. xxv-xxix.
Blümner, *Technologie*, III, p. 227.
Iraq, XXX (1968), p. 58. (Lapis lazuli.)
JEA, XI (1925), p. 144. (Emeralds.)
BMCJ, p. lvii.

Glass

Forbes, A. J. *Studies in Ancient Technology*, V (Leyden, 1957).
Matson, F. R. *Journal of Chemical Education*, XXVIII (1951), p. 82.
Archaeology, XVI (1963), p. 190.
JRGZM, VII (1960), p. 36.

Mycenaean moulds for casting glass

See Vermeule, E. T. *Boston Bull.*, LXV (1967), p. 17.
Evans, *Palace*, I, p. 487, fig. 349. (Knossos.)
Boston Bull., LXV (1967), p. 23, fig. 4. (Knossos.)
BSA, LI (1956), pl. 12e. (Knossos.)
Arch. Rep. (1956), p. 22. (Poros, near Knossos.)
BSA, Suppl. I, p. 150. (Palaikastro.)
Schliemann, H. *Mycenae* (London, 1878), p. 109, fig. 163. (Mycenae.)
Ibid. p. 107, fig. 162. (Mycenae.)
AE (1897), p. 97, pl. 7: 1. (Mycenae.)
Ibid. p. 98. (Mycenae.)
Arch. Rep. (1966–7), p. 9, fig. 13. (Mycenae.)
Boston Bull., LXV (1967), p. 20, figs 1 and 2. (Mycenae.)
Buchholz and Karageorghis, fig. 462. (Mycenae.)
Archaeology, VIII (1955), p. 246, fig. 3. (Chios.)
Furtwängler, A., and Loeschke, G. *Mykenische Vasen* (Berlin, 1886),
    Fig. 20. (Asia Minor.)
Richter, *Met. Mus. Gk. Coll.*, pl. 9, top right. (Provenance unknown.)
Ibid. pl. 8i. (Provenance unknown.)

Faience, etc.

Forbes, A. J. *Studies in Ancient Technology*, V (Leyden, 1957), p. 110.
Stone, J. F. S., and Thomas, L. C. *Proc. Prehist. Soc.* (1956), p. 37.
Perachora, II, p. 461.
Scientific American (November 1963).
Archaeology, XXI (1968), p. 98.
AJA, LXXIII (1969), p. 435.

Gilt terracotta

NS (1940), p. 488, fig. 54.
AE (1937), Pt 3, p. 892.
BMCJ, p. xxxix; pl. 42.
Coldstream, J. N. *Knossos : The Sanctuary of Demeter* (London, 1973)
    p. 171.

6 Greece and the Cyclades 3000–1700 BC

GENERAL

Hood, *APG*, p. 188.
Renfrew, *Emergence, passim.*

Wace, A. J. B., and Blegen, C. W. *Symbolae Osloenses*, IX (1930), p. 28. (Middle Helladic.)

SITES

Troadic

TROY. Schliemann, H. *Ilios* (London, 1880); Schmidt, H. *Schliemann's Sammlung Trojanischer Altertümer* (Berlin, 1902); *Troy*, I and II. First City, *c.* 3000–2000. Second City, *c.* 2500–2200. Third to Fifth Cities, 2200–2000.

TROAD. *Expedition*, VIII (1966), p. 26.

LEMNOS, Poliochni. *Ann.*, XVII–XVIII (1955–6), pl. 5; *ILN*, 3 August 1957. Destroyed *c.* 2200.

LESBOS, Thermi. Lamb, W. *Excavations at Thermi* (Cambridge, 1936). Destroyed *c.* 2200.

Early Cycladic

PAROS, ANTIPAROS, DESPOTIKO. Graves. *AE* (1898), p. 155, pl. 8. 3000–2500.

SYROS, Chalandriani. Graves and citadel. *AE* (1899), p. 77; pl. 10, and p. 123; Sandler, L. F. (ed.), *Essays in Memory of Karl Lehmann* (New York, 1964), p. 63. 2500–2200.

AMORGOS, Dokathismata. Graves. *AE* (1898), p. 154, pl. 8. 2500–2200.

AMORGOS, Kapros, Grave D. *AM*, XI (1886), p. 16; Beil. 1. 2500–2200.

NAXOS. Renfrew, *Emergence*, p. 332.

NAXOS, Louros. Grave. *A. Delt.*, XVII (1961–2), A, p. 104. 2600–2500.

Early Helladic

ZYGOURIES.
Grave 7. Blegen, *Zygouries*, p. 180; pl. 20: 7. *c.* 2000.
Grave 20. Ibid. p. 180; pl. 20: 8, 9.
Houses A and D. Ibid. pp. 183–4; pl. 20: 16, 17.

ASINE. *Asine*, p. 258, fig. 182: 1. 2200–2000.

THYREATIS. Treasure. Greifenhagen, *Schmuckarbeiten*, I, p. 37; pls 1 and 2. As Troy II: 2500–2200.

THEBES. 'Tomb of Zethos'. *AAA*, V (1972), p. 16. 2500–2200.

LEUKAS, Steno. Round graves. Dörpfeld, W. *Alt-Ithaka* (Munich, 1927), p. 217; Beil. 60, 61; *BSA*, LXX (1975), p. 37.

Middle Helladic to 1700

GONIA. Grave 7. *MMS*, III, p. 78; fig. 35.

ZYGOURIES. Grave 1. Blegen, *Zygouries*, pp. 39, 202; fig. 189.

ARGIVE HERAEUM (Prosymna). Graves 17 and 18. Blegen, *Prosymna*, pp. 41, 265.

LERNA. Habitation. *Hesperia*, XXV (1956), pl. 47; XXVI (1957), pl. 42.

ASINE. Grave MH 98. *Asine*, p. 258; fig. 182.

HAGIOS STEPHANOS. Burial 23. *BSA*, LXVII (1972), p. 217.

APHIDNA. Graves 1 and 3. *AM*, XXI (1896), p. 385.

ELEUSIS. Graves. Mylonas, *To dytikon nekrotapheion*, pls 27, 51, 102.

SESKLO. Graves 7, 25 and 28. Wace, A. J. B. and Thompson, M. S. *Prehistoric Thessaly* (Cambridge, 1912), p. 66.

DIMINI. Grave 61. Ibid. p. 82.

DRACHMANI (Elatea). Grave. *AE* (1908), p. 94; fig. 16. 2000–1900.

7 Crete: Prepalatial

GENERAL

Hood, *APG*, p. 188.
Seager, *Mochlos, passim*.

SITES

MOCHLOS. Collective burials. Tombs 1, 2, 4, 6, 16, 19, 21. Seager, *Mochlos*; *BSA*, LXX (1975), p. 101 (re-excavation of Tomb 6). 2500–2000.

ARCHANES. Tomb 3. *PAE* (1972), p. 338; pl. 284. 2200–2000.

HAGIA TRIADA. Tholos B. *Ann.*, XIII–XIV (1930–1), p. 194; fig. 63. 2500–1700. Jewellery as at Mochlos: 2500–2000.

KAVOUSI. Tomb. Hall, *Vrokastro*, p. 184; fig. 107. 2500–2000.

KRASI. Tomb. *A. Delt.*, XII, p. 120; fig. 14. 3000–1900.

LEBENA. Tholos I (Papoura). *ILN*, 6 August 1960. 3000–1900.

PLATANOS. Tholos A, lower level. Xanthoudides, p. 88; pls 15 and 57. 2500–2200.

SPHOUNGARAS. Cemetery ('Early Minoan Deposit A'). Hall, *Sphoungaras*, p. 52, fig. 24. 2500–2200.

TRAPEZA. Cave. Collective burial. *BSA*, XXXVI (1935–6), p. 102; pl. 15. 2500–2000.

8 Crete: Early Palatial

GENERAL

Hood, *APG*, pp. 190, 194.
Xanthoudides, *passim*.

SITES

DRAKONES. Tholos D. Xanthoudides, p. 76; pl. 43. 2000–1700.
KALATHIANA. Tholos K. Xanthoudides, p. 81; pl. 8. 2500–1700.
KNOSSOS, Ailias. Tomb 5. Unpublished. 1800–1700.
KNOSSOS, Mavro Spelio. Pit in Tomb XVII. *BSA*, XXVIII (1926–7), p. 279. 1800–1700
KOUMASA. Tholos B. Xanthoudides, p. 3, pl. 4. 2500–1700.
MALLIA. Tomb. *Études Crétoises*, VII, p. 62; pl. 22, no. 557. 2000–1700.
PHAESTOS (Hagios Onouphrios). Burial deposit. Evans, A. J. *Cretan Pictographs and Prae-Phoenician Script* (London, 1895), p. 105; figs 89–98. 3000–1700.
PLATANOS. Tholos A, upper level. Xanthoudides, p. 88; pls 15 and 67. Jewellery in style of 2000–1900.
VOROU MESARAS. Tholos A. *A. Delt.*, XIII (1930–1), p. 137. 2100–1700.

9 Crete, Late Palatial, and Early Mycenaean

GENERAL

Demargne, P. *BCH*, LIV (1930), pp. 404–21.
Demargne, P. *RA*, VIII (1936), pp. 87–8.
Karo, *Schachtgräber*.
Mylonas, *Taphikos kyklos B*.
Marinatos and Hirmer.
Hood, *APG*, p. 194.

SITES

KNOSSOS.
Palace. Hieroglyphic Deposit. Evans, *Palace*, I, p. 271; Boardman, *GGFR*, p. 34. *c*. 1700.
Palace. Ivory Deposit. Evans, *Palace*, I, pp. 401, 411; fig. 274. 1700–1600.
Palace. Temple Repositories. Evans, *Palace*, I, p. 498, fig. 356. *c*. 1600.
Temple Tomb Deposit. Evans, *Palace*, IV, p. 963; col. pl. 34; Pendlebury, pl. 36. 1600–1500.
Mavro Spelio. *BSA*, XXVIII (1926–7), pp. 243–96. Tombs III, VII and IX. Communal burials, starting in the previous period, and continuing into the next.
Ailias. Tomb 7. *JHS*, LXXIV (1954), p. 166. 1700–1600.
Gypsades. Tomb 18. *BSA*, LIII–LIV (1958–9), p. 252; fig. 35; pl. 60b. 1700–1600.

POROS (near Heraklion). Tomb. *AAA*, I (1968), p. 254; *PAE* (1967), p. 195. Jewellery, 1600–1500.

MALLIA, Chrysolakkos. Communal tomb. *Études Crétoises*, VII, p. 25; *BCH*, LIV (1930), p. 404. 2000–1600. Jewellery probably 1700–1600.

PALAIKASTRO. House. *BSA*, IX (1902–3), pp. 280, 292. 1500–1450.

PALAIKASTRO. House. *BSA*, LX (1965), p. 303. 1500–1450.

GOURNIA. Settlement. Hawes, H. B. *Gournia, etc.* (Philadelphia, 1908), pl. 11, no. E14. Probably 1500–1450.

MOCHLOS. Tomb 22. Seager, *Mochlos*, p. 78; fig. 41; pl. 10. Jewellery, 1700–1500.

HAGIA TRIADA. Tomb 5. *MA*, XIV (1904), p. 723. Jewellery, style of 1500–1450.

PYRGOS. Larnax burial. Evans, *Palace*, II, p. 75, fig. 34. 1600–1500.

SPHOUNGARAS. Pithos burials. Hall, *Sphoungaras*, p. 68. 1600–1500.

THERA, Akroteri. Settlement. Marinatos, S. *Excavations at Thera*, V (Athens, 1972), p. 33; pls 77b, 78a. 1550–1500.

AEGINA. 'The Aegina Treasure'. Tomb robbers' hoard. *JHS*, XIII (1892–3), p. 195; *BMCJ*, XIX, p. 51, nos 683–768; *BMCR*, nos 690–3, 888; *BSA*, LII (1957), p. 42; Higgins, R. *The Aegina Treasure* (London, 1979). Minoan, 1700–1500.

KYTHERA, Kastri.

Deposit. *Kythera*, p. 208, pl. 59. 1500–1450.

Unstratified jewellery. *Kythera*, pl. 84M.

MYCENAE.

Grave Circle B. Mylonas, *Taphikos kyklos B.* Graves with jewellery: 1700–1600, Alpha, Beta, Iota, Nu, Xi, Upsilon; 1600–1500, Gamma, Epsilon, Lambda, Omicron.

Grave Circle A. Karo, *Schachtgräber*. Shaft Graves I–VI. 1600–1500.

Acropolis Treasure. *BSA*, XXXIX (1938–9), p. 65. 1500–1450.

TIRYNS. Chance discovery (two diadems). *AA* (1940), p. 220.

ARGOS, Kaza property. Tomb I. *A. Delt.*, XXVIII (1973), B, p. 102; pl. 100. 1700–1600.

CORINTH. Graves 2 and 3. *Corinth*, XIII, pp. 3, 7–8. 1700–1600.

PYLOS, Englianos.

Tholos IV. *Palace of Nestor*, III, p. 95, figs 190–2. Tomb, 1600–1300; jewellery, 1600–1500.

Grave circle. *Palace of Nestor*, III, p. 134, fig. 225. 1600–1400; jewellery, 1600–1500.

PERISTERIA.

Tholos Tomb 1. *PAE* (1965), p. 113; pl. 129. 1600–1450.

Tholos Tomb 3 *PAE* (1965), p. 114, pls 134–43. 1600–1500.

KAKOVATOS. Tholos Tombs A, B, C. *AM*, XXXIV (1909), pp. 269–328. 1500–1450.

THEBES. Shaft grave. *AAA*, I (1968), p. 10. *c.* 1600.
SKOPELOS. Chamber tomb. *Kr. Chr.*, III (1949), p. 534. 1550–1450.

10 The Mycenaean Empire

GENERAL

Blegen, *Prosymna*, p. 264.
Wace, *Chamber Tombs.*
Wace, A. J. B. *Mycenae* (Princeton, NJ), 1949.
Marinatos and Hirmer.
Hood, *APG*, p. 194.

WORKSHOPS, MOULDS, ETC.

See p. 198.

SITES

KNOSSOS.
Sellopoulo. Tomb 4. *BSA*, LXIX (1974), p. 199. 1425–1400.
Mavro Spelio. *BSA*, XXVIII (1926–7), p. 243. Tombs III, VII and
  IX continued in use from the previous period, probably down to
  c. 1150.
Gypsades. Tomb 7. *BSA*, LIII–LIV (1958–9), pp. 248, 235; fig. 34,
  pl. 60. 1200–1100.
Tomb. *Survey*, no. 149; *BSA*, LI (1956), p. 68. 1450–1400.
Kephala Ridge. 'Tomb of the Alabaster Vase'. *BSA*, LI (1956), p. 79;
  pl. 57a.
KNOSSOS, Isopata Cemetery.
Royal Tomb. Evans, PTK, p. 136. 1450–1425.
Tomb 1. Evans, *TDA*, p. 10; fig. 16. 1450–1425.
Tomb 2 ('Tomb of Double Axes'). Evans, *TDA*, p. 33. 1425–1400.
KNOSSOS, Zapher Papoura Cemetery. Evans, *PTK*. Tombs 7 (1425–
  1400), 21 (1400–1300), 36 (1450–1400), 66 (1400–1300), 75 (no
  dating material), 97 (no dating material), 99 (1300–1200).
KNOSSOS, Palace. Destruction level. Evans, *Palace*, III, p. 412. *c.* 1375.
ARCHANES.
Tholos 1. Side chamber, larnax burial *A. Delt.* (1966), B, p. 412;
  ILN, 26 March 1966. 1350–1325.
Tholos 4. *Ergon* (1975), p. 163; *PAE* (1975), Pt II, p. 260. 1325–1300.
PHAESTOS, Kalyvia Cemetery. *MA*, XIV (1904), p. 505. 1425–1300.
PHAESTOS, Liliana Cemetery. *MA*, XIV (1904), p. 627. 1200–1100.

KAMILARI, Gligori Korifi. Tholos tomb. *Ann.*, XXIII–XXIV (1961–2), p. 98; pl. IV. 1900–1600. Reused 1400–1300 (the date of the gold jewellery).

OLOUS.

Tomb 22. *Études Crétoises*, VIII, pl. 36. 1300–1200.

Tomb 16. Ibid. pl. 47. 1300–1200 (?).

GOURNES. Tomb 1. *A. Delt.*, IV (1918), p. 69; fig. 12. 1300–1200.

PACHYAMMOS. Chamber tomb. *Kr. Chr.*, VIII (1954), p. 399; *BCH*, LXXVI (1952), p. 242. 1400–1200.

PHOTOULA. Tomb. *PAE* (1960), p. 305; pl. 244. 1200–1100.

MOULIANA. Tomb. *AE* (1904), p. 50; fig. 13. 1200–1100.

MYCENAE.

Treasury of Atreus. *BSA*, XXV (1921–3), p. 338; figs 74–6. *c.* 1300.

Tomb of Clytaemnestra. *BSA*, XXV (1921–3), p. 357; figs 78, 79, 81. 1300–1250 (?).

Tomb of the Genii. *BSA*, XXV (1921–3), p. 376; figs 86–9. 1500–1400.

Chamber tombs 1–52. Briefly published *AE* (1888), p. 119. Jewellery in Tombs 2, 8, 25, 28, 31, 42.

Chamber tombs 53–103. Unpublished, except Tombs 91 and 102, for which see Deutsche Forschungsgemeinschaft, *Kretisch-Mykenische Siegel*, p. 115, and *JHS*, XXIV (1904), p. 322. Jewellery in Tombs 55, 66, 68, 71, 75, 76, 78, 81, 84, 88, 91 (1450–1425); 93, 94, 102 (1425–1400); 103.

Chamber tombs 501–24. Wace, *Chamber Tombs*. Jewellery in Tombs 502 (1400–1100), 515 (1450–1100), 518 (1500–1400), 520 (1400–1300), 523 (1400–1300), 524 (1400–1200).

Acropolis, 'Tsountas's House' (shrine?). *AE* (1887), p. 160; pl. 13. 1400–1200.

Acropolis, 'Prinaria Deposit'. *BSA*, LII (1957), p. 199; fig. 1; pl. 37. 13–1200.

ARGOS.

Tomb 6. *BCH*, XXVII (1904), p. 375. 1425–1400.

Tomb 7. Ibid. p. 387. No dating evidence.

ARGIVE HERAEUM (Prosymna).

Tholos. *BSA*, XXV (1921–3), p. 330; fig. 68. 1450–1425.

Chamber tombs. Blegen, *Prosymna*. Tombs 2 (1450–1350); 3, 19, 33, 37, 41 (all 1400–1200); 44, lower stratum (1550–1450); 44, upper stratum (1400–1200).

TIRYNS. 'The Tiryns Treasure'. Tomb robber's cache. *AM*, LV (1930), p. 119. 1400–1100.

DENDRA

Tholos. Persson, *Royal Tombs*, pp. 8–70. 1450–1400.

Tomb 2. Ibid. p. 73. 1300–1200.

Tomb 8. Persson, *New Tombs*, p. 37. 1500–1425.

Tomb 10. Ibid. p. 59. 1450–1400.

ASINE. Chamber tombs. *Asine*, p. 372. Tombs 1, 2, 5, 6. All in use from *c.* 1425–1100.

PYLOS.

Englianos. Tholos III. *Palace of Nestor*, III, p. 73, fig. 169. 1500–1200.

Englianos. Tholos IV. *Palace of Nestor*, III, 95, figs 190–2. 1600–1300.

Englianos. Shaft grave under Palace. *Palace of Nestor*, I, p. 312. 1450–1400.

Tragana. Tholos II, Pit 3. *PAE* (1955), p. 249. 1400–1300.

Rutsi (Myrsinochorio). Tholos II. *ILN*, 6 and 27 April 1957; *PAE* (1956), p. 202, pls 97 ff. 1500–1425.

NICHORIA. Tholos tomb. *Hesperia*, XLIV (1975), p. 76, pl. 20. *c.* 1300.

VAPHEIO. Tholos tomb. *AE* (1889), p. 130, pl. 7; Popham, M. R. *Proceedings of the Third Cretological Congress*, I (Athens, 1973), p. 268. 1500–1400. Most of the jewellery is 1425–1400.

ATHENS, Agora. Chamber tombs. *Athenian Agora*, XIII (1971). Tombs 1 (1425–1400), 3 (1400–1300), 8 (1400–1300), 9 (1425–1400), 14 (1400–1300), 16 (1450–1425), 21 (1425–1400).

ATHENS, Philopappos. Tomb. *Athenian Agora*, XIII (1971), p. 97; *AJA*, XXXVI (1932), p. 64. 1500–1400 (?)

ATHENS, Koukaki. Tomb. Unpublished. (National Museum, nos 7742–9, etc.)

MENIDI. Tholos tomb. Lolling, H. G. *Das Kuppelgrab bei Menidi* (Athens, 1886). 1300–1200.

SPATA. Chamber tomb. *Athenaion*, VI (1887), p. 167; *BCH*, II (1878), p. 185. 1350–1250.

PERATI. Chamber tombs. Iakovidis, S. *Perati : to nekrotapheion* (Athens, 1969–70). Tombs 1, 9, 10, 11, 13, 16, 49, 92, 136, 145, 147, 152, 157; S14, S19, S26, S51. 1200–1100.

THEBES. Kolonaki. Chamber tombs. *A. Delt.*, III (1917), p. 133. Tombs 4 (1350–1250), 15 (1400–1300 and 1200–1100), 19 (1300–1200), 21 (1400–1300), 25 (1300–1200).

THEBES, Palace. *PAE* (1927), p. 43; figs 7 and 8; *ILN*, 28 November 1964, p. 859. Shortly before 1400.

CHALKIS. Chamber tombs. *BSA*, XLVII (1952), p. 49. 1400–1150.

GRITSA. Tomb. *PAE* (1951), p. 148. 1200–1100.

VOLO (ancient Iolkos). Tholos tomb. *AE* (1906), p. 211. 1450–1400.

KEPHALLENIA. Tombs. *AE* (1932), pp. 2–47. 1200–1100..

NAXOS, Grotta, Aplomata.

Tomb 1. *PAE* (1958), p. 228. Mostly 1200–1100.

Tomb 2. *PAE* (1959), p. 180. Mostly 1200–1100.

Tomb 3. *PAE* (1969), p. 139. Mostly 1200–1100.

NAXOS, Grotta, Kamini. Tombs 1–5. *PAE* (1960), p. 329; *A. Delt.*, XVI (1960), B, p. 250. 1200–1100.

SAMOS, Myloi. Chamber tomb. *BCH*, LXXXV (1961); *Arch. Rep.* (1961–2), p. 23. 1400–1300.

MILETUS. Chamber tombs. Greifenhagen, *Schmuckarbeiten*, I, p. 27; pl. 7: 1–4. 1250–1150.

IALYSUS.

'Old Tombs' (British Museum). Furtwängler, H. and Loeschke, G. *Mykenische Vasen* (Berlin, 1886), pp. 1–18, pls A–C. Tombs 4 (1300–1200), 13 (1200–1100), 16 (1400–1300), 19 (1425–1300), 20 (1425–1300), 37 (1425–1300), 38 (1400–1300).

'New Tombs' (Rhodes). *Ann.*, VI–VII (1923–4), p. 86, followed by *Ann.*, XII–XIV (1930–1), p. 253. Tombs 4 (1400–1300), 5 (1300–1200), 17 (1200–1100), 20 (1200–1100), 28 (1300–1200), 31 (1400–1300), 32 (1200–1100), 42 (1200–1100), 53 (1300–1200), 61 (1200–1100), 62 (1400–1300); 67, 70, 71, 80, 83, 84, 87 (1200–1100).

ENKOMI. 'Old Tombs'. *Excav. in Cyprus.* Tombs 19 (1300–1200); 58, 61 (1200–1100); 65, 67, 69, 93 (1425–1300).

ENKOMI. Unstratified. Pierides, *Jewellery in Cyprus Mus.*, p. 17, pl. VIII: 2.

KOUKLIA (Old Paphos). Tomb 8. *BCH*, XCII (1968), p. 162. 1200–1150.

11 The Dark Ages

GENERAL

Kerameikos, V, Pt 1, pp. 183–97.
Desborough, *GDA*.
Snodgrass, A. M. *The Dark Age of Greece* (Edinburgh, 1971).

SITES

ATHENS, Cerameicus.

SM Grave 46. *Kerameikos*, I, pp. 24, 86; *AM*, LI (1926), p. 137; Beil. 6. 1100–1050.

Other SM Graves, with bronze jewellery. *Kerameikos*, I, p. 85.

PG Grave 5. *Kerameikos*, I, pp. 97, 183, 220; pl. 76; Desborough, *PGP*, pp. 24, 49, 79. 1075–1025.

PG Grave 22. *Kerameikos*, IV, pp. 24, 32; pl. 39; Desborough, *PGP*, p. 2. 1075–1025.

PG Grave 25. *Kerameikos*, IV, pp. 25, 33; pl. 39; Desborough, *PGP*, p. 8. 1075–1025.

PG Grave 39. *Kerameikos*, IV, pp. 26, 39; pl. 39; Desborough, *PGP*, p. 37. 1000–900.

SM Grave N 136. Unpublished. 1100–1050.

ATHENS, Agora.

Grave Q8: 6. *Hesperia* XXIII (1954), p. 58; *Athenian Agora*, XIV, pl. 19c. c. 1000.

Grave F9: 1. *Hesperia*, VI (1937), p. 364; fig. 30. c. 1000.

ATHENS, Erechtheum Street.

Grave 1 (1955). Unpublished, but see *Arch. Rep.* (1955), p. 7. 1075–1025.

Grave 7. *A. Delt.*, XXIII (1968), B, p. 56, pl. 31. 1100–1050.

ATHENS (?). The Elgin Jewellery. *British Museum Quarterly*, XXIII (1961), p. 101. Jewellery of 1100–700.

SALAMIS. Graves. *AM*, XXXV (1910), p. 30. 1100–1050.

CORINTH. Grave. *Hesperia*, XXXIX (1970), p. 12. 1100–1050.

TIRYNS. Prison Cemetery. *AM*, LXXVIII (1963), pp. 1–62. Graves 6 (tenth century), 13a (*c.* 1050), 13b (1100–1050), 28 (*c.* 1050).

ARGOS. Phlessas, Grave 5. *A. Delt.*,XVI (1960), B, p. 93; pl. 71. Tenth century.

ASINE. Tomb no. 1970. 15. *Asine*, II, pp. 16 and 18; fig. 24. Tenth century.

VERGINA. Graves. Andronikos, *Vergina*. 1000–800.

HOMOLION. Tombs 1 and 3. *A. Delt.*, XVII (1961–2), B, p. 175, pl. 195b; Desborough, *GDA*, p. 214. c. 900.

SAURIA (Agrinion). Pithos burial. *A. Delt.*, XXII (1967), B, p. 323; pl. 231b. Tenth century.

LEFKANDI. *Lefkandi*, I; Desborough, *GDA*, pp. 67, 188. Skoubris, Tombs 2, 3, 4, 5, 7 (1100–1050); Palaia Perivolia, Tombs 25B (1000–950), 24 (950–900).

SKYROS, Themis. Grave. *AA* (1936), p. 228. 1000–900.

SKYROS, Magazia. Cemetery, *BCH*, LXI (1937), p. 473; *BCH*, XCIX (1975), p. 365. 1000–700.

KNOSSOS, Medical Faculty Cemetery. Grave 200. *Arch. Rep.* (1978–9), p. 46. 1100–1050.

KNOSSOS, Gypsades. Tomb 7. Desborough, *GDA*, p. 116. 1100–1050.

KNOSSOS, Hagios Ioannis. Tomb 5. Desborough, *GDA*, p. 232. c. 900.

KNOSSOS, Tekke. Tomb J. *Arch. Rep.* (1976–7), p. 12. 950–900.

KNOSSOS, Fortetsa. Tombs 6 and 11. Brock, *Fortetsa*. 950–900.

VROKASTRO, Karakovilia. Chamber Tomb 1. Hall, *Vrokastro*, p. 138. Tenth century.

NAXOS, Tsikalario. Cremation. *A. Delt.*, XVIII (1963), B, p. 279; pl. 325. Tenth century.

KOS, Serraglio Cemetery. Unpublished, but see Desborough, *GDA*, p. 176. Tenth century.

ASSARLIK. Tomb B. *JHS*, VIII (1887), p. 69; *BMCJ*, nos 1214–15.
Tenth century.

12 The period of Oriental influences

GENERAL

Coldstream, *GG, passim.*
Reichel, *passim.*
Ohly, *passim.* (Attic.)
BSA, XIV (1969), p. 143.
Laffineur. (Rhodian and Cycladic.)

SITES

Attica

ATHENS, Cerameicus.
Geom. Grave 7. *Kerameikos*, V (1), p. 214; pl. 159. 900–875.
Geom. Grave 41. Ibid. p. 235; pl. 159. *c.* 850.
Geom. Grave 50. Ibid. p. 243; pl. 158. 760–735.
Geom. Grave 72. Ibid. p. 259; pl. 158. *c.* 735.
Grave 290. *A. Delt.*, XVIII (1963), B, p. 29; pl. 29b. 750–735.
Grave 291. *AA* (1964), p. 463, fig. 53. 735–720.
Peiraeus Street. Grave (Berlin). Greifenhagen, *Schmuckarbeiten*, I,
p. 19; pls 3:1, 2:4, and 4:2 and 3.
ATHENS, Agora.
Grave D16: 2. *Hesperia*, XVIII (1949), p. 288; pl. 72. 900–875.
Grave H16: 6. *Hesperia*, XXXVII (1968), p. 77; pl. 32. *c.* 850.
ATHENS, Erechtheum Street. Grave 6. *A. Delt.*, XXIII (1968), B, p. 55;
pl. 31a. 875–850.
ATHENS, Erysichthon–Neleus Streets. Graves 4 (no date); 6, 7, 9
(735–720). *A. Delt.*, XXII (1967), B, p. 80; pls 78–80.
ATHENS, Kavalotti Street. Graves 4 and 5. *A. Delt.*, XX (1965), B, p. 75;
pl. 44. 850–800.
ATHENS, Kriezi Street. Graves 2 (*c.* 800), 7 (850–800), 12 (800–750),
14 (*c.* 800), 16 (750–700), 26 (760–750), 40 (*c.* 800), 106 (800–750).
AAA, I (1968), p. 20; *A. Delt.*, XXII (1967), B, p. 92; pl. 87.
ATHENS, Kynosarges Cemetery. *BSA*, XII (1905–6), p. 91; fig. 12
Eighth century.
ATHENS, Kynosarges Cemetery. Graves 3 (760–750), 9 and 12 (780–760),
18 and 19 (770–750). *AAA*, V (1972), p. 170; *A. Delt*, XXVII (1972),
B, p. 93; pl. 63.

ATHENS (?). The Elgin Jewellery. See above (p. 211).

ELEUSIS.

Isis Grave. *AE* (1898), p. 106; pl. 6:6; Reichel, no. 34. 800–775.

Grave A. *AE* (1898), p. 103, pl. 6:7; Reichel, no. 35. 825–800.

Child's grave (?). *AE* (1885), p. 179; pl. 9: 3–4; Reichel, no. 33; Ohly, pl. 17: 4; Coldstream, *GG*, p. 125, fig. 39a. *c.* 750 (?).

SPATA. Grave 3. *A. Delt.*, VI (1920–1), p. 136; fig. 10; Reichel, no. 32; Coldstream, *GG*, p. 125; fig. 39b. *c.* 730.

ANAVYSOS. Graves 2 (800–750), 51 (*c.* 800). *A. Delt.*, XXI (1966), B, p. 97.

KOROPI. Grave group. *Collection Stathatos*, III, p. 127. 720–700.

BRAURON. Votive deposit. *Ergon* (1962), p. 30; fig. 37.

UNKNOWN SITE (now Los Angeles County Museum of Art). *AJA*, LXXIV (1970), p. 38.

The Peloponnese

CORINTH.

Grave C. *AJA*, XLI (1937), p. 544; fig. 6; *Corinth*, XII, nos 1808, 2000, 2264–5. *c.* 900 BC (?).

Grave F. *AJA*, XLI (1937), p. 545; fig. 7; *Corinth*, XII, nos 1803–7, 1999, 2258–61; Coldstream, *GG*, p. 174. *c.* 750.

Grave D. *Corinth*, XII, no. 1802. *c.* 750 (?)

'Grave group' (in Oxford). Jacobsthal, *Pins*, fig. 15.

'Grave group' (in Berlin). Greifenhagen, *Schmuckarbeiten*, I, pp. 21 ff.; pls 4 : 7–9, and 5 : 1–3. Eighth–seventh century (?).

KLENIA (ancient Tenea). Grave. *AJA*, LIX (1955), p. 126; pl. 40. fig. 14. 830–800.

PERACHORA.

Akraia Temple. *Perachora*, I, pl. 18. 800–720.

Limenia Temple. *Perachora*, I, pl. 84. 740 onwards.

ARGOS.

Grave 16 (875–825), 37 (875–825), 106: 1 (900–875). Courbin, P. *Tombes géométriques d'Argos* (Paris, 1974).

Grave 45 (Panoply Grave). *BCH*, LXXXI (1957), p. 385; fig. 66. Coldstream, *GG*, p. 146. 730–600.

Danaou Street Grave 1. *A. Delt.*, XXVII (1972), B, p. 192; pl. 134. 875–825.

Anapauseos Street. Graves. *BCH*, XCI (1967), 848; fig. 33. 900–700.

'Grave group' (in Athens). *Collection Stathatos*, I, nos 42–5. Style of *c.* 650.

TIRYNS. Prison Cemetery. Graves 7 and 15. *AM*, LXXVIII (1963), p. 1. *c.* 900.

AEGINA.
'Paspara'. Gold band, in Aegina. Unpublished.
North of town (?). *BMCJ*, nos 1217, 1218.
SPARTA.
Temple of Artemis Orthia. Dawkins, *Artemis Orthia*, p. 382; pls. 202–3. Mostly seventh century.
Menelaion. *BSA*, XV (1908–9), p. 142; pl. 8. 630–590.

Central Greece

LEFKANDI. Many graves from Skoubris, Toumba and Palia Perivolia cemeteries. *Lefkandi*, I. From before 900 to 825.
ERETRIA, West Cemetery. *AE* (1903), p. 8; *AM*, XXXVIII (1913), p. 290; Reichel, nos 25–8; Ohly, E1, 2, 4 and 5. Eighth century.
ERETRIA, West Gate Cemetery. Grave 14. Bérard, C. *Eretria, Fouilles et recherches*, III (Berne, 1970), p. 34. *c.* 700.
THEBES (Louvre). *Mon. Piot*, IX (1902–3), p. 148; Coche de la Ferté, pl. 10: 3 and 4; *BSA*, LXIV (1969), pl. 39a.
THEBES, Pyri. Grave. *AE* (1892), p. 219; pls 10–12. 700–675.
THEBES. Grave groups (East Berlin). Bouzek, J. *Forschungen und Berichte*, XVI (1965), p. 161. *c.* 700.
AMPHISSA. Grave. *A. Delt.*, XVIII (1963), B, p. 130; pls 164–5. 750–700
SKYROS, Magazia. Cemetery. *BCH*, XCIX (1975), p. 365. 1000–700.

Crete

KNOSSOS, Lower Gypsades. Tomb (1975). *Arch. Rep.* (1976–7), p. 17. Eighth and seventh centuries.
KNOSSOS, Tekke. Tomb 2 (Tholos). *JHS*, LXIV (1944), p. 84; pls 8–10; *BSA*, XLIX (1954), p. 215; pls 27–8; *BSA*, LXII (1967), p. 57; pls 7–12. *c.* 800.
KNOSSOS, Fortetsa. Tombs I (no date); II, burial 23 (850–825); II, burials 4, 8, 18 (*c.* 700); VII (no date); X, burial 14 (850–825); L (870–850); OD (850–825). Brock, *Fortetsa*.
KNOSSOS, Fortetsa. 'Metaxas Tomb'. *BSA*, LXX (1975), p. 169. *c.* 700.
ARKADES. Tomb L (eighth and seventh centuries), Tomb F1 (seventh century). Pithos 48 (seventh century). *Ann.*, X–XII (1927–9), *passim;* pl. XII.
IDAEAN CAVE. Votive deposit. *AJA*, XLIX (1945), p. 315; fig. 23. Eighth and seventh centuries.
PRAISOS.
Tomb A. *BSA*, VIII (1901–2), p. 243; figs 11–12. Not closely datable.
Tombs 9 and 31. *BSA*, XII (1905–6), pp. 63, 68; figs 3–4. Seventh century.

The Islands

CAMIRUS.
Kechraki. Grave 201. *Cl. Rh.*, IV, p. 350; fig. 388. 680–670.
Kechraki. Grave 210. *Cl. Rh.*, IV, p. 365; figs 409, 410. 625–600.
Papatislures. Grave 11. *Cl. Rh.*, VI–VII, p. 55; figs 53 and 58. 650–625.
Papatislures. Grave 13. *Cl Rh.*, VI–VII, p. 65; fig. 66. 625–600.
Chamber Tomb 82. *Cl. Rh.*, VI–VII, p. 199; fig. 239. *c.* 750.
Votive Deposit. *Cl. Rh.*, VI–VII, p. 340; fig. 86. Mostly seventh century.
Sporadic finds. *Cl. Rh.*, VI–VII, p. 210; figs 252–7.
Grave group (in Berlin). Greifenhagen, *Schmuckarbeiten*, I, pl. 7: 5–7.
IALYSUS.
Grave 23. *Cl. Rh.*, III, p. 53; fig. 44. 700–650.
Grave 45. *Cl. Rh.*, III, p. 73; figs 63–4. 625–600.
Grave 56. *Cl. Rh.*, III, p. 98; fig. 90. 730–710.
Grave 57. *Cl. Rh.*, III, p. 97. 730–710.
Grave 58. *Cl. Rh.*, III, p. 100. 730–710.
Grave 98. *Cl. Rh.*, III, p. 129; fig. 121.
Grave 107. *Cl. Rh.*, III, p. 135; fig. 128. Seventh century.
Grave 112. *Cl. Rh.*, III, p. 139. Seventh century.
LINDUS. 'Couches Archaïques'. *Lindos, I,* nos 270–94. Seventh and sixth centuries.
EXOCHI. Cemetery. *Acta Archaeologica,* XXVIII (1957), pp. 169–81; *AJA*, LXIII (1959), p. 398. Eighth century.
DELOS.
Near Artemision. *Délos,* XVIII, p. 291; fig. 342; pl. 87; fig. 740; no. A 296.
Hieron. *Délos,* XVIII, p. 303; fig. 371; pl. 88; fig. 766; no. A 785.
(Now in Berlin.) Greifenhagen, *Schmuckarbeiten*, I, pl. 10: 2 and 5.
MELOS.
Grave. *BSA*, II (1895–6), p. 75. Seventh century.
Grave(?). *ILN*, 27 April 1940; *AA*, LIII (1938), p. 125. Seventh century.
THERA. Grave 116. *AM*, XXVIII (1903), p. 225; pl. 5. Mid-seventh century.
TRALLES. Becatti, no. 149; *BCH*, III (1879), pls 4–5.
TOCRA. Deposit I. *Tocra*, I, p. 156; pl. 104: 1. Late seventh century.

Eastern Greece

EPHESUS, Artemision. Hogarth, *Ephesus*, pls 3–12; *BMCJ*, p. xxii; *JHS*, LXXI (1951), p. 85. Mostly seventh century.
EPHESUS. 'Grave group'. Greifenhagen, *Schmuckarbeiten*, I, pl. 8: 5–9. 650–600.
SAMOS, Heraeum. *AM*, LVIII (1933), p. 167; Reichel, no. 62. *c.* 670.

SAMOS, West Cemetery. Cremation Burial no. 6. *AAA*, II (1969), p. 203; fig. 3. 650–600.
ASSARLIK. Tomb C. *JHS*, VIII (1887), p. 71; figs 11–12; *BMCJ*, nos 1212–13, 1216; Coldstream, *GG*, p. 97. 800–750.
MYNDUS. *BMCJ*, no. 1245.

The West

SYRACUSE. Grave 404. *NS* (1895), p. 162. Seventh century.
MEGARA HYBLAEA. Grave 240. *MA*, I (1890), p. 890. Seventh century.
GELA. Grave 5. *MA*, XVII (1906), p. 34; fig. 2. Later seventh century.

13 Archaic and Classical

GENERAL

Artamonov, *Treasures*.
B. Met. Mus., XXXII (1973–4), no. 5. Exhibition Catalogue, *From the Lands of the Scythians*.

SITES

ATHENS. 'Tomb of Aspasia'. *JHS*, XXXVI (1916), pp. 258, 288. 450–400.
HALAE. Graves. *AJA*, XIX (1915), p. 425; *Hesperia*, XI (1942), p. 370. Later fifth century.
ERETRIA.
Graves 1–5. *AM*, XXXVIII (1913), p. 296. 475–425.
Grave. Papavasileiou, p. 78; pl. 12: 1.
Grave. *BMCJ*, nos 1653–4. 425–400.
PERACHORA. Limenia Temple. *Perachora*, I, pl. 84: 30, 45.
ISTHMIA.
Temple of Poseidon, Archaic Deposit. *Hesperia*, XXIV (1955), p. 138; pl. 56c. Sixth century.
Lambrou Cemetery. *A. Delt.*, XXIV (1969), B, p. 119; pl. 108. Sixth or fifth century.
DELPHI. Deposit. *BCH*, LXIII (1939), p. 86. Style of 600–550.
HOMOLION. Graves A and B. Miller, S. G. *Two Groups of Thessalian Gold* (Berkeley, Los Angeles, London, 1979), *c.* 350.
KOUTSOMITA. Grave. *Arch. Rep.* (1955), p. 19. 475–450.
MESAMBRIA (North Aegean). Burial jar. *PAE* (1970), p. 74; pl. 107. 375–350.
VERGINA (ancient Aegae). Tomb of Philip II. *AAA*, X (1977), p. 40;

Andronikos, M. *The Royal Graves at Vergina* (Athens, 1978). Shortly before 336.

OLYNTHUS. Robinson, D. M. *Olynthus*, X (Baltimore, 1941).

Graves. Fifth and fourth centuries to 348.

Houses. Shortly before 348.

THASOS. Votive deposit. *Arch. Rep.* (1957), p. 15; pl. 1a.

SAMOS. Grave 45. Boehlau, J. *Aus ionischen und italienischen Nekropolen* (Leipzig, 1898), pl. 15:13. Sixth century.

KNOSSOS, Demeter Sanctuary. Coldstream, N. J. *Knossos: The Sanctuary of Demeter* (London, 1973), p. 130. Fifth century BC to second century AD, some Classical jewellery.

TARRHA (Crete).

Trench 1, Grave 7B. *Hesperia*, XXIX (1960), p. 95: pl. 30a. Mid-fourth century.

Trench 8, Grave 1 (latest burial). Ibid. p. 96; pl. 32. Late fifth century.

IALYSUS, Marmaro Cemetery (1924–8). *Cl. Rh.*, III, pp. 111 ff. Graves 74 (early sixth century), 153 (late fifth century), 155 (early fourth century), 157 (mid-fourth century), 189 (500–475), 254 (*c.* 530).

IALYSUS, Marmaro Cemetery (1934). *Cl. Rh.*, VIII, pp. 105 ff. Graves 5, 10 (mid-sixth century); 35 (later sixth century); 41 (sixth century); 42 (sixth century).

LINDUS. 'Couches Archaïques'. See p. 215. Before 550.

RHODES. Grave 4. *Cl. Rh.*, VI–VII, p. 450; figs 5 and 9. 400–350.

XANTHUS. Unstratified find. Demargne, P. *Fouilles de Xanthos*, I (Paris, 1958), pl. 4; no. 2102.

IASUS. Tombs X and Y. *Boll. d'Arte*, XLIX (1964), p. 206. Style of fifth and fourth centuries.

GORDION. Tumulus burial. *Archaeology*, III (1950), p. 199; figs 5 and 6. *c.* 560.

TARENTUM.

Via Mazzini. Grave. Becatti, no. 313. Sixth century.

Via Principe Amedeo. Grave. Becatti, no. 380. Fourth century.

Via Cagliari. Grave. *AA*, LXXI (1956), p. 203; fig. 4. No dating evidence.

Grave 52. *NS* (1936–7), p. 139; fig. 30. *c.* 350.

CRISPIANO. Grave (?). Becatti, nos 326, 347, 388. Fourth century.

ROCCANOVA. Grave. Becatti, no. 423. Fourth century.

METAPONTUM. Grave. Breglia, nos 74–8. Style of fourth century.

CUMAE. Grave 126. *MA*, XXII (1913), p. 596; Breglia, pl. 9. Mid-fourth century.

MEGARA HYBLAEA.

Grave 16. *MA*, I (1890), p. 806. Sixth century.

Grave 165. *MA*, I (1890), p. 863. Sixth century.

Grave C. *NS* (1954), p. 87,; fig. 9:5. Sixth century.

Grave D. *NS* (1954), p. 90; figs 12, 13. Mid-sixth century.

GELA. Grave 60. *MA*, XVII (1906), p. 50; fig. 22. 550–525.

AVOLA (Sicily). Hoard. *Atti e memorie d. Instituto Ital. d. numis.*, III, p. 25; London, nos 1923. 4–21.1 to 3 and 1963. 2–26.1 (unpublished). 400–350 (?).

OLBIA.

Tomb 81. *AA* (1912), p. 353; figs 41–3. 550–500.

Tomb. *AA* (1914), p. 243; fig. 60; Artamonov, *Treasures*, p. 37; pl. 84. 550–500.

Tomb. *AA* (1914), p. 243; fig. 61. Style of 550–500.

Tomb 76, principal grave. *AA* (1913), p. 198; fig. 39. Style of *c*. 350.

KERCH, Kekuvatsky Tomb. *ABC*, p. 21; Artamonov, *Treasures*, p. 72; pls 268, 269, fig. 141. Early fourth century.

KERCH, Kul Oba. *ABC*, *passim*; Minns, p. 195; Artamonov, *Treasures*, p. 67; pls 199–264. Style of early fourth century.

KERCH, Pavlovsky Barrow. *CR* (1859), pl. 3; Rostovtzeff, *Sk. u. B.*, p. 178; Artamonov, *Treasures*, p. 73; pls 273–8. 340–330.

NYMPHAEUM.

Tombs (Leningrad). *CR* (1877), p. 220; pl. 3; Minns, p. 208, fig. 106; Artamonov, *Treasures*, p. 38; pls 87–106. 450–425.

Tombs 1–5 (Oxford). *JHS*, V (1884), p. 62; Rostovtzeff, *Iranians*, p. 76. Vickers, M. *Scythian Treasures in Oxford* (Oxford, 1979), 450–400.

TAMAN, Great Blisnitza. Minns, p. 423; Artamonov, *Treasures*, p. 73; pls 266–7, 271, 279–315; *CR* as below. Four tombs with jewellery: 'Priestess of Demeter'. *CR*(1865), pls 1–3. 350–325.

'Third Lady'. *CR* (1869), pp. 1–3. 350–325.

'Man's Tomb'. *CR* (1866), pls 1–2. 350–325.

'Burnt Grave'. *CR* (1865), pl. 3. 335–325.

KUBAN. Seven Brothers. Minns, p. 208; fig. 106; Artamonov, *Treasures*, p. 39; pls 107–37; figs 41–72. Tombs in Barrows 2 (475–425), 3 (400–375), 4 (475–450), 6 (450–400).

KUBAN. Kelermes Barrows. Artamonov, *Treasures*, p. 22; pls 4–55. 600–550.

ORDZHONIKIDZE. Tolstaya Mogila Barrow. *Sovietskaya Arkheologiya* (1972), no. 3, p. 268; *B. Met. Mus*, XXXII (1973–4), no. 5, p. 126. *c*. 350.

VELIKAYA BELOZERKA (Ukraine). Barrow burial. *Archaeology*, XXVI (1973), p. 223. Fourth century.

AMATHUS.

Old Tomb 256, Sarcophagus II. *Excav. in Cyprus*, p. 125; *BMCJ*, nos 1644–7. Fifth century.

Old Tomb 88. *Excav. in Cyprus*, p. 119; *BMCJ*, nos 1492, 1617–20 1783, 1784. Sixth to fourth centuries (?).

Old Tomb 211. *Excav. in Cyprus*, p. 123; *BMCJ*, nos 1641–2. Fifth century.

New Tomb 10. *SCE*, II, p. 69; pl. 17. 600–475.

LIMASSOL, Kapsalos. Grave. *BCH*, LXXXVIII (1964), p. 326; fig. 58. 475–400.

MARION.

Excavation of 1886. Tomb 131. Ohnefalsch-Richter, *Kypros*, p. 369; pls 33, 67, 144. *c.* 550.

Excavation of 1886. Tomb 24. Ibid. p. 368; pl. 33; nos 9–15. Ridder, A. de. *Collection de Clercq* (Paris, 1911), nos 1204, 1224, 1504–5, 1542, 1945–7. Fifth-fourth century.

New Tomb 41. *SCE*, II, p. 291; pl. 55. Fifth-fourth century.

New Tomb 46. *SCE*, II, p. 310; pl. 57. Early fourth century.

New Tomb 60. First burial period. *SCE*, II, p. 356; pl. 68. Early fourth century.

Tomb. *Arch. Rep.* (1958), p. 29; fig. 8. Fifth century.

CURIUM. Tomb 73. *Excav. in Cyprus*, p. 82. Fifth and fourth centuries.

VOUNI. Palace. Hoard. *SCE*, III, p. 238; pl. 89:14. Shortly before 380.

DOUVANLI. Tombs. Filow, B. D. *Die Grabhügelnekropole bei Duvanlij in Sudbulgarien* Sofia, 1934; Hoddinott, *Bulgaria in Antiquity*, p. 58. Tombs:

Moushovitsa. *c.* 500.

Koukova. Early fifth century.

Golyama. Mid-fifth century.

Arabadjiska. 450–425.

Bashova. 425–400.

VRATSA. Burial 2. Hoddinott, *Bulgaria in Antiquity*, p. 76. *c.* 340.

TREBENISHTE. Tombs. Filow, B. D. and Schkorpil, K. *Die archaische Nekropole von Trebenischte* (Berlin and Leipzig, 1927); *ÖJH*, XXVII (1932), pp. 1, 106; XXVIII (1933), p. 164; *AA* (1933), p. 459. Later sixth century.

VETTERSFELDE. Grave: Greifenhagen, *Schmuckarbeiten*, p. 61; pls 39–44. *c.* 500.

VIX. Tomb. Joffroi, R. 'Le Trésor de Vix', *Mon. Piot*, XLVIII (1954); Becatti, pl. D. Late sixth century.

14 Early Etruscan

GENERAL

Breglia, pp. 103–25.

Curtis, C. D. *MAAR*, I (1915–16), pp. 63–85.

Dohan, *Italic Tomb-Groups*. (Chronology.)

Karo, G. *St. e. Mat.*, I, pp. 233–83; II, pp. 97–147; III, pp. 143–58.

McIver, *Villanovans*.

Richter, *Etruscan Coll.*

Culican, W. *BSR*, XXIX (1971), p. 1.

Von Hase, F. W. *Hamburger Beiträge zur Archäologie*, V (1975), p. 99. (Origins.)

Idem. *Proceedings of the Tenth International Congress of Classical Archaeology* (Ankara, 1978), p. 1101. (Oriental influences.)

SITES

For poorly published and unpublished material (earrings only) from these and other sites, see Hadaczek, *passim*.

CAERE.

Regolini-Galassi Tomb. Pareti, L. *La Tomba Regolini-Galassi* (Rome, 1947). Mid-seventh century.

Banditaccia, Zone A, Tomb 10, 'Chamber of the Firedogs'. *MA*, XLII (1955), p. 342; fig. 72. 650–625.

PRAENESTE.

Bernardini Tomb. *MAAR*, III (1919), pp. 7–90. Mid-seventh century.

Barberini Tomb. *MAAR*, V (1925), p. 9–52. Mid-seventh century.

VEII, Tre Fontanili. Tomb 2. *NS* (1954), p. 3; fig. 3. Jewellery of seventh-century types.

TARQUINII. Tombs. See Hadaczek, pp. 57, 60. Sixth and fifth centuries.

VULCI.

Tomb(s) (in Munich). Karo, *St. e. Mat.*, II, pl. 2: 2–11; Pinza, G. *Etnologia Antica Toscano-Laziale* (Milan, 1915), p. 144; fig. 94; pl. 2; Montelius, *Civ. Prim. It.*, II, pl. 261. Jewellery of *c.* 650–625.

Polledrara Tomb ('Grotto of Isis'). *BMC Sculpture*, I, Pt 2 (1931), p. 155 and refs; Montelius, *Civ. Prim. It.*, II, pls 265–8. *c.* 625–575.

Tomb (in New York). Richter, *Etruscan Coll.*, fig. 106. Jewellery mostly in style of the later sixth century.

Tombs (in Vatican). *Museo Etrusco Vaticano*, I (Rome, 1842), pls 68–74. Jewellery from unspecified tombs, to be dated stylistically from the sixth to about the first century BC.

NARCE AND FALERII.

Tombs. Karo, *St. e. Mat.*, III, pp. 143–58; Montelius, *Civ. Prim. It.*, II, pls 307–31; *MA*, IV (1894–5), pp. 347–98. Seventh century.

Tombs 42M, 24M, 23M, 102F (in Philadelphia). Dohan, *Italic Tomb Groups*. About mid-seventh century.

BISENZIO. Tombs. *MA*, XXI (1912), pp. 404–98; *NS* (1928), pp. 434–67; McIver, *Villanovans*, pp. 170–4; pl. 32. Early seventh century?

ORVIETO.
Tombs. See Hadaczek, pp. 57, 60. Sixth and fifth centuries.
Tomb 26. *St. Etr.*, XXX (1962), p. 108, fig. 34. 540–515.
MARSIGLIANA D'ALBEGNA, Banditella Cemetery. Tombs 2, 10, 11, 14, 34, 39, 41, 63, 67, 94. McIver, *Villanovans*, pp. 181–92; pl. 35; Minto, A. *Marsigliana d'Albegna* (Florence, 1921), pls 11, 12 and 14. Mid-seventh century.
MARSIGLIANA D'ALBEGNA, Circle of Perazetta. McIver, loc. cit. ; Minto, op. cit. pl. 13. Jewellery of about mid-seventh century.
VETULONIA. Some twenty-seven groups of tombs; and other finds. The tombs listed below are the most important for the study of jewellery. *NS* (1887), pp. 471–531; Karo, *St. e. Mat.*, I, pp. 235–83; II, pp. 97–147; Karo, *St Etr.*, VIII (1934), pp. 49–57; Montelius, *Civ. Prim. It.*, II, pls 178–203; McIver, *Villanovans*, pp. 100–54.
Early group (perhaps 700–660):
Foreigner's Tomb.
Circle of the Bracelets.
Bes Circle.
Circle of the Oleasters.
Circle of the Silver Necklace.
Circle of Pellicie.
Acquastrini Circle.
Tumulus of Val di Campo.
Middle group (perhaps 660–640):
Tomb of the Prince.
Hoard of the Threshing-Floor (Aia Bambagini).
Tomb of the Lictor.
Late group (perhaps 640–620):
Circle of Migliarini.
Graves of La Pietreria.
POPULONIA.
'Tomb of the Intact Dome'. Minto, *Populonia*, p. 137; pl. 28; *NS* (1940), pp. 376–97. Late seventh and early sixth centuries.
'Tomb of the Bronze Fans'. Minto, *Populonia*, p. 139; pl. 30; *MA*, XXXIV (1931), p. 289. Late seventh and early sixth centuries.
CHIUSI. Pania Tomb. Montelius, *Civ. Prim. It.*, II, pls 224, 225; McIver, *Villanovans*, pp. 249–51. Late seventh century.
CAPANNORI. Tomb. *NS* (1893), p. 403. 475–450.
BOLOGNA. Certosa Cemetery. Zannoni, A. *Seavi della Certosa di Bologna* (Bologna, 1876); Montelius, *Civ. Prim. It.*, I, pl. 102; Alfieri, N. and others, *Ori e argenti dell Emilia antica* (Bologna, 1958), p. 37. 525–400. Most of the jewellery is from fifth-century tombs.
MARZABOTTO. Tombs. Gozzadini, G. *Un Antica necropoli* (Bologna,

1865); Gozzadini, G. *Di ulteriori scoperte nella necropoli a Marzabotto* (Bologna, 1870). Sixth century.

SPINA. Tombs. Alfieri and others, op. cit. pp. 43 ff:; Becatti, pl. H. Tombs with jewellery, nearly all *c.* 440–390.

CUMAE. Tomb 104 (Artiaco Tomb). *MA*, XIII (1903), pp. 225–63; Breglia, nos 3–12; Siviero, nos 3, 7–12; Randall-MacIver, D. *The Iron Age in Italy* (Oxford, 1927), p. 169; *Arch. Rep.* (1976–7), p. 44. 730–720.

RUVO. Tombs. Breglia iii, pls 3–6, Sixth-fifth century.

15 Late Etruscan

GENERAL

Breglia, pp. 103–25.
Richter, *Etruscan Coll.*

SITES

PRAENESTE. Tombs (Marini property). *NS* (1897), pp. 254–69. Fourth century.

CIVITAVECCHIA. Tomb E. *NS* (1941), p. 363, fig. 9. Early fourth century.

VULCI. Tombs (now in Vatican). *Museo Etrusco Vaticano*, I (Rome, 1842), pls 68–74, 78, 80, 81, 87–90; Becatti, nos 357, 359–62. Jewellery of *c.* sixth to first centuries BC. See above, p. 220.

POPULONIA.

Tombs. Minto, *Populonia*, pp. 182–3; pl. 47. Jewellery in style of fourth–third century.

Tombs. *NS* (1961), p. 96.

VOLTERRA, Monteriggioni. Family tomb of Calenii Sepus. *St. Etr.*, II (1928), pp. 133–76. *c.* fourth to first centuries BC.

VOLTERRA, unspecified tombs. Consortini, P. L. *Volterra nell' antichità* (Volterra, 1940). Late Etruscan jewellery.

PERUGIA.

Sperandio Tomb. *NS* (1900), p. 554; fig. 2; *JHS*, LXIX (1949), p. 12, n. 53. Fourth century.

Tombs. Shaw, C. *Etruscan Perugia* (Baltimore, 1939), p. 84. Jewellery of fourth–third century.

TODI, Peschiera.

Tomb 1 (in Villa Giulia). *MA*, XXIII (1914), pp. 613–38; Becatti, nos 341, 364, 410, 418. *c.* 300.

Tombs 9, 16 *bis* and 20 (at Florence). *St. Etr.*, IX (1935), pp. 287–303. Tombs 9 and 16 *bis*: third century. Tomb 20: *c.* 300.

CAPENA.
Tomb 179. *MA*, XLIV (1958), p. 175; fig. 48. Late Etruscan jewellery.
Tombs B and E. Ibid. p. 199; fig. 56. Fourth or third century.
SPINA. Tombs. See above, p. 222. Tombs 58 and 169 are of the fourth century.
MARZABOTTO. See p. 221.
ALERIA (Corsica). Tombs. Jehasse, J. and *L. La Nécropole préromaine d'Aléria* (Paris, 1973).

16 Hellenistic

GENERAL

Artamonov, *Treasures.*
Hoffmann and Davidson, *Greek Gold.*
Schreiber, pp. 293–311.

SITES

ATHENS, Lenormant Street. Grave L. *Hesperia*, VI (1937), p. 366; fig. 27. *c.* 150.
ATHENS, Cerameicus.
Incineration (urn no. 4). *AA* (1942), p. 244; figs 15–21; Kurtz and Boardman, pl. 39. Second century.
Sarcophagus no. 33. *AA* (1942), p. 239; fig. 15. Second century.
CORINTH. Hoard. *Corinth*, XII, no. 2055. Later fourth century.
THEBES. Tomb *AE* (1914), p. 128; fig. 9. *c.* 300.
ERETRIA.
Tomb. *AM*, XXXVIII (1913), p. 321; fig. 11; pls 14:6, 16:13. Third century.
'Family Tombs'. Papavasileiou, p. 51. Second–first century style.
'Tomb of the Erotes' (in Boston). *AE* (1899), p. 222; pl. II. Late third century.
Tomb group (in New York). Richter, *Met. Mus. Gk. Coll.*, p. 157. Later fourth century.
ELIS. Tomb of Euxene. *A. Delt.*, XXIV (1969), B, p. 153: pl. 153b. Early third century.
KNOSSOS. Demeter Sanctuary. See p. 217. Some Hellenistic jewellery.
DELOS.
House. *Délos*, XVIII, p. 300; fig. 368. Early first century.
House of Ambrosia. *BCH*, LXXXIX (1965), p. 503. Early first century.
House (Skardhana). *BCH*, XCII (1968), p. 523. Early first century.
RHENEIA. Tombs. *Délos*, XVIII, p. 88; fig. 764. Hellenistic jewellery.
ANTIKYTHERA. Shipwreck. *AE* (1902), p. 162; fig. 10; *AJA*, LXIV (1960), p. 183. 75–50.

IALYSUS, Marmaro. Tomb 32. *Cl. Rh.*, VIII, p. 154; fig. 140. Late fourth century (?).

SARDIS(?). Tomb group (in Pforzheim). Segall, B. *Zur griechischen Goldschmiedekunst des vierten Jahrhunderts v. Chr.* (Wiesbaden, 1966); see also Hoffmann and Davidson, *Greek Gold*, p. 17, and refs. Later fourth century.

KYME (Aeolis). Tomb(s)? *BMCJ*, p. xxxviii, nos 1612–14, 1632, 1662–5, 1670–3, 1709, 1844, 1889–90, 1936–42, 1944–6, 1953–6, 2002–7, 2010–12, 2036–7, 2059–61, 2082, 2097–2103; *BMCR*, nos 352, 577 (?) and 911. Late fourth century (?)

MADYTUS (Troad). Tomb (?). *B. Met. Mus.*, I (1906), p. 118. Jewellery of the later fourth century.

PERGAMON. Tomb. *AM*, XXXIII (1908), pl. 25: 1. Third century.

SYRIA. Tomb (?). *Archaeology*, VIII (1955), pp. 252–9. A collection of jewellery, now in Chicago, from an unidentified site in Syria. Second century (?)

SAMOTHRACE.

Tomb. *Archaeology*, XII (1959), p. 166; fig. 4. Late fourth century.

Tomb. Ibid. p. 166; fig. 5. Third century.

Tomb. Ibid. p. 170; fig. 13. Augustan period.

THESSALY, Demetrias (?). Tomb *Collection Stathatos*, I, nos 217–31. Jewellery of about the later fourth century.

THESSALY, Karpenisi (?). Tomb(s). Segall, nos 28–36; *Collection Stathatos*, I, nos 232–66. Second century(?).

PELINNA (Thessaly). Grave B. Miller, S. G. *Two Groups of Thessalian Gold* (Berkeley, Los Angeles, London, 1979). 200–150.

PALAIOKASTRO. Tomb (?) *AM*, XXXVII (1912), pp. 73–118; *AM*, l (1925), pp. 167–91. First century BC.

KOZANI. Tomb 1. *AE* (1948–9), p. 91; fig. 3. Late fourth century.

AMPHIPOLIS. Tomb. *Ergon* (1958), p. 73; fig. 76. Hellenistic.

SALONIKA.

Tomb. *Arch. Rep.* (1958), p. 13; fig. 15. Second century.

Tomb (?). *B. Met. Mus.*, XXXII (1937), p. 290; fig. 2. Jewellery of later fourth century.

Sedes. Tomb Gamma. *AE* (1937), Pt. 3, p. 866. Later fourth century.

DERVENI (ancient Lete) Graves 3, 4, 5. *A. Delt.*, XVIII (1963), B2, p. 193. 330–300.

ABDERA. Tomb (?) Greifenhagen, *Schmuckarbeiten*, I, p. 34; pls 13–15. Second century (?)

MOUNT PANGAEUS. Tomb (?) Greifenhagen, *Schmuckarbeiten*, I, p. 33; pls 12–13. Early third century (?).

KALLATIS (modern Mangalia). Tomb. Canarache, V. *The Archaeological Museum of Constanta*, p. 39. Second century (?).

ODESSUS (modern Varna).

Tumulus 1. *Bull. de la Société Archéologique de Varna*, X (1956), p. 100; pls 1: 1–3, 2: 1 and 3: 1. Fourth-third century.

Tumulus 2. Ibid. p. 100; pls 2: 2, 3: 1–4. Jewellery of fourth-third century type.

MESAMBRIA PONTICA (modern Nessebar). Tomb. Hoddinott, *Bulgaria in Antiquity*, p. 46; pls 20, 21. Second-century-type jewellery.

GALATA. Tumulus 6. *Bull. de la Société Archéologique de Varna*, VIII (1951), p. 60; figs 103, 112, 113. Fourth-third-century-style jewellery.

KAZANLAK. Tomb. Zhivkova, L. *The Kazanlak Tomb* (Recklinghansen, 1975), p. 25; fig. 6. Late fourth century.

ITHACA. Tombs. *Archaeologia*, XXXIII *AD*, I, p. 3; (1894), p. 36; Williams, *Gold and Silver Jewelry*, p. 147; pl. 18; *AD*, I, p. 3; pl. 12; Stackelberg, O. M. von. *Die Gräber der Hellenen* (Berlin, 1837), pls 73–4. Hellenistic.

SYRACUSE, Dammusi. Tomb. *NS* (1915), p. 187. Late fourth century.

SYRACUSE, Feudo. Hoard. *NS* (1915), p. 234; fig. 37. Late fourth century (?).

MORGANTINA. Cistern. *AJA*, LXI (1957), p. 158; pl. 60; fig. 28. Early second century.

GELA. Hoard. *MA*, XVII (1906), p. 539; fig. 371. *c.* 280.

TARENTUM.

Grave 86. *NS* (1936–7), p. 179; pl. 9: 6. Hellenistic.

Vaccarella, Grave 3. Becatti, no. 405. Third century.

Grave group (?) (in a Swiss collection). Hoffmann and Davidson, *Greek Gold*, p. 266, no. 124. Third or second century (?).

CANOSA. 'Tomb of the Gold Ornaments'. *Iapigia*, VI (1935), p. 225; Becatti, nos 353, 421, 427, 446–8. Third century.

SANTA EUFEMIA (Calabria). *BMCJ*, nos 2113–29; *BMCR*, no. 224; *Ant. Class.*, XLII (1973), p. 552. Early third century.

TRESILICO. Tomb *AA* (1914), p. 198; fig. 9. Third century.

CUMAE.

Tomb (?). *MA*, XXI (1913), p. 712; pl. 113. Jewellery of the late fourth or third century.

Tomb 157. *MA*, XXII (1913), p. 621; pls 114–16; Breglia, pl. 10. Late fourth century.

TEANO DEI SIDICINI. Tombs. *MA*, XX (1910), pp. 6–152, esp. p. 39. Late fourth and early third centuries.

VULCI.

François Tomb. Messerschmidt, F. *Nekropolen von Vulci* (Berlin, 1930), p. 103; figs 79–82. Family tomb, *c.* fifth to first centuries B C. Jewellery belongs stylistically to the end of this period.

Tombs (in Vatican). *Museo Etrusco Vaticano*, I (Rome, 1842), pl. 74.

Jewellery stylistically third to first centuries B C. See above, pp. 220 and 222.

VOLTERRA, Poggio alle Croce. Tomb A. *St. Etr.*, XXVII (1959), pp. 258 f. ; figs 6 and 7. 225–50 B C.

VOLTERRA, Monteriggioni. Family tomb of Calenii Sepus. *St. Etr.*, II (1928), p. 133. Fourth to first centuries B C. Urn 16, late third century.

PERUGIA. Tomb 30. Urn of Tannia Caia. Conestabile, G. *Monumenti di Perugia*, III (Perugia, 1855), p. 133; pl. 7–23, no. 9. *c.* second century B C.

BETTONA. Tomb. *NS* (1916), p. 16; fig. 19. Second century.

TODI, Peschiera. Tombs 9 and 20 (at Florence). Third century. See above, p. 222.

ANCONA.

Tomb 3. *NS* (1902), p. 460; fig. 29. Late fourth to first centuries.

Tomb 1. *NS* (1910), p. 349. Third–second century.

FILOTTRANO. Tombs. dall' Osso, I. *Museo Nazionale di Ancona* (Ancona, 1915), pp. 233, 234, 237, 285; Becatti, no. 303. *c.* fourth–third century.

MONTEFORTINO. Tombs 8, 23 and 32. *MA*, IX (1901), pls 3, 5 and 8. 300–250.

CURIUM.

Old Tomb 69. *Excav. in Cyprus*, p. 85; *BMCJ*, no. 1784. Late fourth century.

Old Tomb 80. *Excav. in Cyprus*, p. 83; *BMCJ*, nos 1728–9. Late fourth century.

MARION.

New Tomb 9. *SCE*, II, p. 206; pl. 38. 325–150.

New Tomb 58 (latest burial). *SCE*, II, p. 345. 345; pl. 64. 330–200.

New Tomb 60. *SCE*, II, p. 356; pl. 68. Early fourth century.

APHENDRIKA. Tomb 33. *R. D. Ant. Cyp.*, *1937–9*, p. 62; pl. 31: i (5). Third and early second centuries.

TOUKH-EL-QUARMOUS (Egypt). Tomb. Rostovtzeff, *SEHHW*, I, p. 390; pl. 47; *Collection Stathatos*, I, p. 82. *c.* 300.

TANIS (Egypt). House. Petrie, W. M. F. *Tanis*, I (London, 1885), p. 34; pl. 12: 45. First century B C.

KERCH, Quarantine Road. (The letters of identification given to these tombs are the present writer's.)

'Tomb A'. *ABC* p. 20; Schefold, *Meisterwerke*, p. 63. *c.* 330.

'Tomb B'. *ABC*, p. 35; Rostovtzeff, *Sk. u. B.*, p. 188. *c.* 250.

'Tomb C'. *ABC*, p. 20; *AdI* (1840), pls A-C; Rostovtzeff, *Sk. u. B.*, p. 186. *c.* 250 (?)

'Tomb D' *ABC*, p. 19; *AdI* (1840), pls A-C; Rostovtzeff, *Sk. u. B.*, p. 189. *c.* 250–225.

'Tomb E'. *ABC*, p. 19; *AdI* (1840), pls A-C; Schefold, *Meisterwerke*, p. 139.

TAMAN, Great Blisnitza. See p. 218. The graves of the 'Priestess' and the 'Third Lady' and the 'Man's Grave' overlap this period and the preceding. The 'Burnt Grave' falls entirely into this period; *c.* 330–320.

TAMAN, Artjukhov's Barrow. *CR* (1880), pls 1–4; Minns, p. 433; Rostovtzeff, *SEHHW*, III, p. 1411; *JRGZM*, V (1958), pp. 94 ff.; *Sovietskaya Arkheologiya*, no. 3 (1960), pp. 46–58. Second century.

TAMAN.

Tomb. *AA* (1913), p. 179; fig. 2; Jacobsthal, *Pins*, p. 70. Later fourth century.

Tomb. *AA* (1912), p. 335; fig. 19. Later fourth century.

KUBAN, Karagodeuashkh. Tomb. Minns, p. 217; Artamonov, *Treasures*, p. 79; pls 316–20. Later fourth century.

17 Roman

All dates in this section are AD.

GENERAL

Pfeiler.

Brailsford, *Antiqs of Roman Britain*.

Schreiber, pp. 293–311.

Coche de la Ferté, E. *Antique Jewellery from the Second to the Eighth Century* (Berne, 1962).

Vermeule, C. C. 'Numismatics in Antiquity: The Preservation and Display of Coins in Ancient Greece and Rome', *Revue Suisse de Numismatique*, LIV (1975), p. 5.

PRE-IMPERIAL ROME

Bloch, R. *The Origins of Rome* (London, 1960).

Gjerstad, E. *Early Rome*, II (Lund, 1956).

Ryberg, I. S. *An Archaeological Record of Rome from the Seventh to the Second Century* BC (London and Philadelphia, 1940).

TECHNIQUES

Gummerus, H. *Klio*, XV (1918), p. 256.

Roman Crafts, pp. 43 and 53.

MUMMY PORTRAITS AND PALMYRA SCULPTURES

Parlasca, K. *Mummienporträts und verwandte Denkmäler* (Wiesbaden, 1966).

Shore, *Portrait Painting*.

Mackay, D. 'The Jewellery of Palmyra and its Significance', *Iraq*, XI (1949), p. 160.

SITES

POMPEII AND HERCULANEUM. Houses. (1) Breglia and (2) Siviero, *passim*; Pfeiler, no. I. First century AD to 79.

BOSCOREALE. House. *Mon. Piot*, V, pp. 263–74; Pfeiler, nos III and IV. As for Pompeii and Herculaneum.

PETESCIA (Sabine Hills). Greifenhagen, *Schmuckarbeiten*, I, p. 77; pls 57–61. Early first century.

ROME. Sarcophagus of Crepereia Tryphaena. Becatti, no. 525; Pfeiler, no. XXVII. Sarcophagus in style of later second century.

ACAMPORE. Incineration. *Fasti*, I (1946), no. 1928; figs 61–3. Coins of second and third centuries.

ZARA. Tombs. *ILN*, 9 January 1932, p. 50; fig. 9. First century.

LYON. Tomb. Comarmond, A. *Description de l'écrin d'une dame romaine trouvé à Lyon en 1841* (Paris and Lyon, 1844); Pfeiler, no. XXXVI. Coins to 211.

VILLARDU. Sambon, A. *Collection de M. Guilhou: Objets antiques* (Paris, 1905). Lots 198–208. Third century.

BEAURAINS. Treasure, Bastien P. and Metger, C. *Le Trésor de Beaurains*. Wetteren, 1977. Early fourth century.

BONN. Girl's tomb. *Bonner Jahrbücher*, CLXI, p. 319. Mid-third century.

BACKWORTH. Tomb. *BMCJ*, nos 2738–40; *BMCR*, nos 451, 460, 461, 636, 943; Pfeiler, no. XIX. Coins to 139.

SOUTHFLEET. Child's grave. Brailsford, *Antiqs of Roman Britain*, p. 28; pl. 1: 7; *Jewellery Through 7000 Years*, no. 170. c. 300.

RHAYADER. Tomb. Brailsford, *Antiqs of Roman Britain*, pp. 14, 28. Uncertain date.

CARDIFF, Sully Moors. Tomb *BMCR*, nos 203, 544, 796–7. Coins to 306.

CARLISLE, Newtown. Tomb. Brailsford, *Antiqs of Roman Britain*, p. 28. Coins to 180.

CASTLETHORPE. Tomb. *Archaeologia*, XXXIII (1849), p. 348; *BMCR*, no. 1162. Coins, 138–69.

ILCHESTER. Tomb. *BMCR*, no. 267. Coins, 222–35.

NEW GRANGE. Tomb. *Archaeologia*, XXX (1844), p. 137; pl. 12; *BMCJ*, nos 2744, 2795–6. c. 200.

SLAY HILL SALTINGS (Kent). Tomb. *BMCR*, nos 1164–6. Coins of Marcus Aurelius (161–80).

ATHENS.

Tomb. *Hesperia*, VI (1937), p. 366; fig. 27. Roman date.

Bathing establishment. *Hesperia*, XVIII (1949), p. 226; pl. 46: 6, 7, 8. Before 300.

NEA ANCHIALOS. Tomb I. *A. Delt.*, XXIV (1969), B, p. 230, pl. 230. Second–third century.

PEIRAEUS. Tomb. Segall, nos 93–8; Pfeiler, no. VII. Early first century.

SIPHNOS. Graves 14 and 23. *BSA*, XLIV (1949), pp. 80 ff. ; pl. 31; Pfeiler, nos X and XI. Coins of 75–80.

CURIUM, Hagios Hermogenis. Tomb 8, Burial 4. *AJA*, L (1946), p. 449; pl. 45; Pfeiler, no. VIII. Early first century.

VASA (Cyprus). Tombs. *R. D. Ant. Cyp.* (1940–8), pl. 3:5 (no. 53). First to third centuries.

SHURAFA (Egypt). Cemetery. Petrie, W. M. F. and Mackay, E. *Heliopolis, Kafr Amman and Shurafa* (London, 1915), pl. 52.

TEKIYA (Yugoslavia). Hoard. Mano-Zissi, D. 'Les Trouvailles de Tekiya, Musée National Beograd', *Antiquité*, II (1957); Pfeiler, no. XII. Coins to Domitian (81–96).

TENÉS (Algeria). 'The Tenés Treasure'. Heurgon, J. *Le Trésor de Tenés* (Paris, 1958). Jewellery of the fourth century.

ELEUTHEROPOLIS (Palestine). Tomb. *Journal International d'Archéologie Numismatique*, X (1907), p. 230; pl. 7; Pfeiler, no. XV. First and second centuries.

ALEPPO. Hoard. Greifenhagen, *Schmuckarbeiten*, I, p. 73; pls 53–6. 250–300.

NINEVEH. Tombs. *British Museum Yearbook*, I (1976), p. 47. Early second century.

TYRE. *Bulletin du Musée de Beyrouth*, XVIII (1965), p. 61; Pfeiler, no. XXXIII. First and second centuries.

TARSUS. 'The Tarsus Treasure'. *Revue Numismatique*, XIII (1868), p. 309; *BMCR*, nos 188, 268, 801. Coins to 243.

DOURA EUROPOS. Hoard. Baur, P. V. C. and Rostovtzeff, M. I. *Excavations at Doura Europos : The Second Season* (New Haven, 1931), p. 78; pls 15, 44–6. Coins of the third century.

KERCH.

Tomb. *CR* (1881), p. 46; pl. I: 10; Pfeiler, no. XIII. Coin of Kotys I (45–62).

Tomb. Minns, p. 407; fig. 295; Pfeiler, no. XIV. First century.

ARMAZI (Georgia). Tomb 6. Mongait, A. L. *Archaeology in the USSR* (Harmondsworth, 1961), p. 221, pls 13b, 14; Pfeiler, no. XXVIII. Second–third centuries.

EMESA (Homs). Tombs. *Syria*, XXIX (1952), p. 204; XXX (1953), p. 12. First century.

ESKISEHIR (Central Turkey). Tomb. *AJA*, LXXVIII (1974), pl. 54.
  First century.
LÜLEBURGAZ (Turkish Thrace). Tomb. *AA* (1941), p. 123; Pfeiler, no.
  XVII. Second century.

GENERAL INDEX

GEOGRAPHICAL INDEX

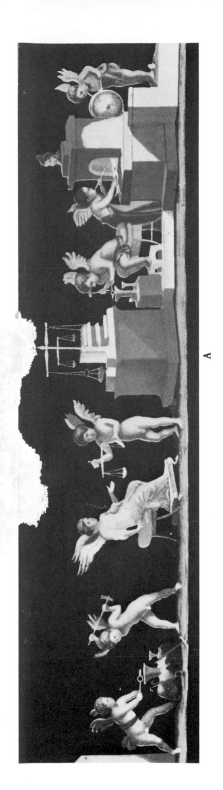

A

B

C

D

E

I TECHNICAL PROCESSES

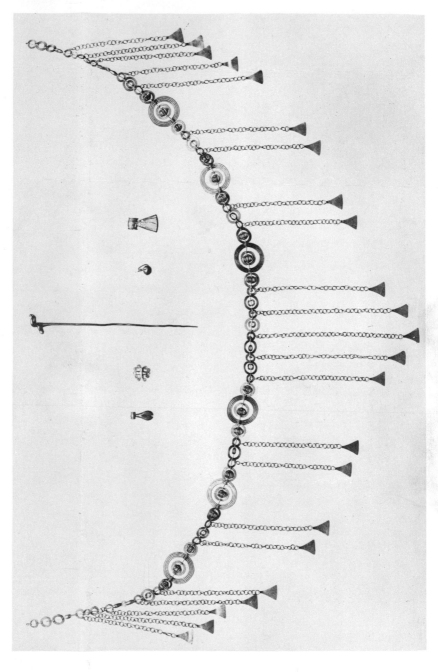

A

B

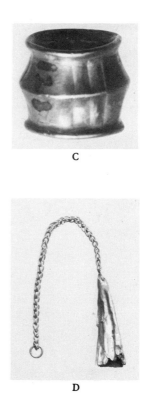

C

D

3 MINOAN PREPALATIAL JEWELLERY. ABOUT 2200 BC

A

B

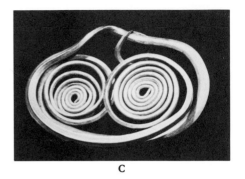

C

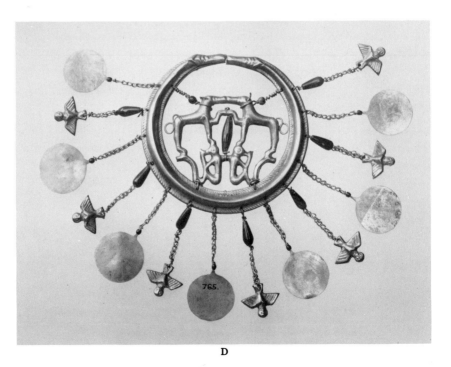

D

4   MINOAN AND MYCENAEAN JEWELLERY. 1700–1500 BC

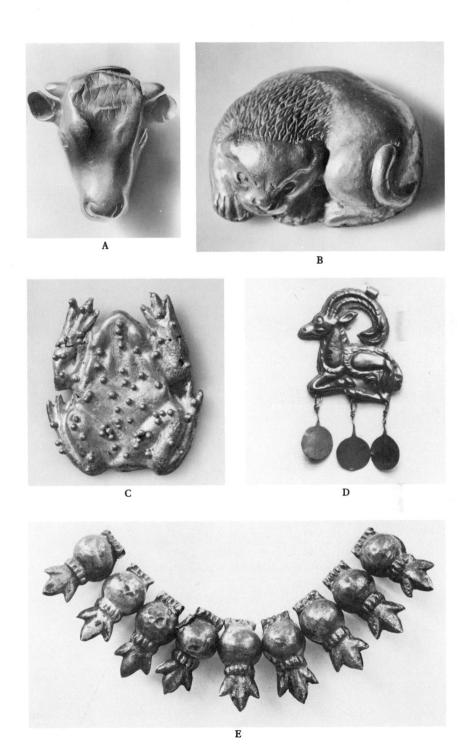

A

B

C

D

E

5   MINOAN AND MYCENAEAN JEWELLERY. 1700–1450 BC

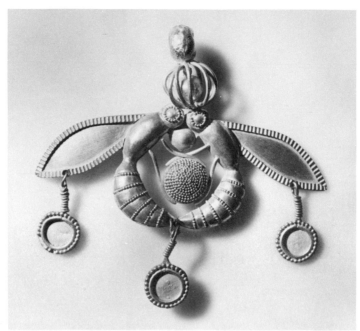

A

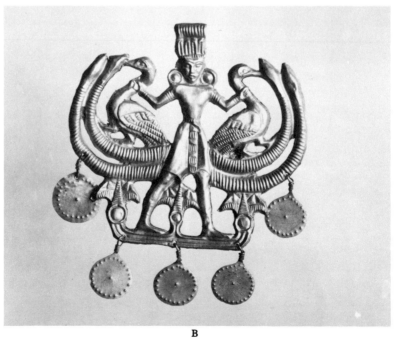

B

6 MINOAN JEWELLERY. 1700–1600 BC

A

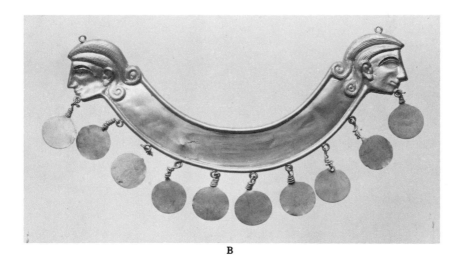

B

7   MINOAN AND MYCENAEAN JEWELLERY. 1700–1500 BC

A

B

C

D

E

F

G

8   MINOAN AND MYCENAEAN JEWELLERY. 1700–1500 BC

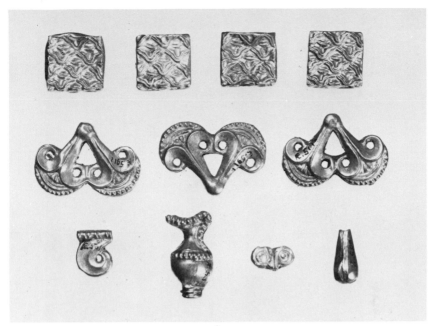

A

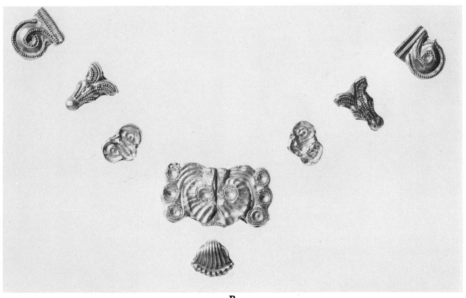

B

9   MYCENAEAN JEWELLERY. 1450–1300 BC

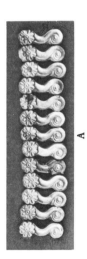

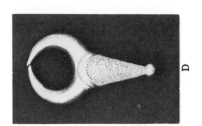

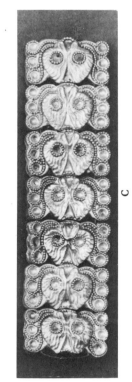

IO   MYCENAEAN JEWELLERY. I450–I200 BC

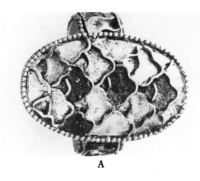

A

B

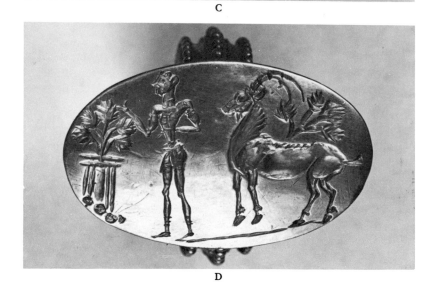

C

D

II MYCENAEAN FINGER RINGS. 1450–1200 BC

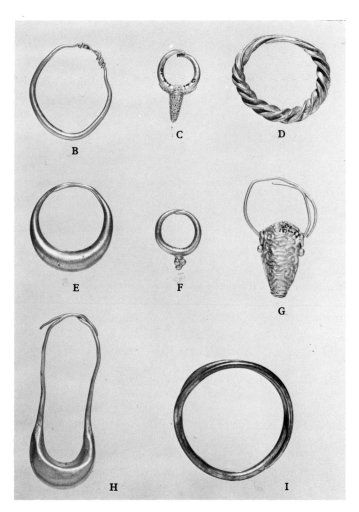

12   CYPRO-MYCENAEAN JEWELLERY.   1400—1100 BC

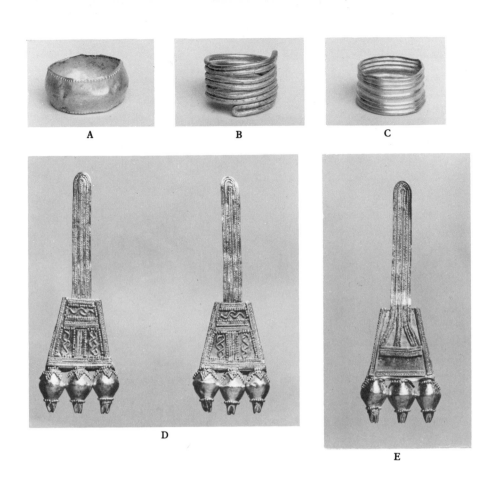

A   B   C

D   E

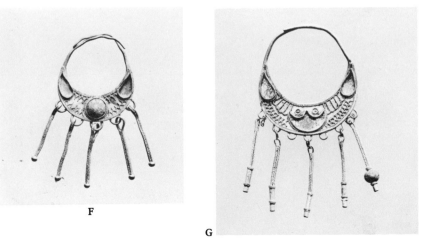

F   G

13   GREEK JEWELLERY: ATTIC. 1100–750 BC

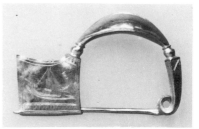

A

B

C

D   E

14   GREEK JEWELLERY: ATTIC. 800–750 BC

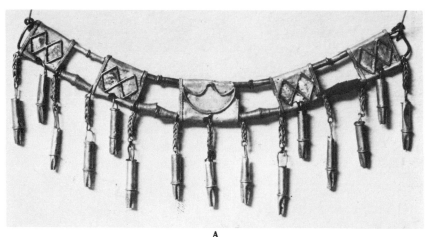

A

B

C

D

E

F

15   GREEK JEWELLERY: ATTIC. 750–700 BC

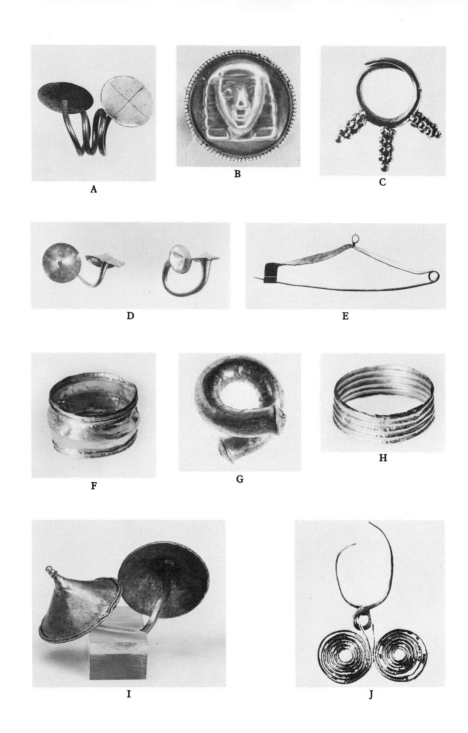

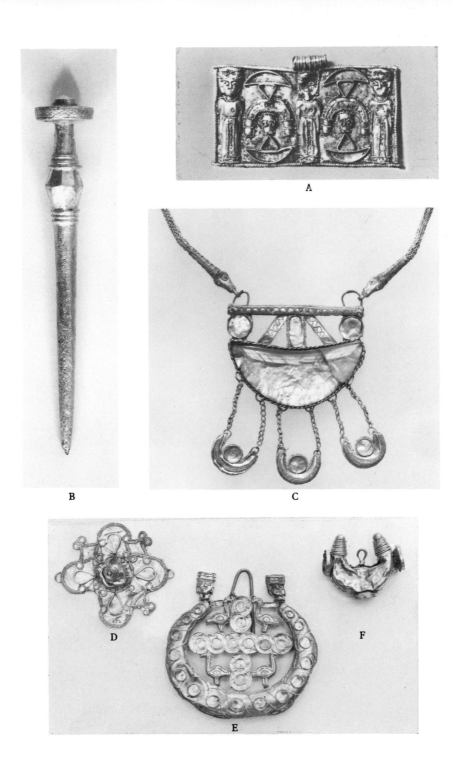

17   GREEK JEWELLERY: CRETAN. 800–700 BC

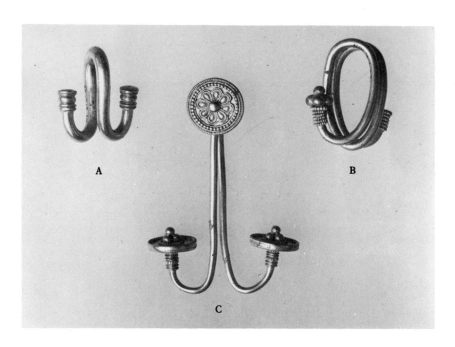

A

B

C

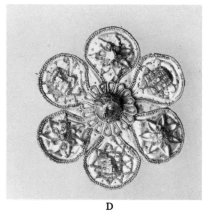

D

E

18 GREEK JEWELLERY, THE ISLANDS. 700–600 BC

19 GREEK JEWELLERY, THE ISLANDS. 700–600 BC

A

B

C

D

E

A

B

C

D

E

F

20   GREEK JEWELLERY, THE ISLANDS. 700–600 BC

21   GREEK JEWELLERY: EPHESUS. 700–600 BC

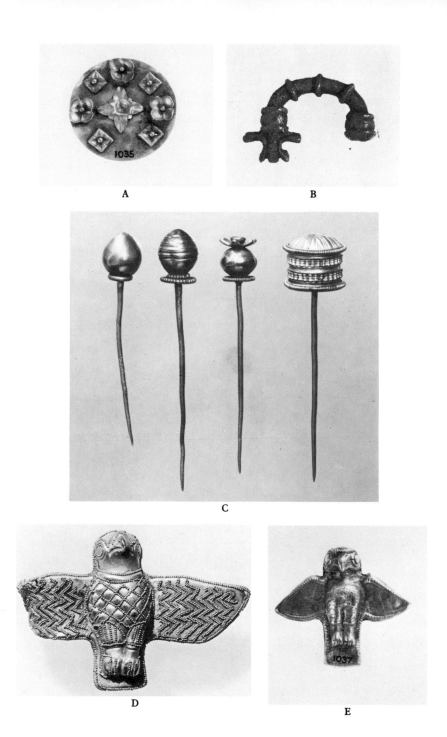

A

B

C

D

E

22   GREEK JEWELLERY: EPHESUS. 700–600 BC

23   GREEK WREATH. 350 BC

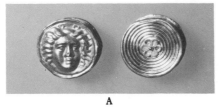

A

B

C

D

E

F

24   GREEK JEWELLERY. 500–400 BC

A

B

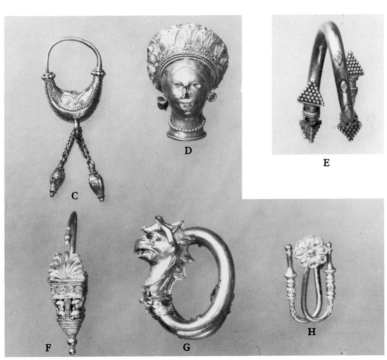

C

D

E

F

G

H

25　GREEK JEWELLERY. 450–330 BC

26 GREEK NECKLACES. 500–400 BC

27 GREEK NECKLACES. 450–400 BC

28   GREEK NECKLACE. 400–350 BC

29   GREEK PENDANT. 375–350 BC

A

B

30   GREEK BRACELETS. 500–350 BC

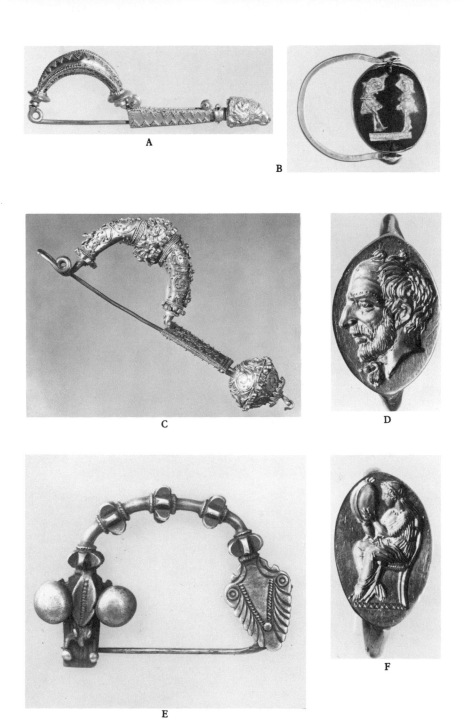

A

B

C

D

E

F

31 GREEK RINGS AND FIBULAE. 550–350 BC

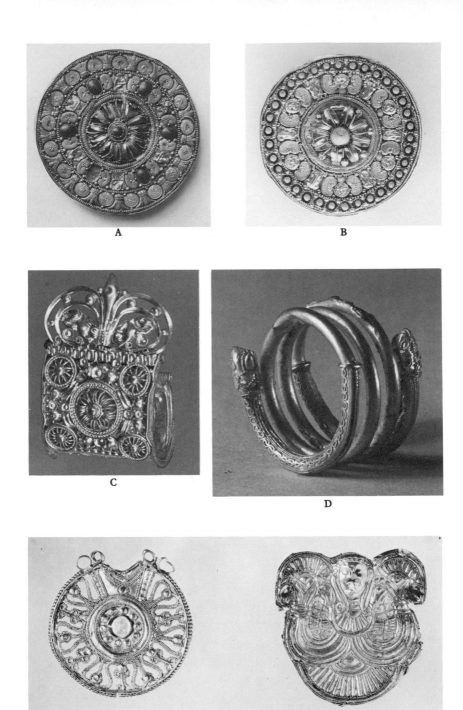

A

B

C

D

E

F

32   ETRUSCAN JEWELLERY. 700–500 BC

A

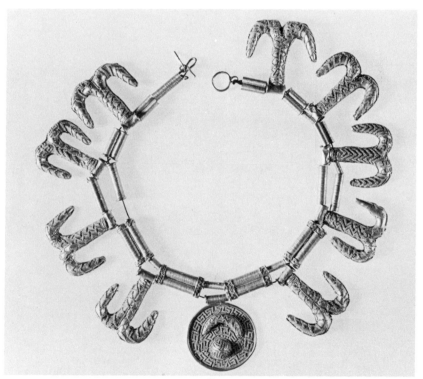

B

33 ETRUSCAN NECKLACES. 700–600 BC

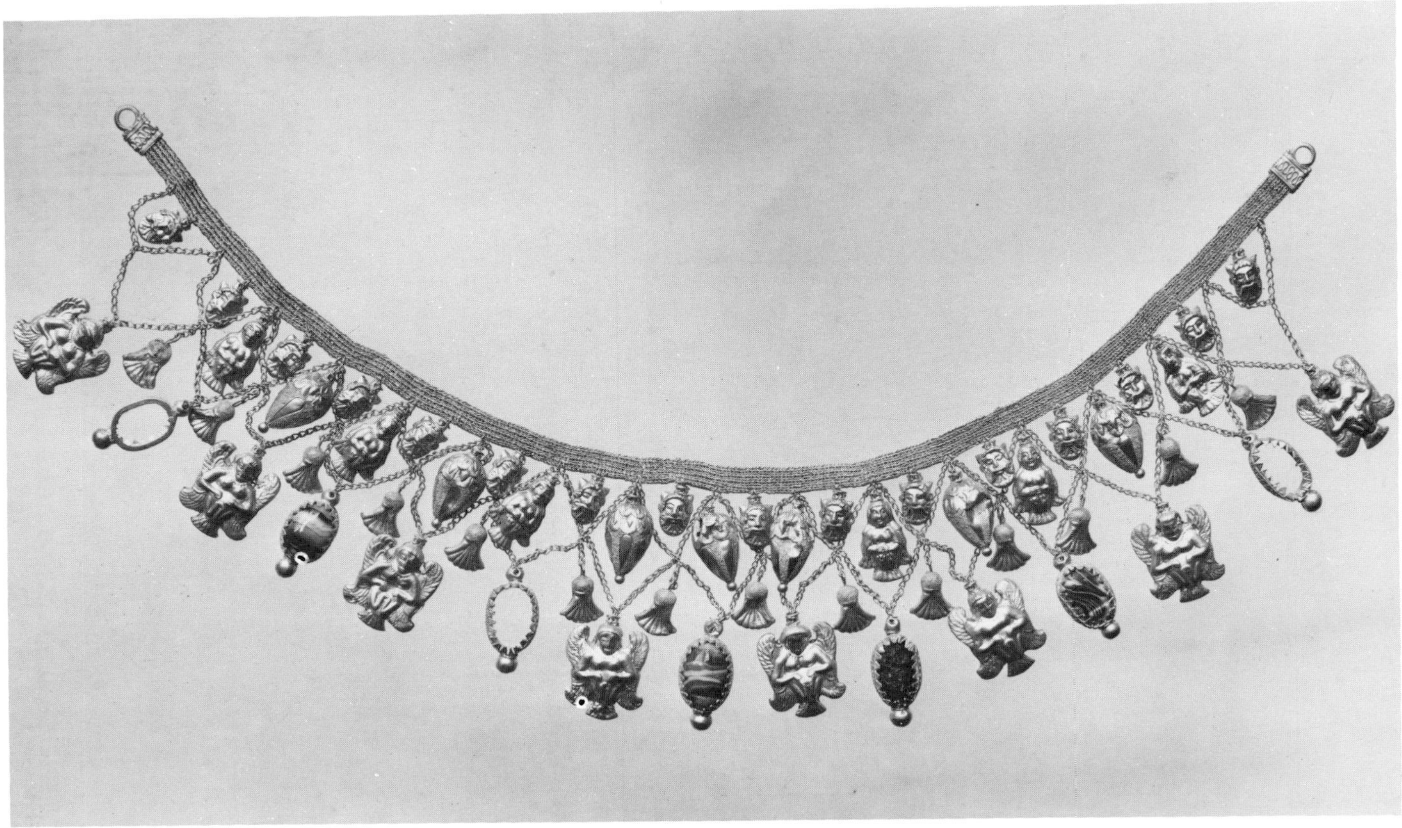

34 ETRUSCAN NECKLACE. 500 BC

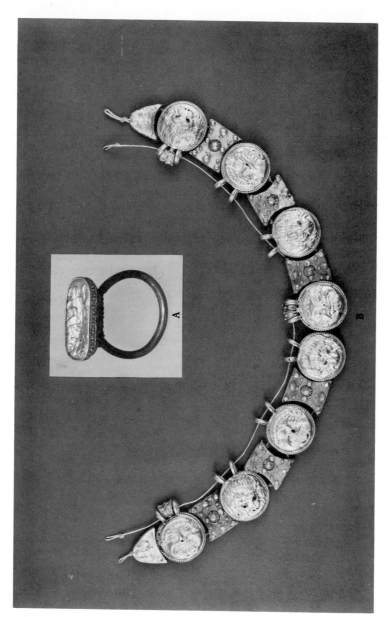

35 ETRUSCAN JEWELLERY. 625–500 BC

A

B

36 ETRUSCAN BRACELETS. 700–600 BC

A

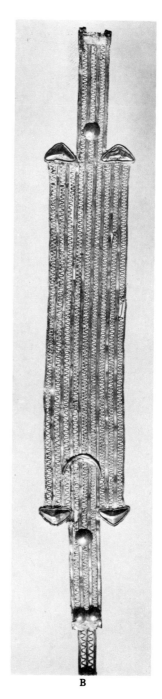

B

37 ETRUSCAN BRACELETS. 700–600 BC

38 ETRUSCAN FIBULAE. 700–600 BC

A

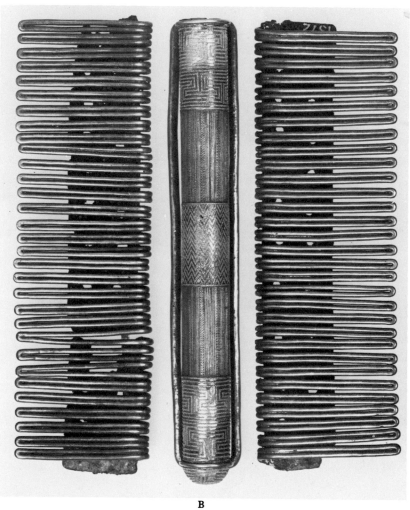

B

39   ETRUSCAN FIBULAE. 700–600 BC

40   ESTRUSCAN FIBULA. 700–600 BC

A

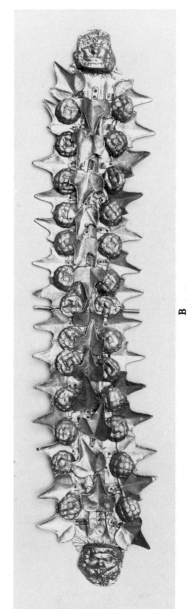

B

41 ETRUSCAN WREATHS. 400–250 BC

A

B

C

D

42 ETRUSCAN JEWELLERY. 400–250 BC

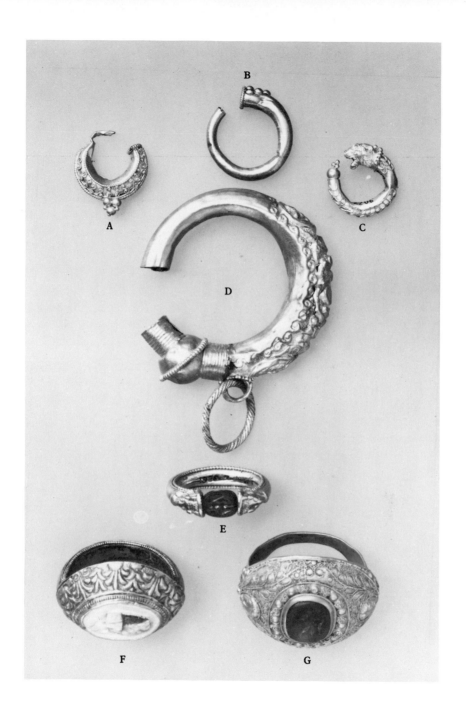

43 ETRUSCAN JEWELLERY. 600–250 BC

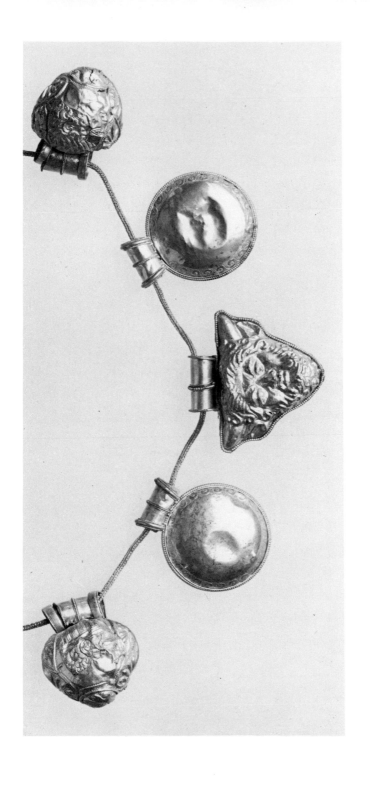

A

B

C

45 HELLENISTIC DIADEMS. 330–150 BC

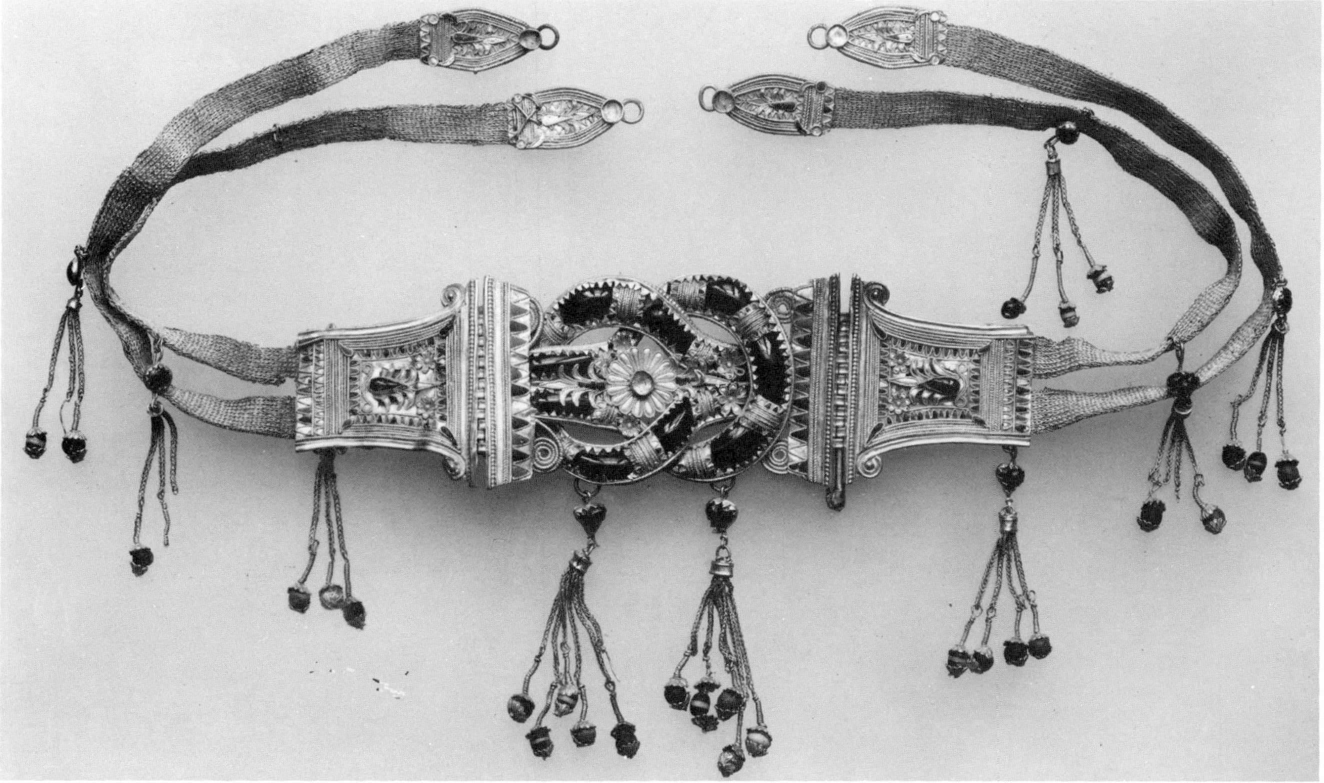

46 HELLENISTIC DIADEM. ABOUT 200 BC

A   B   C

D   E

F   G   H

I   J   K

47 HELLENISTIC EARRINGS. 330–27 BC

A   B   C

D   E

48   HELLENISTIC EARRINGS. 330–27 BC

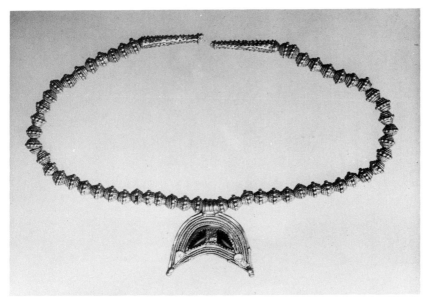

A

B

49   HELLENISTIC NECKLACES. 200–100 BC

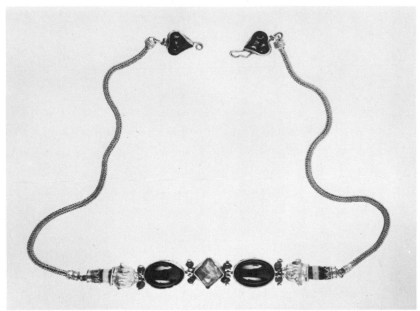

A

B

50   HELLENISTIC JEWELLERY. 200–100 BC

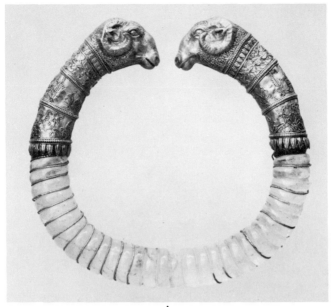

A

B

C

51 HELLENISTIC BRACELETS. 330–100 BC

A

B

52 HELLENISTIC MEDALLIONS. 200–100 BC

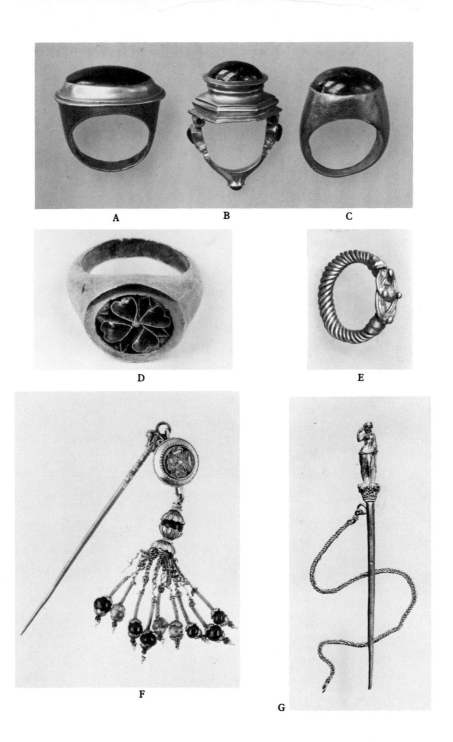

A B C

D E

F G

53 HELLENISTIC JEWELLERY. 300–27 BC

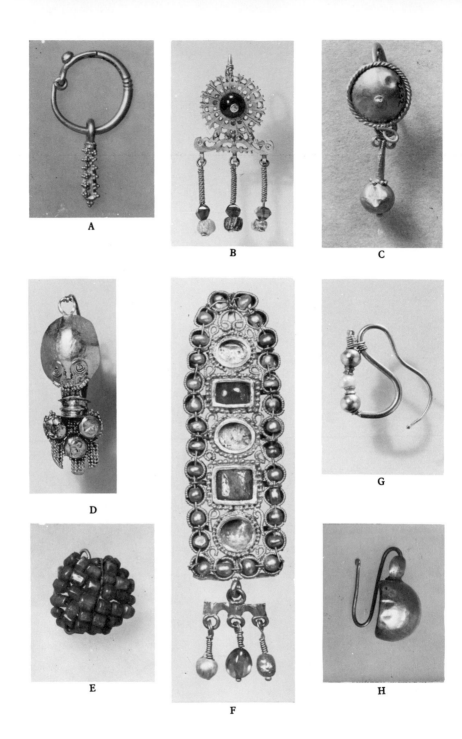

A

B

C

D

E

F

G

H

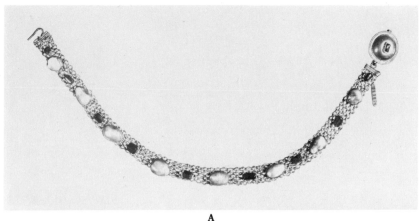

A

B

55 ROMAN NECKLACES. 27 BC–AD 100

56   ROMAN NECKLACE. AD 50–150

A

B

57 ROMAN NECKLACES. AD 50–150

58 ROMAN NECKLACES. ABOUT AD 200

A

B

59   ROMAN PENDANTS. AD 250–350

A

B

60 ROMAN BRACELETS. 27 BC–AD 50

61 ROMAN BRACELETS. 27 BC–AD 250

A

B

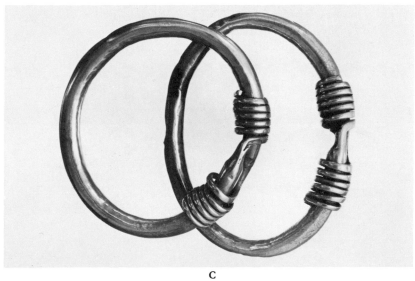

C

62   ROMAN BRACELETS. AD 50–250

A

B

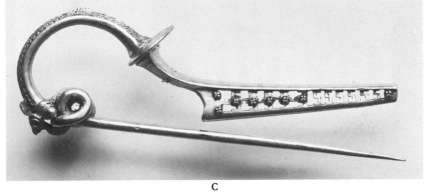

C

63 ROMAN JEWELLERY. AD 50–350